The metaphoric process

'If the philosophy of language is to have a future, it   t.
the perspectives opened up by Gemma Corradi !   ork.

Margaret Whitford, *Queen   . ry   .d Westf.   .   . ege,*
University of London

'... an original and lucid analysis of metaphoric language and its influence on the individual's emotional experience. The book represents an important and eminently useful contribution to psychoanalytic understanding.'

Otto Kernberg, *International Psychoanalytic Association*

'An original contribution to the vast literature on metaphor . . . Its scholarship from Aristotle to Davidson is impeccable. The writing is brilliant, and the quality of argumentation is impressive. I strongly recommend it.'

Avrum Stroll, *University of California, San Diego*

Praise for *The Other Side of Language*:

'A particularly valuable feature of the work is the delicate but sure-footed sensibility and psychological penetration of the author, which wins from a thoroughly rigorous philosophical analysis a host of ideas and suggestions for the philosophy of life and even for psychology itself – a rare combination.'

Brian McGuinness, *University of Oxford*

'Gemma Corradi Fiumara's vast project . . . shows a rare mastery in the domain of linguistic philosophy and especially in the area of encounter between analytic philosophy and hermeneutics.'

Paul Ricoeur, *University of Chicago*

Gemma Corradi Fiumara is Associate Professor of Philosophy at the Third University of Rome and a full member of the International Psychoanalytic Association. Her writings include *Philosophy and Coexistence* and *The Symbolic Function: Psychoanalysis and the Philosophy of Language, The Other Side of Language: A Philosophy of Listening* was published by Routledge in 1990.

The metaphoric process

Connections between language and life

Gemma Corradi Fiumara

London and New York

British Library Cataloguing Publication Data
A catalogue record for this book is available from the British Library.

Library of Congress Cataloging in Publication Data
A catalogue record for this book has been requested.

ISBN 0–415–12624–X (hbk)
ISBN 0–415–12625–8 (pbk)

To my husband Romano Fiumara,
in loving memory

Contents

1   Connections between language and life

AN INTERPERSONAL APPROACH TO METAPHORICITY

Books dealing with metaphor frequently start out with Aristotle's celebrated discussion of this figure of speech. To shift the focus of attention from a mainly formal outlook to a more interactive approach to human metaphoricity we will also invoke the Aristotelian view of metaphor, but in conjunction with revealing aspects of his social philosophy. As a preliminary, we should note that as soon as we recall our Greek origins we can see that our linguistic tradition is not so distant from a Platonic legacy 'demonstrating' that one cannot grasp the truth via any corporeal senses but must employ the mind in the form of 'pure and unadulterated thought'.[1] And although in contemporary philosophy we have gradually substituted language for the notion of 'pure thought', and words for 'concepts',[2] a subject–object cognitive model still seems to prevail; this model does not ultimately allow for the developments we seek through work that might originate in our coexistence with nature and culture, rather than in an abstract rationality intent upon controlling the world.

More 'physiologically' inclined than his predecessor – and thus not entirely preoccupied with the purity of thinking – Aristotle proclaims, 'The greatest thing, by far, is to be a master of metaphor. It is the one thing that cannot be learnt; and it is also a sign of genius.'[3] Thus the naturalist philosopher, reacting to Platonic transcendence, insists that our metaphoric potential is, by far, 'the greatest thing' in language – indeed a sign of 'genius' for creativity and survival. And yet it is even more interesting that Aristotle's treatment of metaphor can be significantly reconnected with aspects of his social philosophy tacitly aiming to safeguard some form of Platonic 'pure thought'. He seems to suggest in a great variety of ways that 'slaves' must speak 'plainly' before their masters, and thus abstain from the 'genius' of metaphor. He explicitly repeats that 'it is not quite appropriate that fine language should be used by a slave.'[4]

Imaginative linguistic links may indeed serve to influence world-views and, obviously, slaves are not supposed to compete with their masters, even in 'metaphoric' terms. If we regard the 'slave' as an emblematic figure standing for whoever has insufficient contractual power in whatever situation, the injunction to avoid 'fine language' and not to engage in metaphor can be equated with the prohibition even to envisage changes in conceptual structures. To ensure that slaves remain constrained in such a stable way that the burden of their own submission does not weigh on the masters but is conveniently placed upon the slaves themselves, it is an essential pre-emptive condition that they be persuaded to speak plainly, to avoid fine language, and keep their minds confined within one vocabulary. Granting permission to address their 'superiors' metaphorically would be comparable to recognizing slaves' capacity to migrate from one epistemic context to another, while their 'own' (imposed) vocabulary is confined to producing self-confirming prophecies supporting the social epistemology from which it emanates.

It is equally interesting that in spite of such a clear indication by the celebrated thinker of what is a salient function of language – 'by far the greatest thing . . . and a sign of genius' – the topic of metaphor has been systematically ignored throughout the centuries. Perhaps in the early stages of our western culture priority has been wisely accorded to the sort of rationality which could generate a productive tradition of objectivity. But our philosophy might now appear sufficiently consolidated to allow itself a fuller reflection on the nature of our specific human 'genius' and a more daring approach to the question of rationality and meaning. Significantly, indeed, Quine argues that 'the absence of an adequate study of imagination in our theories of meaning and rationality is symptomatic of a deep problem in our current views of cognition. The difficulty is not a matter of mere oversight. The problem is far more distressing, for it concerns our entire orientation toward these issues, based as it is upon a widely shared set of presuppositions that deny imagination a central role in the constitution of reality.'[5] The paradigms of rationality are in fact still regarded as organizing forms which transcend the structures of affective experience. And although it is usually granted that metaphorical projections may be part of our mental processes in creating novel connections, such attempts are typically regarded as 'psychological' antecedents, 'obviously' irrelevant to the construction of our ways of reasoning.

A live language which shares in the organismic domain as well as in the conscious and willed levels of the mind, is as problematic for the philosopher as it is for the individual; thus, in order to regulate the varied richness of language, the prevalent human tendency is to acquire (often idealized) standards of normative linguistic behaviour. Reliance on the literalness of cultural concepts may, however, conceal the danger of devaluing all those inner experiences that could, perhaps, be expressed metaphorically but certainly not in the terms of commensurable standards. On the other hand, reaching for, or prefiguring, a future stage of philosophical maturity, we could appreciate that creative processes may have their own as yet unknown lawfulness which may be often obscured, and even distorted, by our stringent requirements for intellectual formalization. At this prefigurative stage we may nevertheless reacknowledge and explore the profound dimensions of beliefs and desires.[6] I am thus arguing in favour of a transition from the cultural narcissism of isolated intracommensurable epistemologies, to a metaphoric weaving of inter-epistemic circuits attempting to connect non-homogeneous domains. The special contribution of an inchoate philosophical culture could help us rethink the terms of an interepistemic debate by creatively providing ever new metaphoric instruments.

Like most myths, perhaps the story of Babel is two-sided.[7] On the one side, it tries to indicate the impossibility of attempting bold constructions while maintaining the comfort of a universal communication. On the other side, the myth evokes the nostalgia for an ideal, original condition which putatively existed and which has had to be relinquished in the process of developing more complex and diversified constructions. Such an ideal antecedent state may be thought of in terms of total unequivocal communication. Like other myths pertaining to the story of human linguisticity, it proclaims the need for an emancipatory separation as a condition for the development of what might be regarded as more powerful forms of world control. And yet the suspicion remains that the laborious quests for truth at the core of our philosophical games might be thought of as capable of ultimately 're-establishing' an ideal condition of total communication in our technological era;[8] such an 'ideal' might explain our inexhaustible search for truth conditions and standards of meaning. Our longing for a 'lost' condition of unequivocal language might be what sustains our persistent search for standards of accurate representation and objectivity. Should the flourishing research on truth conditions reach a cluster of conclusive convergences, the result might be sufficient virtually to reproduce a pre-Babelic structure of successful communication.

What is remarkable in philosophical writings is that, usually, in order to typify areas in which regular and predictable descriptive behaviour is *not* at work, authors tend to conjure up examples of absolute strangers, such as extragalactics, 'savages', or slaves, in Aristotle's time. The hypothesis of such interlocutors is probably more comfortable than the idea of segregated parts of the mind; ultimate strangers, moreover, may be less disquieting than fellow speakers in our own phatic community 'uttering sentences' from too distant points in the life cycle, or from unacceptable styles of life operating at the periphery of the regular and regulative (language) games.

Metaphor frequently inhabits the margins of discourse and its potential incivility generates concern for its management. There is a subliminal anxiety which results from the difficulty of maintaining the boundary between 'proper' terminology in the face of metaphorical boundary-crossers; and the way in which the superbly elaborate analyses of philosophical literature are conducted might even suggest an effort of *containment* and a problem of *mastery*. The very idea of transportability of words, notions and features could be a threat to the dignity of our mainstreams of philosophy, in the sense that certain ideas might not only be out of place but out of control.[9]

As increasingly cosmopolitan relations and survival problems for our global village will inevitably reverberate in philosophy, special difficulties may emerge for our rationality to cope with; at the same time, previously unacknowledged resources may be activated for the construal of 'alien' world-views. Surely we are interdependent in terms of telematics and currencies, in terms of the air we breathe and the water we drink, but we are even more subtly and profoundly linked by the language we create and live by. This entails an awareness of the potential threat of linguistic involution: a degradation which might jeopardize the development of a meaningful relation between nature and culture, world and language, deforming the relationship itself into a parasitic, destructive pattern. Just a few decades ago the notion of ecology was rarely invoked, while our fashionable language now resounds with worrisome expressions related to the deterioration of the planet we inhabit. And yet there is no comparable concern for the potential degradation of our linguisticity, our symbolic habitat and transpersonal cultural home.[10] Even though we do not have conceptual instruments that can adequately diagnose any such degradation, there is no way of excluding the trend, which can be all the more pervasive because we cannot properly articulate it, and as dangerous as it is capable of concealment.

In a Rortyan perspective, a clearly codified area of thought, whether among persons or within the same individual, could almost be regarded as an epistemology within which we can conveniently operate.[11] Thus the development of some reasonable interaction between different epistemic languages, or between differently speaking aspects of the same mind, stands out as one of the main challenges that the human sciences must face. Language, in fact, poses its major problems at the level of interlinguistic construal and interaction; and the recognition of these difficulties will continue as long as the desire for personal and cultural growth is strong enough to make us persist in the metaphoric attempts to reconnect different languages and create interepistemic links.

DEVALUATION *AND* EMPLOYMENT OF METAPHORS

Books dealing with metaphor also frequently quote from Hobbes's work to demonstrate his disapproval of metaphoric expressions; but then, it is equally instructive to remark in his writings a concomitant devaluation *and* employment of metaphors. In his criticism he compares metaphors to 'senseless and ambiguous words', to 'ignes fatui' and also suggests that reasoning with metaphors is like 'wandering amongst innumerable absurdities', only conducive to 'contention, and sedition, or contempt'.[12] He also writes: 'Inconstant names can never be true grounds of any ratiocination. No more can metaphors, and tropes of speech.' Thus 'In reckoning and seeking truth, metaphors are not to be admitted.'[13] These assertions could be juxtaposed to remarks deriving from his original interest in mechanical constructions: 'Why may we not say that all *Automata* . . . have an artificiall life? For what is the *Heart*, but a *Spring*; and the *Nerves*, but so many *Strings*; and the *Joynts*, but so many *Wheels* . . . ?'[14] He thus both suspects and makes use of metaphor, thereby obliquely inviting exploration of such an interesting coincidence. But it would be futile to ask why Hobbes fails to see that he both uses *and* criticizes metaphorical language because this attitude, in fact, represents a general cognitive predicament: humans appear to be constantly engaged in striving to optimize the equilibrium between their ineliminable metaphoricity and literalness.

A comparable attitude can be recognized in twentieth-century logical positivism, which goes as far as to divide all discourse – roughly – into three distinct types: logical propositions, factual statements, and nonsensical expressions. As is known, to the category of nonsense it not only assigns the assertions of traditional metaphysics but also metaphorical expressions, meaningful discourse being confined to the domains of logical and empirical statements. But then, if we ask in which way the logical positivists characterize these two meaningful realms of discourse and their interrelation, we realize that they do not use an entirely literal language and that expressions drawn from the putative domain of 'nonsense' are frequently invoked. The theories of the empirical sciences are in fact described as originating from 'erstwhile uninterpreted postulates containing "primitive" concepts.'[15] And even in the formal domain of logic metaphorical expressions are used, such as 'logical atoms', 'molecular propositions', 'meaning as picture', or 'nomological nets'[16] – as derived from the piscatorial tradition. And if we ask what is the relation between the formal and empirical realms, Smith points out that in logical positivism the formal component of theory needs to be 'tied' to the observable elements by means of what are variously described as 'links', 'anchorings', 'chains of sentences', and 'bridge principles'.[17] The metaphorically articulated rules of correspondence are thus established to connect the abstract concepts of the postulates with the empirical concepts of the observation language in such a way that the factual–empirical significance may 'seep upward'[18] to the originally quite abstract concepts of the postulate system. As in the case of Hobbes, then, disparagement and employment of metaphor seem to converge in the development of the enterprise.

INTERACTIVE AND REPRESENTATIONAL CONCERNS

A concern for the metaphoric constructs which concur to shape intersubjective relations *and* our experience of nature seems to imply different levels of our linguisticity: our metaphoric potential, in fact, does not entirely unfold in an area of public linguistic lucidity since it involves the 'obscure' depths of our affectual life as well as our intellectual and formal achievements. This concern requires, therefore, an effort to explore the metaphoricity of human creatures living from infancy to senescence 'within' one mind (intellect, self, spirit, consciousness, ego . . .) where affects and reasons are inextricably interwoven. And even though a comprehensive 'logic' capable of accounting for both affects and deductions, for life and abstractions, has not yet been expressed in human culture, it is possible that the mode of being which may generate this new rationality is already at work. It is not impossible that in Neanderthal times some members of the human community may have thought 'Greek', that some of our contemporaries may think 'Neanderthal', and others still, think 'future'. Pristine originality can be an illusion, since germinal ideas may inconspicuously be at work well before a conventional founder proclaims them with sufficient persuasiveness to elicit recontextualizations. Official founders may utilize the full implications of ideas that precursors lived by, albeit with a scarce grasp of their 'revolutionary'[19] force.

Questions of interaction – of which cognition is a superb variant – refer to a complex of links which constantly point to both the *development* of knowing subjects and to the *construction* of possible realities – a construction which obviously does not entail that material reality is 'mind- dependent'.[20] Hence, in the present approach, language is not only viewed as constitutive of our cognitive efforts but, indeed, of our whole being. The embodied relations influencing our ontogeny can be viewed as offering a more fruitful and encompassing scope than the questions of accurate representation. And if language becomes excessively disembodied it might unnoticeably be indifferent to life and death, construction and destruction, inasmuch as the representationalist preoccupations associated with objectivity of meaning come to absorb most of our 'philosophical' concerns. A conviction that the essential characteristic of language is its capacity to represent the way things are is, historically, typified by Frege, Russell, Tarski, Carnap, the early Wittgenstein, and by thinkers with comparable tendencies: possibly the derivatives of profound inclinations which surface in the form of irreducible epistemological stances.

Once an ontogenetic, life-dependent, perspective is adopted, a more interactive communicational dimension is inevitably disclosed in which language appears as a process rather than as a system – a process which helps us focus more holistically. We can thus incline toward appreciating the complexity of linguistic dynamics rather than positing a 'system' that communicators would allegedly employ in cognition. The comprehensive relevance of interpersonal contact is indirectly illustrated by Quine where he strives to explain the indeterminacy of translation by suggesting that a translator would constantly revise a manual in the light of successes and failures of communication:

> And wherein do these successes and failures consist, or how are they to be recognized? Successful negotiations with natives is taken as evidence that the manual is progressing well. Smooth conversation is further favorable evidence. Reactions of astonishment or bewilderment on a native's part, or seemingly irrelevant responses, tend to suggest that the manual has gone wrong.[21]

And perhaps another reason why theories, or definitions, of metaphor are ultimately inadequate is probably linked to their resistance to the idea that metaphor is primarily a process. If 'To know is to represent accurately what is outside of the mind', to understand the nature of knowledge we must remain confined to the task of ascertaining the way in which the mind is able to construct such representation.[22] Rorty suggests that, in fact, 'The picture which holds traditional philosophy captive is that of the mind as a great mirror, containing various representations – some accurate, some not – and capable of being studied by pure, nonempirical methods. Without the notion of the mind as mirror the notion of knowledge as accuracy of representation would not have suggested itself.'[23]

In a representationalist perspective the meanings of our sentences would be given by the conditions that render them determinately true or false. Indeed, a view of language so restrictively circumscribed that it could distort the nature of our linguistic life. It is a view of language that does the best it can in striving to connect the complexity of life to its view of the world through what, after all, are the only kinds of connections it understands: reference, truth, instantiation, exemplification, satisfaction, and the like. Human language could also (or instead) be viewed as a bodily, interactive, constitutive process emanating from communicative practices; a process to be somehow differentiated from the more circumscribed representationalist concerns, intent upon analysing which sorts of true statements, if any, stand in representational relations to non-linguistic items. In Stewart's view, the same linguistic phenomenon cannot be both constitutive and representational;[24] it cannot be both a way of being which is constitutive of humanity and of its interaction with the world, *and* a system instrumentally employed by already-constituted humans capable of accurately representing reality. 'Insofar as language is a way of being, humanity gets accomplished in it or via it. But the claim that language instrumentally represents something else presupposes humans who are already constituted and capable of intending and representing. Thus either humans come-into-being linguistically, or they are already "in being" and then consequently "use" language. But both claims cannot be coherent.'[25] The distinction between a linguistic domain, on the one side, and the domain of things and thoughts, on the other, probably harks back to the Aristotelian assessment of a representational way of human functioning: 'Spoken words are the symbols of mental experiences' says Aristotle, 'and written words are the symbols of spoken words.'[26] A 'logic' of correspondences is thus tacitly advocated which obscures the background of our personal interactive exchanges while bringing cognition into focus – a logic which ultimately tends to establish a basically semiotic account of language.

Of course the representational accounts of language do not entirely coincide, as they differ in important ways, and semiotically oriented authors would accept some claims made in complementary literature and reject others.[27] But despite their differences, representationalist thinkers share the view that language is primarily a semiotic system, that is a system of signs representing or signifying something else. These outlooks presuppose a fundamental ontological dichotomy which separates the sign from the signified, the name from the named and word from thought. Once the representational choice has been made, a structural *a priori* is established which tends to perpetuate a fracture between the linguistic world and the world of things and thoughts.

METAPHOR AS PROCESS

What is advocated is the creation of more permeable boundaries in our philosophical discourse inasmuch as we can no longer start out from 'philosophical language' as if antecedent life conditions were irrelevant to the development of such language. Barth critically points out that much of our philosophy cognitively operates in a *social-solipsistic* style 'in which physical objects may be of importance as such but where *no* verbal contact or other sign contact between humans occur, *or are taken into consideration*'.[28] Conversely, the present inquiry is inspired by an outlook on life and language which assumes their reciprocal interaction. Any concept of either life or language that does not account for their interconnectedness will probably fail to yield more than superfluous artefacts; these have little to offer to an inchoate philosophical culture pursuing the quest for a language not only conversant with intraepistemic deductions but also capable of interepistemic communicative efforts. The sort of approach we seek to develop may ultimately challenge the map of an internalized culture whose order relies upon 'unbreakable' distinctions between domains which are customarily classified as either experiential or formal, synthetic or *a priori*, bodily or mental, instinctual or rational – in an endless sequence of comparable and irreducible oppositions.

Once the existence of two divided realms has been posited, they somehow increasingly appear as composed of different elements, and philosophy is thus confronted with the task of explaining how units in one world relate to elements in the other. In the perspective of a mind-as-mirror-of-nature metaphor, the question is answered with the indisputable claim that one set of units somehow represents, signifies, or symbolizes the other.[29] In this way language becomes *primarily* characterized as a semiotic system consisting of structures which represent the rest of reality. This sort of language may tend to form pictures of the world – nature, persons, culture – widely useful in controlling it, and to eschew world-views inviting dialogic exchange and mutual enrichment. Although western philosophy has largely described language as a signifying system emanating from an impersonal logic, work can be done within the scope of an alternative characterization of language, in which it is regarded as the derivative of a personal logic and of an unbreakable unity of listening and speaking. A comparable interdependence between reading and writing is also generally obscured. Danto points out that there are philosophical texts which, if true, would entail their own logical illegibility; and he remarks that it is inconceivable that philosophers would have fallen into such incoherences if they had not, as it were, forgotten that their texts, in addition to being representations of a kind of reality, were things to be *read*. The price we pay for rendering this relationship unseen in the current style of writing is that it 'enables' us to depict worlds in which readers cannot fit.[30] The initially plausible aspiration to overcome the features of a pre-reflective knowledge that makes things appear to us as they do and not as they 'really' are, can tacitly induce a good measure of rigidity in the legitimized domination of whatever epistemological approach is in force. In the human sciences we are made to flee the participatory approach under the pressure of an assumption that any object of inquiry must be something not from any particular (interactive) point of view but, virtually, 'in itself', practically indicating that it must comply with the locally most prestigious way of assessing cognitive relations. It is thus perfectly plain, in Danto's view, that the implied vision of philosophical knowledge, of the form of life evolved to pursue it, and the form of literature most suited to represent it, derive from the view of reality, life and literature that Kuhn counsels us to regard as 'normal science'.[31]

Indeed, once two separate worlds are given, one is repeatedly led to ask how units of one relate to items in the other. The ostensive way of answering the question has been, of course, surpassed, criticized and revised. And yet, the suspicion remains that it inconspicuously affects our research policies more than we can appreciate. Stewart expresses this suspicion by suggesting that 'unfortunately, rather than re-examining the basic assumption that words function representationally, scholars typically have looked for ways to salvage their semiotic analyses.'[32] He also remarks that the ontological difference basic to the symbol model is quite widespread despite protestations to the contrary, and in spite of the fact that the semiotic characterization of the nature of language cannot be coherently applied to concrete instances of the phenomena it purports to describe.[33] An alternative to representationalist concerns may instead be developed by exploring human linguisticity more in its relational function than in its semiotic uses. The propensity of semiotic accounts implicitly to induce a schism between two realms seems moreover to distort the sense of the term 'world' as we can understand it, in an ontogenetic perspective where, basically, the 'world' is the domain that we inhabit.

Possible human worlds[34] are collaboratively constructed and transformed through the unbreakable interaction of listening and speaking. This does not imply that interlocutors typically agree or concur in world shaping enterprises. Even though conflict is pervasive, disagreement is largely relational and thus collabora-tive, in a sense; for, indeed, in the language of Davidson, 'widespread agreement is the only possible background against which disputes and mistakes can be interpreted.'[35] Of course self-delusion tempts us at every turn and we must ask how, if not by public observational methods, we can guard against the illusions of sheer subjectivity. Thus the question of how to be independent of cognitive stereotypes and yet avoid the distortions of subjectivity, represents a way of framing a central human problem.

Although a thorough description of the syntactic and logical structure of meta-phor would surely prove enlightening, its omission need not be fatal for our present purposes. In fact the enforcement of such a prerequisite would probably imply a dependence upon whatever form of epistemic literalness may prevail at a given moment, and consequently a refusal to explore anything for which we do not have a sufficiently shared philosophical vocabulary. And metaphorization perhaps defies exact definitions because it is not so much a concept or an object but rather a complex process. In consideration of the numerous attempts to define metaphor, Martin-Soskice has suggested that anyone who has grappled with the problem of metaphoric expressions 'will appreciate the pragmatism of those who proceed to discuss it without giving any definition at all';[36] she even mentions a scholar claiming to have found more than one hundred different definitions, which may constitute only a part of those which have been formulated.[37] There are probably good reasons, then, to proceed with broader views since enough evidence emerges from the vastness of literature to support Cooper's suggestion that 'usually one gains rather than loses by employing "metaphor" in a generous way.'[38]

THE METAPHORIC MATRIX OF THEORIES

Theories of knowledge might be regarded as ideas about the structure of the interactions that are operative in the 'mind' of those who create the theories. These internal structures may be referred to as 'implicit theories' because they exist in some sense in our world-view without being explicitly formalized in such a way that they can aspire to the status of proto-theories. And even though we may not be aware of having implicit theories that we think by, it may be fruitful to hypothesize that explicit theories originally arise from implicit ones. Even theories that are empirically derived may have their origin in implicit models inasmuch as these initially generate our choice of tests and hence define the domain of possible causal factors and of possible areas of concern. When a question is being posed, or a problem identified, it is our philosophical right to ask why just *that* question is being asked. That there cannot be an explicit, appropriate or consensual reply is no reason for not continuing to inquire why a certain question is being asked in the sense of being privileged with respect to other possible questions.[39] That meaning grows out of use is an increasingly accepted and often sloganized point even though its practical implications are often unsuspected; for, indeed, as contexts of use are invariably contexts of life vicissitudes, it becomes necessary to ask what people are trying to do, and *why*, in whatever context. This line of inquiry may open new perspectives on the creative and metaphoric roots of our cognitive concerns.[40]

If metaphor is indeed 'a sign of genius',[41] the generation of implicit theories is highly to be valued. In order to emphasize the creative agility of the mind striving towards innovative connections, Galileo has had to argue laboriously against opponents who supported their theses with an abundance of quotations from the classics. Galileo claims, in fact, that the discussion of a difficult problem cannot be made analogous to the task of carrying loads: in this case many horses would carry more sacks of wheat than one horse only. And in this case, of course, he would agree that a profusion of discourses should be more effective than a single one; 'but a discussion is more like running than carrying, and thus a single Berber horse will run better than a hundred Friesians'.[42]

It is our metaphoricity rather than our semantic use of discourse which enables us to create novel perspectives of whatever reality we inhabit and to experience it largely as a unity, as a whole, even though all its parts are not always exactly in place. We do cope with our world by constantly attempting to relate parts to whole in order that integration and connection can be made functional criteria. And although implicit models and theories are not literally true of the world, they are somehow significant in indicating possible connections in the world. Perhaps they do not actually indicate but rather offer ways of coping with it. Arbib and Hesse express this possibility by suggesting that the reliability of models for prediction depends on analogical relations between diverse natural systems and on the fact that 'they *exhibit* rather than *state*, *show* rather than *say*.'[43] In fact, what can be stated depends on the classificatory resources already present in the language, and any observation language is theory-laden with that implicit classification. Our implicit classifications can be construed as the seminal metaphors of an age, emerging from profound affectual and cognitive experiences in which the complexity of our life vicissitudes is symbolically condensed. Contemporary philosophers are often engaged in detailing theories of metaphorical meaning. But a fuller account of the metaphoric function requires a comparably detailed discussion of our personal metaphoric thinking. Kittay suggests that as more contributions converge on this topic we shall probably recognize that metaphoric thinking is 'as fundamental as inductive and deductive reasoning in formulating hypotheses, providing explanations, forming categories, generating predictions, and guiding behaviour'.[44]

According to Kuhn's general argument[45] there is practically no difference between the function of the paradigm as a guiding conceptual pattern in scientific procedure and that of the root metaphor as a conceptual guideline in world hypotheses, except the more restricted scope of the former. And the support provided through the growing body of literature on the pervasiveness and indispensability of metaphor has induced more philosophers to grant Goodman's claim that metaphor 'permeates all discourse, ordinary *and special*'.[46]

The paradox of a metaphor is that it seems to affirm an identity while also somehow denying it. At the dawn of our philosophical history we see Thales affirming that 'All things are water'; in so doing he seems to be stating an identity while probably also acknowledging that the identity is not so obvious and that the difference is more conspicuous. He creatively claims an insight beyond the conventional view of things in such a way that it becomes incumbent on his philosophy to show how the 'identity' can be justified. Thus his metaphor becomes the 'root', or implicit theory, of his philosophical enterprise, and remains vitally connected to it.[47] Johnson is a representative of those who criticize the often claimed disjunction between an alleged 'context of discovery', involving psychological processes for generating new theories, and a 'context of justification' in which we reconstruct the internal logical relations of a theory.[48] The way in which the theory is developed is incorrectly regarded as having no influence upon the context of justification, as if rationality only consisted in tracing out formal relations that obtain among concepts and propositions. And this is supposed to be independent of the preliminary vicissitudes – or 'accidental' precedents – of the logical constructions; it is admitted that the content or material that we are reasoning about will somehow affect the nature of the conclusions drawn, but this is not supposed to affect the structure of rationality as such. It remains a puzzling fact that the theories of meaning and rationality dominant today do not offer any serious treatment of metaphoric imagination. We will not find it discussed in any of the standard texts on semantics or in any of the most influential studies of rationality. These works will of course acknowledge that imagination plays a role in discovery, invention and creativity but they never investigate it as (co)essential to the structure of rationality.[49] And yet this point has been amply conceded in the sense that it is generally agreed that the entire personality of a scholar is involved in research efforts. But even though this outlook is traditionally admitted, we hardly ever confront the task of thinking out the theory behind it, almost as if the enterprise were too challenging and might have devastating effects on any of our favoured dichotomies, such as, for instance, between affects and reason, cognition and participation. We commonly admit that it takes the whole person to do creative research work, but we are not to ask just how inquiry interdigitates with the live personality of the scholar.

In Aristotle's words, 'It is from metaphor that we can best get hold of something fresh.'[50] But metaphors do not necessarily exhibit their metaphoricity on the surface, and what sounds like verbal imagery may turn out to be a structural hypothesis of how a question that we heretofore lacked words for is to be understood. And, indeed, one of the ways in which the metaphors of our cognitive and interactive pursuits can be distinguished from poetical metaphors is to recognize their function of inchoate explanatory devices – even though the boundary between the poetic use and the heuristic use must ultimately remain vague. Thus by becoming more aware of the metaphoric roots of our theories we may be clearer about some of the specific questions that our theories generate.[51] The more contextualistic modes of thought seem now to introduce enough distance between the instruments of cognition and what they cognize, and thus almost come to regard sets of categories as inchoative metaphors.

Like any vigorous metaphor, the assertion itself may appear to be nonsense; confronting a novel linguistic figure we may feel paralysed in our expressive habits and try to find the points of connection between the two terms of the metaphor in order to make sense of apparent nonsense and thus appreciate its heuristic use as an agent of discovery. How a metaphor can invite, direct, and control exploration of a context in which new knowledge is implicit, though not yet manifest, is one of its salient functions. At the same time the use of a metaphor may re-order stored information in such a way that it may affect cognition. It not only activates connotations already present but quiescent; it introduces into its terms semantic features not previously available. 'When I am convinc'd of any principle, 'tis only an idea which strikes more strongly upon me', we read in Hume's celebrated *Treatise*.[52] In fact a powerful metaphor may complete its work so effectively as to obliterate its own traces. And as we test the utility of an emerging scheme we will learn to apply it in contexts other than those in which it originated. The novel 'entities' will be named by means of some neologism only when they materialize distinctly enough to be pointed to: unless a new relation is clearly understood it cannot be named. But a new relationship is precisely what we were unable to understand properly. Leondar remarks that a configuration half-perceived, a relation faintly grasped, or a concept newly emergent must be, first, named metaphorically.[53] Of course once such a newly discovered phenomenon is well understood and extricated from its originating context, the metaphor will vanish into the literal lexicon, its heuristic work completed. Through a growing awareness of the pervasive use of metaphors we may come to perceive our imaginative construction of reality (with its derivative structures of meaning) as distinct from the claim that a successful empirical test (with its feedback loops) is what conclusively warrants the acceptance of our basic view of the world.[54] An easier acceptance of this differentiation may enable us to explore a continuity in model-making which connects an expanding variety of different domains.

2   The life of language

AN EVOLUTIONARY PERSPECTIVE

To try to contextualize the discussion we could say that a small part of the known universe is inhabited by living beings, distinguishable from inanimate matter by a constellation of peculiar functions; the historical continuity of these functions we call life, and human language is one of its expressions. Since we are living creatures it is only natural that our dialogic practices and inferential patterns would emerge from our functioning as human beings; and thus philosophical attention to our biological condition should in no way be construed as an oblique devaluation of our unique capacity for the abstractions and formalizations in which we constantly progress. As we consider that life itself carries the flux of language we also notice that the study of metaphor may reinforce an awareness of the evolutionary nature of human linguisticity. By seeking to unravel the originary sources of our epistemic unfolding, metaphoric language offers precious avenues of access to the realm of our query.[1] These original sources operating in the recesses of our cultural functioning could be relinked with public language in the effort to reach for an integrated comprehension of our evolving rationality. With an increasing permeability of cultural borders, moreover, the prospect of the forthcoming years may require our views to become interrelated as parts of a coexistential philosophy.[2] As our ecosystem may be imperilled and as a global economy can be approaching, various principles of interdependence no longer constitute pious slogans but evolutionary opportunities.

Current fascination with the topic of metaphor may be associated with a growing interest in the linguisticity of living creatures as distinct from – roughly – the more 'normal' language of books; along with interest, however, there is a tacit fear of actually approaching the language of life and becoming involved with its innumerable challenges. According to Bateson, for instance, the emphasis on metaphor seems singularly appropriate to biology, for in his view it constitutes the language of nature, relationships, and historicity. Metaphor directs attention to similarity in structure across realms or events; it represents the logic of evolving organisms, and of structures by which different levels soar to further degrees of complexity, each level in a sense metaphoric for the other, thus creating what Bateson labels the 'pattern which connects'.[3]

By coming to appreciate metaphoricity we become confronted with a living language partially approachable in terms of metabolic and evolutionary processes; we can thus view language as an expression of life and alive itself – subject to growth and development, deterioration and extinction.[4] This general outlook also emerges from the later Wittgensteinian interest in forms of life. Referring to the 'countless different kinds of use of what we call "symbols", "words", "sentences"', Wittgenstein says: 'This multiplicity is not something fixed, given once for all; but new types of language, new language-games, as we may say, come into existence, and others become obsolete and get forgotten . . . Hence the term "language-*game*" is meant to bring into prominence the fact that the *speaking* of a language is part of an activity, or of a *form of life*.'[5]

Considering in conjunction forms of life and modes of language, Wheelwright suggests that what basically matters in human metaphoricity is the psychic depth at which the things of the world, whether actual or fancied, are transmuted. The transformation process that is involved might be described as a semantic motion, the idea of which is implicit in the very word 'meta-phor'. The motion, *phora*, that the word implies is a symbolic motion – the double imaginative act of outreaching and combining that essentially marks the metaphoric process.[6] Language itself is a bringing together of diversities into a unity of meaning which is contextually supported, something like a metabolic process at the symbolic level. Human metaphoricity enhances the practice of connecting diversities by juxtaposing terms which are distinct and incongruent with respect to the conceptual frame relative to which the expression is metaphorical. Thus language cannot possibly remain unaffected by time, for if it were it would be something all too detached from living creatures; what one can say is that it is remarkably stable and changes very slowly. This seems a plausible assumption; otherwise we would have to suppose that our remote ancestors had the same logical structures we now use and that linguistic structures will not vary in the possible future of humanity. In any case it would seem a category mistake to call something permanent, or timeless, when in fact it is only very stable – as locally defined, of course.

Referring to the suggestion that the meaning of words changes in accordance with transformations of our cognitive condition – such as when, for instance, we acquire more knowledge about the subject matter – Putnam remarks that this 'would not allow any words to *ever* have the same meaning, and would thus amount to an abandonment of the very notion of the word "meaning"'.[7] But this extreme view can be modified if we reflect that the notion of relative stability is not identical to the idea of permanence and that language – as an expression of life – is not immutable. If we can say that even stars have a 'life' cycle in the sense that they are born and die, we would not be so surprised by the constant transformations of logic and language – however easily they go unnoticed.

To the extent that we cultivate an awareness of belonging to the biological history of the planet we might be able to develop the sort of openness that allows us to reconnect our biological and dialogic dimensions. Whenever our phylogenetic depths are not taken into sufficient account as an inseparable aspect of the human condition we may become confined into an abstract sort of philosophical knowledge that does not measure up to the task of linking with our predicament of living creatures. It is an increasing effort of self-acceptance that makes it possible for us to acknowledge ourselves as the 'Aristotelian' 'rational animals'. As the rational component is normally focused upon and privileged in intellectual traditions, we are faced with a rationality that tends to be split off from biological history. As soon as we recognize our 'animalness' we have made the first step toward overcoming our animal condition – even without denying it. We can not go beyond our animal state by ignoring it or by refusing to attend carefully to the biological history that beats within us;[8] and acceptance is possibly the only method that allows us to do so.

As the boundaries between figurative and literal statements are perceived as *less* distinct and impermeable, and as awareness grows of metaphoric expressions evolving into literal, formal ones, we become increasingly confronted with the life cycle of our linguistic forms. Since successful metaphors range from being new-born and entirely innovative, to being worn out and extinct into literalness, we can only think of a qualitative gradient as a possible description of the distance extending between the two extremes. Metaphor is both continuous with, and distinct from, literal language. Thus the status of literalness is not a matter of universal agreement but rather a question of degree in terms of prevalence, familiarity and context.[9]

We generally disregard insensible perturbations in shifts of meaning and concentrate on conspicuous and enduring regularities. The current limits of these regularities fix the limits of the areas of meaning; and where the explanatory power of standard sense comes to an end, so does semantics. One can perceive the weakness of boundaries as a tacit threat which may sanction disquieting transformations.

If language has a life cycle and if it is not a permanent representational-semantic instrument to which we may pay a tribute by declaring it *a priori*, then it shares the precariousness, vulnerability and historicity of our own living condition. Our attention, however, is not so much directed to problems of the comparative degree of metaphoricity or literality of any linguistic form, but rather to the evolutionary quality of the language we inhabit as both living creatures *and* 'philosophers'.[10] If one could ultimately argue for the thesis that all language is evolutionary and metabolic, then both literal and metaphoric aspects, or phases, would appear as equally essential, just as stability *and* change are necessary features of living structures.

Once an utterance is produced, it becomes a public property whose management is not governed by what the speaker did or did not have in mind. As to the general question whether metaphors retain their metaphorical nature on dying, there is virtually unanimous agreement that once they are incorporated into literalness they are no longer metaphors. Cooper remarks that the more we forget that they are being used instead of a literal equivalent, the more a metaphor is extinct and the more it is alive in the vocabulary of a standard epistemology.[11] Fowler suggests that we might call this the 'amnesia scale', while Newmark points out still a different scale made up of qualifications such as 'dead', 'clichéd, 'stock', 'recent', 'original': here it looks as if age is the measure and this he calls the 'geriatric scale'.[12] The life cycle which goes from metaphor to idiom has been similarly described by Hobbs in terms of an identifiable sequence.[13] Creative and alive in the first phase, a word belonging to one conceptual domain is extended to another domain and inferential paths allow it to be interpreted; in the subsequent phase the metaphor is sufficiently familiar for the interpretive path to become established and less complex; in the third phase the metaphor is described as being already 'tired', indicating that a direct link is formed between the two domains; in the fourth and final phase the metaphor is extinct and one can no longer trace the metaphorical origin of the expression. A literal locution is thus conceived of as a way of denoting the object, action or event that was once only metaphorically connotated as such.

Metaphors, of course, may not have a cognitive content although they may originate a great deal of cognition. They can be a cause of surprise at the same level as a natural surprise except that a surprising metaphor may have sufficient success to fully develop, that is, undergo a metamorphosis whereby it subsides as a linguistic novelty and survives as literal language. At this point of its complex life cycle it may be said to convey some commensurable truth. Indeed a metaphor has to become extinct to obtain a satisfactory theory of how it works in the form of a widely shared paraphrase of the original metaphor. When Lakoff and Johnson point to *everyday* locutions such as 'defeat an argument' or 'attack a position',[14] a crucial question emerges regarding the metaphorical age or 'biological' status of such expressions. One may wonder whether they are sufficiently alive to count as metaphor or sufficiently extinct to appear as literal locutions. And a dead metaphor is such to the extent that it has been successfully absorbed into any of the standard epistemologies. The distinctive difference is probably due to the degree of familiarity of any such locution and thus it is a matter of use, attachment and hierarchization of values. In this sense, then, the metaphoricity of language is more dependent on our bio-cultural vicissitudes than upon analytical and formal adjudications. As is known, in such expressions as 'the north and south wings of the building' or 'the branches of physics', the figurative sense has entirely disappeared, and only an act of imagination could resurrect it.

THE LIFE OF LANGUAGE

As we commonly say that metaphors are born and that they pass away into literal language, we can admit that we are somehow inclined to think in terms of a life of language. And yet it might be objected that a recognition of birth, maturation, and death does not suffice to think legitimately of language as an expression of life because the biological phenomenon of procreation should also be recognizable: the idea of reproduction, in fact, is generally included in the notion of life. Should such a stringent requirement be indicated, we could invoke Peirce, who goes as far as to attribute to language reproductive capacities. And however we may interpret his suggestions, there certainly seems to be a propensity actually to think in terms of a life of language. For in fact Peirce dares ask: 'Has the word any such relation as that of father and son?'[15] Indeed he seems to attribute to language the complete and full capacities of life by seeing in it even the potential for parenting. He writes:

> Perhaps the most marvellous faculty of humanity is one which it posseses in common with all animals, I mean that of procreation. I do not allude to the physiological wonders, which are great enough, but to the fact of the production of a new human soul. Has the word any such relation as that of father and son? If I write 'Let *Kax* denote a gas furnace', *this sentence is a symbol which is creating another within itself. Here we have a certain analogy with paternity; just as much and no more as when an author speaks of his writings as his offspring, an expression which should be regarded not as metaphorical but merely as general.*[16]

Thus, in his view, the fertility of language does not so much belong to the realm of metaphoric constructions but rather to the domain of common beliefs. And he further insists:

> It may be our knowledge of the relation of parentage is not sufficient to say positively, but it may be that there is a great analogy to the parental relation. If it be so, then as one of these symbols affords the content and the other the sphere of the new symbol, one parent ought to give the *feelings*, the other the *energies* of the child.[17]

In these remarks he seems to regard linguistic links as a connubial, procreational enterprise – no less than that.

Resonating with these suggestions we could no longer afford to regard the functions of language as inanimate objects of research, detached from the sort of life which generates them and separated from the challenges of survival. And in Einstein's view, even knowledge seems to exist in two forms: 'lifeless, stored in books, and alive, in the consciousness of humans. The second form of existence is after all the essential one; the first, indispensable as it may be, occupies only an inferior position.'[18]

If we now concede a measure of coextensiveness between the notions of linguistic life and animate existence, we would also appreciate that the idea of organic unity is frequently used as an epistemic criterion, instrumental for the comparative attributions of value in the most disparate disciplines; thus we presumably resort to the idea of life in order to create valuational guidelines.[19] Over a disparate array of situations the *degree* of organic unity seems to express our intuitive notion of the degree of intrinsic value. Nozick suggests that, in fact, the idea of organic unity usually functions as the common strand to value across different domains.[20] Within the theoretical realm we quite often refer to the phenomenon of organic unity: a good theory is one that closely links (in explanatory fashion) diverse and apparently disparate data via its tightly unifying relationships. Similarly – in Nozick's view – one general and unified theory tends to appear more valuable, other things being equal, than a group of separate and discrete theories on the same topic. In the perspective of the individual person, sentience and then consciousness add new possibilities of unification over time and at a time, and self-consciousness being an 'I', appears as an especially tight mode of unification.[21]

In this outlook, change, novelty, and the breaking of bonds may come to appear as the destruction of premature unities.[22] In fact, whenever new and unexpected dimensions are introduced, a greater diversity can be integrated, for it would not be so extraordinary to unify a few closely resembling elements.[23] Old structures are discarded in order that new and more complex paradigms of unification can be introduced. The common purpose of the most disparate processes of transcending limits would thus function as an effort to reach a new and higher degree of organic unity. Metaphors are at the same time holistic and analysable, in Coulmas's view, for they are basically composed of freely occurring units whose global meaning cannot be reduced simply to the meanings of these units.[24] Nozick, of course, does admit that it is difficult to know how 'to take account of the thematic material in a measure of diversity, and of thematic relations in a measure of unifiedness'.[25] And yet he suggests that holding fixed the degree of unifiedness of the material, the degree of organic unity varies directly with the degree of diversity of the material being unified. And also:

> Holding fixed the degree of diversity of the material, the degree of organic unity varies directly with the degree of unifiedness (induced) in that material. The more diverse the material, however, the harder it is to unify it to a given degree.[26]

Empirical psychologists and neuroscientists are often puzzled by 'philosophical' questions and perhaps wish no one would ask them, even though researchers persist in obliquely asking them: these are the questions of 'organic unity' that ultimately motivate the enterprise and tacitly support its morale. The biochemical problems of neurotransmission or the questions of hemispheric dominance present their own intrinsic interest, to be sure, but if there were no hope that integrating enough data about our brains might lead to knowledge of our own minds' life, enthusiasm for such reaearch would not be as lively as it is.

A LANGUAGE FOR LIFE

Certain areas of culture seem 'cognitively' to cope with life problems so efficiently as to relieve other domains of thought from these burdens. Such 'lesser' areas of our culture almost protect the lucid intraepistemic games of the 'higher' branches by steadily coping with existential vicissitudes and foreign affairs on their behalf. It is unlikely that any epistemology will begin to cope with problems of external relations and of its own inner depths as long as the more hermeneutic disciplines will laboriously perform this function. If the 'lesser' philosophical language were to monitor its inclination to be hyperfunctional and to solve problems for the sedate and solemn epistemologies, it is possible that the more 'serious' (lucid and coherent) intellectual domains of culture too might have to confront their hypo-functional policies. Eventually, certain areas of philosophy may no longer avoid an increasing number of difficult questions on the grounds that they are peripheral and not to the point; such issues, in fact, are usually described as tangentially connected, insufficiently clear, unfocused, inappropriately articulated, excessively controversial, etc.

When cultural conditions are relatively stable, our western rationality exhibits a fair equilibrium between hermeneutics and epistemology. One is versatile, imaginative, and sensitive; the other is well identifiable, lucid, and coherent. When problems arise, however, coexistence is transformed into a challenge. Indeed, the higher status of epistemology is commonly unchallenged in a culture whose technology largely enables us to cope with and control our world. As long as hermeneutics will secretly covet and pursue the 'superior' status of epistemology, the latter will be able to afford to function in its dignified independence and will repeatedly proclaim its inviolable boundaries of rationality.[27] And this is still another reinforcing function performed by the hermeneutic disciplines – thus a task from which epistemology is relieved.[28] Should hermeneutics stop tacitly admiring epistemology, and become creatively concerned with its own potential, it is possible that the 'superior' domains will begin to acknowledge their vital needs for contacts, closeness, and fertile coexistence. Hence, the situation we face does not so much induce us to question the status of either one of the areas, but rather the interactive relation between the two.

The role of metaphoric language is more suited to the safeguard of a general reasonableness then to the affirmation of an autonomous rationality. There are life situations in which humans resort to metaphoric expressions designed to maintain a dialogic continuity and to relinquish identifications with 'autonomous' epistemic constructions. Indeed, dominant streams of culture may achieve control but not quite autonomy because, by themselves, they cannot confront the conditions of dependency which derive from our belonging to life. The illuminating function ascribed to certain epistemic aspects of our rationality is often dependent upon the auxiliary functions performed by the lesser aspects of culture, those in charge of 'humanizing' our knowledge. The dominant rational styles may thus come to recognize that their intellectual freedom – coming forth in the translucent coherence of arguments – is only operative within circumscribed domains of literalness. In order to stabilize domination, standard epistemologies need increasingly to delegate the tasks of creating links with alien domains. The most significant interactions may derive from the necessity to depend upon functions which are at the same time needed and denied.

The propensity for abstractions entailing the elimination of an increasing number of 'irrelevant' variables almost seems to confer an absolute freedom in the struggle for intellectual dominance and success. And yet, whatever epistemic dominance we could envisage, it would virtually operate in a vacuum, increasingly detached from life. The lesser aspects of culture fulfil innumerable tasks from which the dominant areas of rationality are relieved. The question is whether it is necessary to deal with these indispensable servants who cannot too easily be ignored or eliminated. Even though a tradition of literalness allowing for convenient internal communication creates the setting for peaceful working conditions, at the same time it requires a symbiosis with other areas of culture performing functions of linkage. Within normal knowledge no confrontation is ever invited with alien languages, styles and assumptions. Their celebrated rational independence is not so much proclaimed as it is out of the question. And in these traditions one may opt for migrating to a different domain of literalness without even attempting to develop metaphoric connections that may reveal serious problems of translation, linking and coexistence.

If knowledge was originally a successful human response to the difficulties of survival, it is now transformed into a human production which expands in an autonomous fashion and which unhaltingly develops on its own terms; and even if we draw from such expanding intellectual wealth, we frequently recognize that it is of little avail in coping with the challenges of self-creation or with the more serious problems of human coexistence.[29] The distinctively rational knowledge which differentiates itself from the 'soft minded' approaches is not so strong as it would like to appear. It is in fact the sort of thinking that succumbs most easily when confronted with the slightest pressure from the vestiges of the reptilian brain that operates alongside cognitive structures in human beings. The major theatres of western rationality are periodically shaken by horribly destructive festivals which unfold with total indifference toward the 'powerful' thinking that finds itself incapable of resisting the achaic mechanisms of human nature. This powerful thought nevertheless resumes its usual logomachies as soon as the period of terror has come to an end.

The lack of hospitality to this sort of issue may be due to an unobtrusive shift of the whole outlook, a shift from the construction of communicative meaning to the processing of detached information. But, in fact, as Davidson points out, the concept of meaning would have no application if there were not cases of successful communication 'and any further use we give to the notion of meaning depends on the existence of such cases'.[30] One may otherwise come to believe that computation is the ruling outlook and that computability is a necessary feature of a good theoretical question: a well shaped philosophical question should thus enable us to order, combine and commensurably compare our precoded information. And yet the system that does all these things can be deaf and blind with respect to whether the language which is dealt with is 'words' from an infant (actually the non-speaker) or from a moribund (actually approaching silence rather than argument). It is almost as if a tacit revulsion for any contact with life and historicity secretly dominated our epistemic culture. There is hardly any point in attempting to describe the tremendous advantages of cognitive developments in both hominization and individual ontogeny – which indeed constitute the subject matter of a profusion of contributions. This evolutionary story is generally celebrated in such a way as to ignore the problems that it creates. These problems are likely to be overlooked because they do not pertain to the sort of language that successfully advances in the mainstream of accredited epistemologies – thus creating forms of scholasticity ever more detached from the complexities of human life.[31]

Theories of psychology and epistemology provide the current historical manifestation or 'appearance' of our mind's life. But then, an excessively detached way of looking at language not only conceals the life of language but also remains unaware of this concealment. Indeed an excessive gap between linguistic analysis and linguistic life remains largely unnoticed and as a consequence philosophers may see through their instruments of inquiry no more than the literal facts of whatever epistemology is current. A tradition of inquiry may ultimately become a screen which not only conceals the fact that our linguistic life is reduced to an artefact, but also obscures this concealment. Of course we are inclined to think that the mind's life is at the heart of our inquiries and that it is constantly being reflected through different disciplines. But one may also suspect that not only is linguistic life con-fused (etymologically, poured together) with whatever is the dominant epistemology, but also that it is reflected in the way in which a culture organizes its self-perpetuating strategies. Thus we may presume that the way in which an age constructs its view of the world and of human interactions basically represents our philosophy of language; this philosophy, in turn, makes the world a reality of reflection, the product of its way of mirroring things – especially when accurate representation is its ultimate concern. The thematization of language no longer indicates a sharp separation between modern linguistic knowledge and ancient linguistic ignorance, as a way of dividing the absence of a linguistic awareness from its presence:[32] it may simply enhance a new appearance of linguistic life. The different disciplines exploring language generate a contingent appearance of linguistic life; that is the way in which our live linguisticity comes to appear in different domains of research. Our philosophies of language thus function as the producers of the contemporary version of the life of language.

We could tentatively define philosophical maturity as the relinking of intellectual operations with the embodied core of interpersonal and inner experiences. In spite of the classical separation of the two modes – epitomized in the distinction between the celebrated pure reason and practical reason – recent concerns inaugurated by the study of metaphor reflect a move towards a reintegration of the two approaches. Such a reintegration can be conducive to a broader recontextualization of intellectual processes, such that it might include the operations of affects and profound beliefs.

Our metaphoric efforts represent ways of trying to inhabit fields which previously appeared as opaque and unapproachable. But then, once we inhabit a certain area of culture, whether it is the most objectively quantifiable or the most speculative, it remains a singular struggle not to regard our vantage point as yielding the more realistic and more correct version of the 'true nature' of whatever is being investigated. Despite our best scientific education, we may experience a fundamental disinclination to reorient our perspective in order to accommodate that of our interlocutor. And yet, whatever it is that induces this difficulty, it in fact constitutes the sort of issue which we regard as worthy of the utmost attention. It may be especially difficult, for instance, to abandon the conviction that ours is the more correct approach to 'truth', especially when a discrepancy emerges regarding the way in which we are individually perceived. In psychoanalytic culture this difference of perception constitutes the central axis of transference: another's view of ourselves is as interesting and as revealing as our own. If we shift our attention to listening more accurately to the metaphoric allusions directed to us, we may learn more about our interlocutor's inner world and even about ourselves. And whenever there is a measure of struggle, however evanescent and remote, it may be an indicator that we are trying to guide the other to look at reality our way. And the sort of reality which emerges from the discrepancy between 'standard' perceptions and personal perceptions is usually metaphorically conveyed. There may thus be a new opening for philosophy the moment we become more concerned with the discrepancies than with the topic of discussion itself.[33] And this is not due to a lack of interest in coherence or truth conditions but to an equal interest in the specifics of inner linguistic life.[34]

Although creativity involves the construction of novel combinations, creativity is also required in the process of construal – in the courage of choosing to construe, rather than waste, the metaphoric attempts of interlocutors. What we call originality can be much less the act of the first one to generate a thought than the readiness of the second to 'choose' to develop the value of what he listens to. But, of course, it may not be the case of all interactive co-operations that the construers are more the geniuses than the generators of enlightening metaphors. Indeed some creative minds rarely offer poor suggestions and their construers ultimately reproduce what they receive. In still other cases the generation of new ideas can be highly erratic in its deployment, thus demanding the rigour of accurate and perceptive construers. There appears to be a metabolic exchange between fertility of imagination *and* interpretive construal; a process of creation seems to require both and seems, moreover, subject to fluctuations in how much of each gets done by each collaborator.

THE LIMITS OF A 'LIFELESS' PHILOSOPHY

While, in a sense, our organism is the most abiding presence in our lives, it is also marked by its 'cultural' absence; as it has often been remarked, our western culture almost seems characterized by a disembodied style of knowledge. A tendency toward disembodiment may also be seen as a central strain of our intellectual history: from the Platonic emphasis on the liberated soul to the Cartesian focus on the *cogito* experience, from the Kantian transcendental apparatus to the logico-linguistic turn of philosophy, our cultural heritage gravitates toward a vision of the human self within which an 'immaterial' rationality tends to prevail. Our bodily condition is relegated to a secondary and frequently oppositional role while an incorporeal reason is systematically brought into focus. Part of current linguistic philosophy seems tacitly to support the view of an immaterial language emanating from some alien organism, ultimately unrelated to human linguisticity. The Cartesian portrayal of our extended being as the negative aspect of knowledge is often strengthened by the experiential prominence of our organism precisely at times of crisis or illness. And of course this dualism can be easily strengthened by a selective blindness and deafness towards anything or anyone associable with the subrational, 'negative' polarity located in the *res extensa*.[35]

Forms of subtle and pervasive dualism are the heritage of an ontology in which the irremediable separation of mind and body mandates a separate philosophical discussion for whatever can be regarded as cognitive, representationalist and logical. A joint thematization of metaphor and life may however provide a potential mode of escape from the excesses of dualistic cognitive constraints. In so far as our living organism is restricted to its physicalist, 'hardware' description, those aspects of behaviour involving linguistic representation and cognition are necessarily upgraded and segregated into an incorporeal area which we call the mind.[36] And this is what a joint thematization of language and life can finally subvert. If our biological existence is an instrument of experience, then one need not ascribe cognitive capabilities to a disembodied mind.

The induced 'experience' of an abstract thought and of a lifeless language provide a powerful frame for the idea of a rational mind as incorporeal. In the ensuing philosophy the life of a thinker is conceptually and experientially effaced. This is conducive, in turn, to the view of language as a disembodied activity engaged in by an incorporeal mind. Ideally, in an adequate philosophical contribution no evidence of authorial presence should transpire: it ought to be a sample of pure argumentation, to the production of which an author should sacrifice all personal identity. According to Danto this implies a vision of ourselves as vehicles for the transmission of impersonal 'truths' and a vision of philosophy as constituted of isolatable, difficult, but not finally intractable problems, which, if not altogether soluble by means of neat papers, can be brought closer to resolution.[37] 'The paper is then an impersonal report of limited results for a severely restricted readership, consisting of those who have some use for that result, since they are engaged with the writers of the paper in a collaborative enterprise, building the edifice of philosophical knowledge.'[38]

Expressions suggesting our physical disappearance enhance models of disembodied and lifeless rationality. The more this outlook is accepted and valued, the more our linguistic modes of experience are oriented into a 'lifeless' direction. And our western reverence for a disembodied language shapes a variety of cultural experiences whereby a structuring loop is established. Our belief in the detachment of language and life induces further disassociative expressions such as a generalized propensity to abandon personal language in favour of public linguistic forms. This in turn intensifies our experience of language as dissociated from life, thus confirming the initial premiss in the style of self-fulfilling prophecies. Such a divisive outlook, moreover, can be primarily intended for domination rather than for knowledge, as if the ultimate purpose were not so much accurate representation as easier ways of control. A disembodied language exhibits an arrogance which contaminates our relations to other animate or inanimate creatures. If language is identified primarily with intellection, then obviously infants and animals, plants and water do not have one. 'Mindless' creatures can thus be regarded as mere objects of knowledge or as targets of indoctrination by a superior representationalist language. This outlook that holds us captive may be employed to justify all manner of appropriation and control. As Leder points out, 'The Cartesian conceptual "death of nature" helps us lead to the real destruction of our ecosystem.'[39]

All of these difficulties may effectively be eschewed by simply ignoring pain, growth, illness; by denying life altogether and producing a philosophy which has

ng to do with it. It is in fact the painful body that emerges from disappearance
ecome a thematic object. Leder remarks that pain exerts a power that reverber-
s throughout experience and which transforms our relations with both the world
and ourselves: 'There is a disruption of intentional linkages and a constriction of
our spatiality and temporality to their embodied center. The painful body emerges
as alien presence, its telic demand reorganizing around its ongoing projects of
interpretation and repair.'[40]

By jointly thematizing life *and* metaphoricity a different scenario can eventually
emerge. Cooper acutely remarks that to go about uttering wildly false sentences in
the knowledge that this is what they are is to add an activity to be assimilated to
other things we just do: 'Metaphor, after all, does present a problem, for on most
accounts of why we speak, metaphor should not occur at all.'[41] This is so probably
because the cognitive accounts that we seek, or produce, are so segregated from a
caring concern for our life cycle that they are non-vital and non-maturational: they
are just-sophical. If instead of identifying with 'professional scholars' we invoked
images of 'thoughtful adults' concerned with new-born infants and dying elders,
we would probably think that metaphorical talk is all that matters. We customarily
draw examples from narrow standard situations, usually remote from the enigmatic
complexities of our lives. It is possible that a different linguistic repertoire could
generate a different philosophical discourse. If we hypothesize a philosophical
practice stipulating that examples can only be drawn from marginal situations as
distinct from 'normal' styles of life and standards of mental health, then profoundly
different philosophical concerns might come into focus.

It is true that severing language from life is incongruent with many aspects of
lived experience; and, as such, this variant of classical philosophy functions to the
detriment of attending to the life-world. And yet it is from the very experience of
our life-world that this dualism is first brought forth. It is precisely our corporeal
condition which gives rise to experiences that lend our dualist account apparent
support. This 'support' appears to be convincing in an outlook of body effacement
in which language appears almost as if it were the perfect substitute for the classical
purity of the mind. When our customarily absent body becomes the focus of
thematic attention it is often as the result of another sort of absence: that of a desired
or 'normal' state of the body's unproblematic unity with the self.[42] And as life
poses problems in times of disruption we further associate our embodied condition
with negativity and compulsory situations. This outlook generates a hidden and
powerful gestalt which tacitly rules our intellectual vicissitudes. To use Wittgenstein's metaphor, we may have become ensnared inside a view of language as
something disincarnate and lifeless: 'A picture held us captive. And we could not
get outside it, for it lay in our language and language seemed to repeat it to us
inexorably.'[43]

As metaphoricity and life are jointly thematized a different scenario of open
systems is gradually emerging. In exploring our linguistic vicissitudes we can in
fact make use of two different approaches: one deriving from a tradition of closed
systems, and one emanating from the necessity of open systems. The first type of
model can easily be linked to the mainstream intellectual heritage, whereas the

other recently thematized approach is perhaps seeking some organizing theoretical model which might account for its complexity and possible inscrutability. In fact if we think of our beliefs and desires as linked to a symmetrical, all-or-nothing logic rooted in our unconscious life, we will understand that they can be projected towards infinity, and that it can be necessary to *fight* for them as they constitute 'immense' vital issues.[44] In this view it becomes easier to appreciate the pervasive nature of the common metaphor explored by Lakoff and Johnson: 'Language is fight.'[45] Indeed it is, if we accept that language is a biological expression of our ethological life.[46] If we keep in mind the symmetrical logic of our instinctual, unconscious life it becomes likewise easier to understand why in all areas of culture, including philosophy, idealizations (and ensuing conflicts) are tacitly at work no matter how careful we are in constantly making a show of critical detachment.[47] In idealization the individual self tends toward the infinitely small while an abstract entity – thinker, theory, school – is endowed with quasi-infinite greatness in one way or another.

In a perspective of open systems, Danto suggests that we should not overlook the way in which philosophy functions as literature does, not in the sense of extravagant verbal artefacts, but as engaging with readers in striving towards some sense of organic unity.[48] Literature, in fact, can be regarded as being about the reader at the moment of reading through the process of reading. In his view the texts require the act of reading in order to be complete, and it is as readers of a certain type that philosophical texts address us all; the variety of philosophical texts implies a correspondingly great variety of possible kinds of readers, and hence of theories of what we are in the complex attitude of reading something.[49] The propensity to neglect the reader is a derivative of an inclination to leave creatures of the sort readers exemplify outside of the situation which the text purports to cope with. Some outlooks almost constitute examples of such an oversight, as if supported by a view of philosophical writing which renders the reader nearly evanescent; it is a view which sustains a sort of 'disembodied professional con-science', in Danto's language. He also remarks that science can get away with this largely because even when it is about readers, it 'is not about them as readers and so lacks the internal connection philosophical texts demand because they are about their readers *as* readers'.[50] If we rotate the discussion in this sense, then we come to appreciate an inescapable live relationship between any living beings engaged in *philo*sophy in its real sense.

We could ask if only works of art are autobiographical or if cognitive pursuits as well reflect diverse channels for expressing one's experience of life. Possibly even the most formal and regulated strivings of humans are aimed to try to endure beyond the limited moment and ultimately to fulfil a dream of immortality. Life's vicissitudes can perhaps be operative in shaping even the highest intellectual achievements of a culture. And the project of achieving a transcendental rationality is possibly first suggested by the inherent finitude of our life cycle. The 'idealist' project may in fact represent a way out of the challenges of our embodied condition. Traditional philosophy attempted to inquire into the ultimate principles and inermost structures, tacitly assuming a status quo of reality and of its objectivity.

Overwhelmed by the inexorable power of nature, original ontologies sought in the notion of 'being' an ever present principle suitable to encompass whatever may be the case. Modern philosophers shifted the quest for the basic principles to the constitutive power of the mind, which has come to be systematically regarded as essentially abstract, almost transcendent, detached from the survival concerns sustaining human understanding. Our life as organisms has thus been ignored inasmuch as it has been denied any role in the development of the 'intangible' logico-linguistic connections. *And even questions of gendered thinking can only appear as totally inappropriate in a lifeless philosophy.* The mind has, thus, come to be regarded as providing the explanation of how the world emerges within the 'transcendental' circuit of human functioning, one in which nature is seen as an ever self-renewing constructive project of knowledge. In a lifeless perspective the clarity of the contrasts between different views of the world would thus depend on regarding epistemic schemes as fixed, and on supposing that changes may come about by simply redistributing truth values over different sentences.

LANGUAGE AS METABOLIC PROCESS

That we fail to regard language as part of (human) life is possibly due to a common perspectival 'error' whereby we also fail to consider human creatures and their cultural institutions as relatively temporary and evolving aspects of hominization: thus the 'enthusiasm' for metaphoric language, which has characterized the last decades, may be tacitly derived from a desire to relink (structures of) language *and* (forms of) life. Interest in metaphor may thus indicate the emergence of new perspectives within which to discuss our global intellectual functions throughout the life cycle of individuals and cultures. In our western tradition these functions have been described primarily by reference to logical or objective forms, and generally contrasted with affectual, organismic processes. Recent contributions, on the other hand, seem to suggest that theories based on the assumption of the primacy of representational ways of knowledge offer an incomplete and possibly distorting picture of our experience.[51] Rather than continuing basically to identify mental life with functions of objective cognition, emerging theories of thought and language can be seen as rooted in a duality of modes: interactive and representational. And even though these modes may often appear to be incompatible and in competition, still they are essential to our being, and virtually function in a synergic relationship. Live metaphors inspiring innovative thought and metaphors extinguished into the formalities of literalness are constant witnesses of the metabolic nature of our culture. A balanced dialogue between the two styles is what possibly sustains our striving toward intellectual maturity. It has frequently been noticed that a new mode of thinking tends to be expressed in figurative language. In an evolutionary perspective the term 'metaphor' should not be taken in its more restricted sense of figure of speech, but rather as an indicator of our cultural metabolism, for, obviously, it is not just a simile with the omission of the preposition 'like'. It is rather the use of one part of experience to illuminate another, to help us approach something that only seems to exist if we can somehow symbolize it and use the symbolization. And the metaphorical element, or term, may ultimately be absorbed into what it is a metaphor of. But this is no surprise because in our sequence of metaphoric extensions we tend actually to shape the cultural world we wish to inhabit.

Certain excessive theories of empiricism may conspire with dreams of a comprehensive logic to direct attention away from the facts of linguistic ambiguity and of the transformational processes of language; they generally induce us to gravitate towards a more formal analysis of language in terms of exact and stable meanings. But, when (relative) stability is tacitly and erroneously equated with some sort of permanence, then, of course, the function of human metaphoricity is aptly eschewed, devalued, and regarded as auxiliary or decorative. The perplexity engendered by any form of scholastic turn-over is not due to a recognition that cultural life is inconceivable in a static way, but to the frustration of the culturally induced desire for some permanent basis of philosophical departure, whether in language or in facts; this is a basis that we could use as an Archimedean point for a global control of our view of the world. The fact that we are living creatures participating in an evolving culture attracts our attention predominantly at times of serious crises, reminding us of human finitude and of the potential extinction of life. For it is at such times that we linguistically try to articulate the force of our physical condition and strive to exhibit its role in experience. But then, a maturing philosophy reorganizing itself to be hospitable to the 'alien' presence of metaphor becomes open for disquieting in-depth movements in which even time boundaries vanish as the distancing 'space' of time seems to disappear. Indeed, Wordsworth's much quoted metaphor, 'The child is father to the man', presents a conflation of times and relations before the mind can accommodate it, logically and chronologically, as the conflation of times and identities in the life cycle of a single individual. Explanatory efforts detached from metaphoricity would be difficult to conceive, for in order to try to describe the unknown, we must resort to concepts that we know, and that is the basic effect of metaphor: an unusual juxtaposition of the familiar and the unfamiliar. Arbib remarks that one may, for instance, try to convey an understanding of the brain in terms of two common approaches such as the cybernetic metaphor: 'Humans are machines', or the evolutionary metaphor: 'Humans are animals'. [52] But of course, it would be unjustified to suppose that one may thus downgrade the differences as we, in fact, invent metaphors in order really to learn something from the putative similarities. Thus, when he calls his book *The Metaphorical Brain*, Arbib does not imply that the understanding of the brain that it affords will be any less 'real' than that afforded by other books; rather he tries to make explicit the aid that metaphor constantly provides, and to lessen the risk of misunderstanding that results whenever an implicit metaphor is mistaken for reality.[53] Our failure to make explicit, or even look for, the aid that a seminal metaphor provides, not only induces us to mistake an implicit metaphor for reality but also unwittingly to strive to impose such an error on our interlocutors. We may thus be tacitly perpetrating an endemic violence of which we are scarcely aware.

An interactive metaphoric view of theoretical models may synergically function with the persuasion that all observation is theory-laden. In this perspective it is difficult to think that some observational uses of language are irreducibly literal and constant with respect to the transformations of our linguistic contexts. Equating interactive and metaphoric processes, Arbib and Hesse claim that 'scientific revolutions are, in fact, metaphoric revolutions'[54] and that 'The interaction view sees all language, including the scientific, as dynamic.'[55] But then, the term 'dynamic' may sound a rather defensive, timid way of expressing what is urging us on in our culture, namely the growing 'fearsome' awareness that language is not only dynamic but actually alive as an essential aspect of the life of our minds and cultures. 'Dynamic' could be a rather neutral adjective borrowed from the vocabulary of mechanics, whereas the term 'living' is more dangerously linked with our temporary habitation of history, our participation in the immensity of life, and our inexorable finitude. Language is thus more complex and multidimensional than we are prepared to admit. Although aspects of it may be amenable to explanation in terms of logical deductions, algorithms or syntactical combinations, we increasingly come to appreciate that even these features of our linguisticity do interact with affectually generated metaphorical processes. And this is probably one of the fascinating challenges emerging at the climax of the linguistic turn.

In a synoptic view we could regard as metaphorical the variety of messages which are exchanged between different aspects of our living structure, each endowed with its own code and specific organization. In this view we could come to think of metaphoric links as extending from our biological metabolism on to the life of our minds. We could for instance think of our unconscious dynamics as enhancing the generation of metaphoric messages in terms of strategies for their expression; however unaware we may be of them, they constitute the links which reconnect nature and culture. Our biological nature projects itself into culture which in turn generates metaphoric guidelines for the inhabitation of our world. But then, it is a world that is now primarily cultural in the sense that the 'existential' dangers are feared as much as biological crises. An awareness of embodied affects thus seems a condition for our attempt to reach for a more integrated view of ratiocination. It is not a matter of arguing about the prevalence of the literal over the metaphorical, or of the digital versus the analogical, or of the normal as against the revolutionary since all of these issues can be regarded as co-essential aspects of an evolving rationality. Our reasoning involves in fact preconceptual and non-propositional structures of experience that can be metaphorically projected and propositionally elaborated to shape our human ways of thinking. Metaphorical projections of our physical condition are not arbitrary but rather are significantly determined by our biological functions and affectual vicissitudes. Experience in this context is thus to be regarded in an open sense so as to include emotional, biological and historical dimensions. The nature of our embodiment helps us create the metaphors through which we organize multiple experiences. Our thinking cannot be viewed as 'pure reason' inasmuch as it is a derivative of our ways of coping with contingent problems of self-formation. Inasmuch as we are living beings there cannot be too much pure reason. Our thinking is even often inconspicuously ancillary to behaviour, beliefs and desires. To try honestly to explore our human thinking is to come to terms with the biological conditions from which it derives and with the practices in which it is implicated. The abstract study of our thinking is as exact and coherent as it is detached from life's vicissitudes. But then, *in vitro*, rationality could be a sad travesty of our living thought.

A no-ownership theory of thought may ultimately undercut even our concept of self. Far from demonstrating the existence of a mind distinct from the body, Cartesian-like arguments render the concept of mind redundant. In Eiser's view, once we allow for the possibility of disembodied arguments and experiences (or indeed insist that these forms of language are the only topics worthy of philosophical attention), we add nothing by trying to argue that these thoughts belong to a disembodied mind.[56] It is not simply contingent that the mind is 'in' the body as it is not a substance that could be extracted from a living creature without damage. It can thus be misleading to consider linguistic interactions as if they were in principle immune from the living condition from which they emanate.

3   The interdigitation of fields

In an attempt to explore questions of interconnections between heterogeneous domains we could initially invoke Davidson's view of metaphor. He basically indicates that metaphoric language consists of a special use of literal meanings aimed to intimate or suggest something that might otherwise be ignored;[1] a 'something' that comes to 'exist' because a certain language generates it. And as Cavell notes, Davidson's account has the virtue of linking the *verbal* to the *non-verbal* arts[2] – two non-homogeneous modes of human ingenuity.

But the domain of the 'non-verbal arts' may include a wide spectrum of non-propositional manifestations ranging from our quasi-biological interactions to affectual vicissitudes, from organismic experiences to developments of image schemata. To the extent that we regard our metaphoric potential as one of the instruments for coping with life we may come to see metaphor as actually connecting such dissimilar human domains as the verbal and the non-verbal: an approach which is strongly suggestive of a 'metabolic' view of language as an emanation of our embodied condition.

Heterogeneous as they may be, even stimuli deriving from external sources and images emerging from our psychic depths are commonly thought to interdigitate in our different ways of shaping reality. Laboriously struggling with the question of imagination as a function of knowledge, Kant is forced to admit that the schematizing activity of imagination 'must be *pure*, that is void of all empirical content, and yet at the same time . . . it must be *sensible*.'[3] And no two factors more alien than external derivatives and transcendental schemes possibly emanating from the deeper strata of the self could be proposed as coessential in our perceptual activity.

Writings belonging to the 'species *loosely ruminative* and *comparative-historical* rather than to the species *strictly argumentative* and *systematic-analytical*'[4] may be generally regarded as more hospitable to the interdigitation of heterogeneous discourses; in one such enterprise Strawson brings together Hume's and Kant's view of imagination, arguing that for both philosophers imagination is conceived as a 'connecting or uniting power',[5] thus, basically, as a metaphoric 'force' capable of linking non-homogeneous domains.

'The metaphoric sentence expresses a proposition [says Cavell] but the *seeing as* response that it inspires is not a propositional attitude.'[6] But then, something which is not a propositional attitude may refer to the immense variety of human vicissitudes that emanate from our organismic nature. Then, indeed, life and language may be seen as interacting in a process which is more metabolic on the side of life and more metaphoric on the side of language.

We may recall that the word 'theory' etymologically derives from the Greek verb *teorein*, to see – so deeply ingrained is our western visual metaphor. But then, if metaphors inspire our way of seeing things, by inducing ulterior 'seeing-as responses', they also influence our subsequent ways of theorizing about the world; a circuit is thus created linking the propositional domain to the non-propositional aspects of our mind's life, which in turn generates further propositional develop-ments.[7] Metaphors, then, seem to transform not so much our intellectual beliefs as the way we perceive situations – and thus relate to them. By creating statements that prompt ulterior insights we may be induced to see a fact in a different scheme; and if the 'seeing as' response that is generated by a metaphoric proposition is not a propositional attitude, it might be any of the affectual attitudes that shape, or even constrain, our outlook on life. In this sense, then, propositional and non-pro-positional expressions are to be viewed as inextricably interwoven in our cognitive growth.

As Johnson points out, a distinction is often drawn between an alleged *context of discovery*, involving psychological processes for generating new ideas, and a *context of justification* in which we reconstruct the internal logical relations of a theory.[8] The *way* in which the theory is imagined and developed is generally regarded as having no influence upon the context of justification – as if reasoning only consisted in tracing out the formal relations that obtain among words, mental representations, concepts and propositions; such logical reconstruction and evalu-ation of rational judgements is thus inaccurately supposed to be independent of their preceding events, almost as if the antecedents of a theory were a purely accidental set of circumstances.[9]

In connection with the 'seeing as' response mentioned by Cavell, it is worth recalling that Wittgenstein is particularly impressed by the case where images undergo a change of aspect under one's very eyes, the case where one is suddenly struck by a new aspect of the situation. Significantly, Strawson pauses to wonder why this does impress Wittgenstein so much: to see a different aspect of a thing, in this sense, 'is, in part, to *think* of it in a certain way, to be disposed to *treat* it in a certain way, to give certain sorts of explanations or accounts of what you see, in general to *behave* in certain ways.'[10] And Wittgenstein makes several attempts to produce expressions which may enlighten just such a relation; he says, for instance: 'Hence the flashing of an aspect on us seems half visual experience, half thought';[11] 'Is it a case of both seeing and thinking? Or an amalgam of the two, as I should almost like to say?';[12] 'What I perceive in the dawning of an aspect is not a property of the object . . . It is almost as if "seeing the sign in this context" were an echo of a thought. "The echo of a thought in sight" – one would like to say.'[13] Besides these formulations, which he calls 'metaphors', Strawson makes his own expressive attempts by suggesting that 'the visual experience is *irradiated* by, or *infused* with, the concept; or it becomes *soaked* with the concept.'[14]

And the more we wonder about 'seeing as', the less we can rest with the customary connections – thus inclining to go as far as actually to envisage a Wittgensteinian 'amalgam' of propositional and non-propositional experiences. An 'amalgam of seeing and thinking' seems to indicate a disposition to conceive of such links as creating a logic of continuity. This way of thinking could challenge the map of an internalized culture that depends upon 'unbreakable' distinctions between domains – domains classified as either experiential or formal, synthetic or *a priori*, bodily or mental, instinctual or rational, in an endless sequence of comparable and irreducible dichotomies.

If we can develop a view of our relations with things and persons as more complex and intriguing than the one induced by an 'avoidant' style of dichotomies, we would then become involved with a variety of revealing interactive activities which indeed incline toward an inchoate 'logic' of interdigitation and continuity between hitherto alien domains. And as 'aliens' are somehow disquieting, it is perhaps not so much a problem of acumen but rather a question of courage and probity.

After lengthy passages which Wittgenstein devotes to the discussion of *seeing as* and of changes of aspect, he finally remarks that 'We find certain things about seeing puzzling because we do not find the whole business of seeing puzzling enough.'[15] The whole discussion, then, points to 'a peculiarly intimate link between the momentary perception and something else; but the "something else" is behaviour, and so the upshot seems remote from the peculiarly intimate link we laboured to establish in connection with Kant's use of the term "imagination" . . . *But is it really so remote*?'[16] But if we can identify an authentic opening in philosophy, allowing for links between propositional and non-propositional domains, the path is then open for the exploration of innumerable and *not so remote* exchanges between language and life. If we begin to thematize areas of propositional language regarded as capable of inducing phenomena that are not propositional, an eventful theoretical connection is established between language and life – the relationship we are ultimately concerned with, even though in different degrees of remoteness. A metaphorical statement, for instance, can be regarded as capable of making an inchoate person see – or fail to see – life as worth attempting, or the world worth exploring. Conversely, the unnoticed philosophical avoidance, and consequent misuse, of our metaphoric functions may induce an epistemic degradation that eventually affects visible forms of cultural life.

We may recall in this context Cavell's suggestion that a metaphoric use of language could be regarded as a case of saying something literally false which none the less inspires a revelation. She says,

> Most theories attempt to account for this interesting fact by attributing two meanings to a metaphor so that it may be literally false yet metaphorically true. Davidson, however, is as insistent on the revelatory power of metaphor as he is in denying that we can put together some propositional contents that capture it.[17]

From a synoptic view of this approach one could reasonably deduce that language, mind and action are inseparable and that efforts to understand them in isolation are ultimately bound to fail.[18]

The thematization of metaphor tells us, moreover, that an exploration of this joint dynamics is both possible and desirable, almost as if our reach should regularly exceed our grasp, for if it did not it would be pointless as an inquiry. And, indeed, internal deductions performed within a homogeneous, standardized discourse could be a task that computational devices might perhaps accomplish in our place.

THE QUESTION OF BOUNDARIES AND LINKS

If we think of general questions of the type 'Which areas of research should have priority?,' 'What should we find out?' and 'Which method of inquiry should be developed?', a possible reply could be that there is a whole world yet to be discovered not so much of fertile fields of research but of *relations among* areas of knowledge.[19] Unless epistemological immigration and emigration should be decreed a matter of mere contingency, the question is how we can move from one epistemology to the other and which are the metaphoric processes for adequately doing so. What we have not filled in yet are the blanks of knowledge on how epistemologies may interdigitate, and this is perhaps an even greater challenge than the progressive elucidation of local problems.

It is significant, for instance, that Bruner acknowledges with gratitude that it was a highly *diversified* community of researchers[20] which reinforced his conviction that the boundaries that separate such fields as psychology, anthropology, linguistics and philosophy are only matters of administrative convenience rather than of intellectual substance. A metaphoric perspective thus appears eminently open not only to interdigitation among disciplines but also to the interaction between prevalently 'normal' and 'revolutionary' forms of research.

The sort of philosophical lucidity applicable to regular and predictable linguistic behaviour is not equally suited to the kind of linguisticity emerging in areas outside stabilized domains of literalness. For instance, as soon as we shift our discussion from the perception of things to the perception of persons we are induced to recognize that it necessarily involves some *attitude* towards the other even if it is an attitude of detatchment. It is therefore impossible, claims Berenson, 'to construe the seeing of a person in a certain way, such that the perception is *separated off* from . . . attitudes and feelings'.[21] Both foci of attention are unquestionably illuminating with no necessity of logically establishing which is the 'foundational' one. The question of foundations depends, I believe, upon the way we choose to place the punctuation in the preliminaries of our philosophical discourses.

If we regard literalness, and truth conditions, as the starting point of our approach, metaphoric languaging could then be viewed as a subsequent derivative. On the other hand, if we begin our discourse with a view of language understood as tradition and form of life, we would then come to regard domains of univocity as no more than relatively stable areas of consensual linguistic behaviour against the historical horizon of hominization.

However lucid and finely elaborate, philosophical contributions relying on the assumption of a dichotomy between affects and cognition might silently become obsolete. In a Wittgensteinian perspective, for instance, criteria of truth presuppose agreement in judgements – an agreement which we are still too reluctant to explore thoroughly. This is a point that can be illustrated by a synoptic remark of the *Philosophical Investigations*: 'So you are saying that human agreement decides what is true and what is false? – It is what human beings *say* that is true and false; and they agree in the *language* they use. That is not agreement in opinions but in forms of life.'[22] Here again a problematic combination of heterogeneous features is invoked since the actual interdigitation of verbalized opinions and forms of life, of *logos* and *bios*, is probably one of our main, unresolved concerns.

And even attempts to define metaphors in terms of literal language (itself constituted by faded metaphors) appear to some extent circular as, indeed, the literal defining language emerges from a metaphoric ground: thinkers can often argue for the literalness of the language we use by ultimately invoking terms of just the type whose literalness is in question.

There is a customary belief that identificatory questions must be answered before ones of cultural or substantive order are raised. And yet neat identificatory questions that are not in part circular are perhaps a rarity. It would be tedious and sterile if all discussions of metaphor had to await preliminary adjudication of analytical disputes regarding all of the terminology. And this prescriptive claim for the identification of issues is perhaps induced by the super-valuation generally attributed to the more prestigious, extinct, metaphors which have become incorporated into literalness. The enforcement of such a prerequisite would probably imply a dependence upon whatever form of literalness may prevail at a given moment and consequently a reluctance to explore authentically anything for which we do not have a sufficiently shared scholasticity. The enforcement of such a prerequisite, moreover, is not explicitly demanded as it is tacitly presupposed *per se*, with no reference to the complex 'logic' it represents.

Circumscribed areas of literalness in which the notions of meaning can thrive are necessary and illuminating; they, in fact, constitute the basis of much analytical and empirical knowledge. These structures of relative stability are essential for any complete development and full utilization of those pristine seminal metaphors which have originated such structures. And yet, at this point in our epistemic itinerary, we may regard ourselves as sufficiently mature to appreciate that stability is not to be equated with permanence (or delusional eternity) and that cognitive boundaries are instrumental in the creation of structure rather than of autarchic forms of isolation.

Without intending to underestimate the cognitive relevance of syntactical and formal relations of language, we are interested in the all-too-neglected aspects of function and context. This same focus of attention is significantly expressed by Bruner, who goes as far as suggesting that the subtlety and complexity of syntactic rules leads him to believe that such rules can only be learned *instrumentally*, as instruments for carrying out certain priorly operative functions and objectives –

which are certainly not propositional in nature. 'Nowhere in the higher animal kingdom', he remarks, 'are highly skilled and recombinable acts ever learned "automatically" or by rote, even when they are nurtured by strongly developed biological predispositions.'[23]

A humanistic education is generally praised as long as we carefully avoid the question of just *why* it ought to be appreciated. Apart from the minor gains of an increase in performative literacy, the 'actual' value of what is called a well-rounded education remains persistently unexplored and even questions regarding the purely 'cognitive' results of a humanistic background are systematically ignored: we all 'agree' that it is something of the greatest maturational value but rarely ask in which specific ways it contributes to generating an improved cognitive performance. The answers that we envisage to such unavoidable questions tend to suggest that the scope of what we call a humanistic education basically contributes to enhance the 'maturation' of our metaphoric potential. In fact we can only *facilitate* such growth because metaphoricity is a 'sign of genius' and 'the thing that cannot be learnt from others'.[24]

In one of his articles Davidson seems to go as far as to suggest that metaphor should be regarded as the paradigm of linguistic interpretation. And if we accept this view then we should realize that we have abandoned not only the ordinary notion of language, but also that we have '*erased the boundary* between knowing a language and knowing our way around the world generally'.[25] Although it is increasingly acknowledged that there are not only boundaries but significant continuities between mastery of a language and 'knowing our way around the world', language is too important a human capacity and too influential upon life to allow us to rest with the general notion of 'simply' erasing a boundary. The tremendous ontogenetic relevance of language requires us to make further attempts to reach an acceptable view of the interaction between life and language. Generally speaking, while some theories of language are too exclusionary, some other views may come to be all too inclusive: a boundary-dependent sort of theorizing. In fact we are perhaps unwittingly trapped in the immemorial notion of boundary, in the sense of an isolating device; indeed it is one of the key principles of a pristine logic of classes[26] inspiring western tradition. Perhaps it is not a problem of either erasing boundaries between 'knowing a language *and* knowing our way around the world' or of developing a more adequate theory of language which can maintain appropriate limits with regard to our involvement with life. Through a 'forthcoming' philosophical maturation which is invoked from disparate sources, we can perhaps erase boundaries by stipulating links. We do not so much need better theories for pre-defined domains of inquiry as we need to develop connections with 'alien' domains of knowledge or behaviour. Where boundaries persistently determine problems, there we should strive to create links of varying degrees of appropriateness. We need contractual, 'connubial' or stipulative connections which somehow indicate reciprocal distinctions rather than separations.

JUVENILE AND ADULT COGNITIVE STYLES

The question that guides the present discussion is not so much which might be the best epistemology to be inhabited but how we can move from one epistemology to another, or how we can best create metaphoric links among them. Thus the evolutionary conditions from which hominization derives and the cultural foci providing its symbolic instruments should be seen through the ontogenetic events that bring these two powerful forces into contact.

It has been suggested that meaning and cognitive content are coextensive and also that metaphors bear no direct cognitive content. Officially, it is also recognized that live metaphors are necessary for fostering the growth of knowledge even though they do not convey information before being absorbed into literal language. And yet the flourishing study of metaphor that we are witnessing bears testimony to our incipient capacity to recognize that there is a life cycle of language such that even our linguisticity is ultimately recognized as an emanation of life. And even though language is capable of shaping and transforming the structure of human culture, its original links with our biological condition cannot be ignored.

If we are concerned with the *life* of our rationality rather than with a timeless section of it, and view our thought processes as correlates of self-creation projects, we may come to perceive an inner maturational course. In it we partly abandon our original metaphoric propensities in order to achieve some degree of epistemic literalness; but as soon as we can proceed to high levels of sophistication and complexity, we can afford to regain our full metaphoric potential. The mastery of a standard language, or epistemology, may result in a symbiosis with it and a consequent idealization of the self by the identification with collective intellectual processes. As a phase of an intellectual cycle it may indeed represent a necessary passage. And yet such a developmental sequence may usher in difficulties from the point of view of the 'maturation' of our thinking. The opposition between principles and desires, thoughts and affects inherent to a 'juvenile' phase of rationality may be unwittingly conducive to an 'adult' view of philosophy haunted and constrained by literalness, conventionality and rigidity. And unless we are capable of tempering our epistemic literalness with tolerance of metaphoric expressions, our 'juvenile' pattern of powerful rationality may ultimately induce forms of 'adult' irrationality. The quality of intellectual maturity, therefore, is somehow different from that of earlier phases of rationality inasmuch as it may better integrate metaphoricity and literalness.

The tradition that regards our reasoning as purely conceptual and algorithmic could be integrated with a dependency upon metaphorical extensions of non-propositional mental structures. Although our rationality can transcend the way in which humans live, and regard itself as operating in a domain virtually free of affectual constraints, it is now perhaps sufficiently adult to become hospitable to deeper and further dimensions which are in no way detrimental to its standard products. Culture, then, could be viewed as offering schemes of concatenation which tell us what can be linked with what. And we come to absorb these associative possibilities through those extended metaphors which *suggest* the nature of coherence, probability and sense within our inner world.

Metaphor is potentially revolutionary in the sense that what is at stake is a profound turn whereby the general notion of truth as correspondence only becomes one of the components of the vast problem of language and reality. Indeed a turn whereby we recontextualize our view of knowledge around further foci of attention, such as for instance appropriateness, fertility, utility or heuristic value. As is known, metaphors also provide for the redescription of domains already seen through one metaphoric frame in terms of another. 'Such redescriptions can have disruptive effects on previously complacent ways of looking at the world.'[27] And there are metaphoric recontextualizations more suited to be inserted in the life cycle of a cultural development rather than in a relatively stable enclave of linguistic commensurability.

Knowledge is not 'lifeless' as it can be the sort of knowledge that is also suited to nurturing and nourishing, to caring and tolerating, improving and preserving. An 'unimpassioned' use of our cognitive functions may be characterized by tacit aims *extracted* from that complex activity of knowledge, such as for instance control and (contemptuous) detachment. Just as Athena sprang fully armed from the head of Zeus, so our prevalently representationalist knowledge seems to claim a parthenogenic birth from the brains of a logos-father; a high-level, noble 'birth' unquestionably entitling it to ignore the vicissitudes of life. This characteristic, moreover, may be an essential key to its success as it provides an approach of great attractiveness to a power-dependent and territorially inclined cognitive culture.

Attention to metaphoric processes of language focuses instead upon the life-course and metabolism of our linguisticity. By seeking to unravel the original sources and motives of the unfolding of culture, language of course offers an incomparable access. But then what sort of language or what parts of it? The sort of language from which examples are customarily drawn in 'normal' philosophy seems to avoid – almost as if it were an antecedent 'statutory' stipulation – the language of infancy and senescence, of pathology and creativity, of silence and pseudo-language, indeed, the spectrum of linguisticity which we strive to recuperate.

Metaphoricity does not in fact derive from sheer cognitive competence but rather from a sort of affectual empathy – the 'genius' Aristotle speaks about in his view of metaphor. And although geniality is a different way of dealing competently with language, it is not entirely distinct from it since boundaries between genius and competence, metaphor and literalness are temporary, shifting and often interwoven.

Thinkers may coherently function within their epistemology although they may not really develop any form of reflective language for it. A rudimentary metalanguage is possibly best differentiated in the interepistemic space where a plurality of epistemologies (be they philosophical schools, hermeneutic methods, or logical propensities) is more conveniently acknowledged. A reflective language is then not to be viewed as a *super*-structure for adjudicating controversies but as an inchoate maturational dialogue emerging from attempts at interacting with diverse vocabularies.

INTEREPISTEMIC LINKS

The inchoate philosophy we pursue is primarily concerned with the means we could develop in order to move from one 'epistemological' position to another. We are not concerned, then, with the quest for the best forms of reasoning but with the relationship which could be created among different conglomerations of rationality. And because of its 'genius'[28] for linking alien domains, human metaphoricity is probably one of the salient resources for attempting connections between different schools of thought or intellectual factions.

When the question of such interactions is not addressed, the relations which none the less predominate and which philosophy cannot yet thematize may well be of a hierarchical, colonizing, adversarial or avoidant nature – thus quite different from the philosophical ideal of the intraepistemic style. The characteristics of openness and lucidity through which philosophy legitimizes its status in culture seem to be confined to intraepistemic concerns; these same features are perplexingly neglected whenever reference is made to extra-epistemic enterprises or to interepistemic relations. Significant areas of epistemic agreement 'should' ultimately live in isolation from one another in such a way that 'proper' philosophy may primarily apply to domestic concerns and be excluded from the preoccupations of foreign affairs. And it is precisely this view that is difficult to conjugate with the idea of a maturing philosophy.

Under some provisional circumstances the practice of isolating a discipline from external considerations may serve its peculiar purpose of enhancing its inner cohesion and refinement; in a 'permanent' perspective, though, isolation can trivialize the research and transform itself into a sterile addiction. Concisely, Midgley remarks that 'The supposed rigour of isolationism is a fraud.'[29]

The narcissism of groups makes us blind to whatever dynamics obtain between different 'factions'; and if we could focus our attention on the in-between spaces, we might even discover that some of the epistemic features we praise are created by differentiating interepistemic assumptions which we cannot easily appreciate. An epistemic enclave, moreover, cannot properly reflect on itself but can be urged to do so when reached by external metaphoric links; these may induce some mirroring and comparative assessments. Perhaps we do not have sufficient instruments to process in our thinking whatever dynamics may occur in between epistemic conglomerations. The in- between logical spaces, in fact, may often be hospitable to the most archaic sort of relations. Our interepistemic relations are often intractable – 'unthinkable' – because they are too difficult to listen to affectually and are therefore kept at a distance from the reassuring sentential workings of our mind. But then, how could we elaborate on something that does not even reach our consciousness or come across as a problem? And yet, we can think of our interepistemic vicissitudes only to the extent that we do not entirely think through our favoured epistemology.

Of course, one could remark that different schools of thought actually scrutinize other philosophical outlooks and thus the insulation of epistemic areas is not to be dreaded or regarded as a serious problem. The point, however, is that whatever is taken to be a studied object tends to become an entity with regard to which the studying agent becomes somehow transcendent. And the first to study the other automatically seems to acquire a higher epistemic status inasmuch as it functions as the 'author' (and authority) of knowledge. The creation of a studied 'other' is simultaneous with the insurgence of the transcendent theorizer who can thus even appear to 'exist' outside of temporal vicissitudes and contingencies. A dominant epistemological enclave may even invent metaphoric ways of symbolizing its own relation to the rest of culture. And yet the vital point is the enhancement of primary metaphors, that is of the sort of language in which *any* particular culture may represent relations external to itself. Unless we recognize the need for disparate cultures to be able to represent their own relation to other epistemic areas in their own specific ways, and not according to a generalized model, a devaluing hierarchy will ultimately tend to prevail.[30] If we *simply* 'live by' metaphors and maintain the complex dynamics of metaphorization vulnerable to obscurity we perpetrate an illicit naturalization of what is in fact an effort to symbolize interactions or representation. And because metaphoric constructions have a structuring effect upon the otherwise unrepresentable interepistemic events, this rather important distinction between natural and symbolic conditions should not be disregarded.

A misleading philosophical education silently assumes the task of curing students of unprofessional ways of thinking, of that vital epistemophily which is conducive to asking unfamiliar questions. If this 'correction' is explicitly attempted, learners can of course detect it and behave consequently. But if it is never made explicit 'philosophy' can ultimately be equated to a sophisticated form of epistemological indoctrination.[31] It is difficult for philosophers to realize how much of their restraining influence is conveyed through the subliminal expressions of their guiding assumptions rather than through argument proper. And yet, the measure of the insight which any contribution provides lies primarily in the richness and variety of the novel questions which it forces on our attention, and in its capacity to reveal significant connections between features or fields that previously appeared entirely independent.[32] The disposition to create links between diverse perspectives so as to allow a measure of cross-fertilization is thus one of the functions of our metaphoric potential.

Interepistemic discussions implying different underlying metaphors are usually regarded as futile and 'frustrating'. And yet, in the sort of philosophy which we try to develop, these conditions turn out to be uniquely challenging and constructive. Conversely, intraepistemic debates inspired by a single metaphor tend to produce a sufficiently endorsed literal language in which we may operate by means of a calculus of propositions or appropriate algorithms: the sort of work that artificial intelligence might virtually perform. Intraepistemic knowledge thus not only avoids 'frustrations' but bestows upon us the gratifying experience of elaborating coherent knowledge and justifying the legitimacy of territorial expansions onto different areas of research. It is to be hoped that a maturation of philosophy may teach us to endure intellectual frustrations and ultimately come to appreciate that the battling interactions in which we seem to talk past each other may actually reveal the more fertile fields of research – and perhaps the sort of enterprises that artificial intelligence could not equally well perform.

If philosophical debates are not so fruitful it is perhaps because their profound nature so often goes unrecognized. Scholars occasionally talk past each other without even noticing that they are doing so. On the other hand, in order to 'avoid' such outcomes philosophers may tend to circumscribe their discussion within homogeneous epistemic frames securely inspired by one and the same basic assumption. As is well known, comparisons of our theories with alternative ones derived from the same metaphor are usually ' fruitful', whereas comparisons with theories emanating from different metaphors can be systematically 'frustrating'.[33] Referring to research in theories of intelligence Sternberg argues that even intra-metaphoric discussions may be less meaningful than scholars believe, inasmuch as both linguistic elucidations and experiential operations which we view as suitable to identify the 'best' theory may actually accomplish no more than to distinguish among alternative instantiations of a given metaphor. Indeed a theory of intelligence may be correct in some respects, but its correctness is predicated on the varying applicability of the root-metaphor underlying it.[34]

We confront 'intractable' problems to the extent that we think of rationality as an entirely intraepistemic emanation of particular systems of propositions and concepts; if we cannot think of rationality in terms of interepistemic strategies whereby humans aptly migrate from one set of concepts and beliefs to another, we are indeed prone to meet an impasse of intractable problems. In such a restricted view we may confuse the laborious rationality of theorizing with the logicality of inferences within particular theories. Toulmin, for instance, argues that philoso-phers have failed to recognize theories as formal abstractions deriving from a historically developing enterprise whose rationality lies primarily in its procedures for conceptual transformation; the history of science has thus been treated 'as a chronicle of successive propositional systems, whose comparative logicality has provided the only measure of rational acceptability'.[35] The popular computational metaphor of knowledge tends to envision the mind as a computing device and often analogizes the processes of intelligence to its operations – or software; and of course this is a view of knowledge probably more suited to the discussion of intraepistemic problems than to the thematization of interepistemic questions. Perhaps we could let our computational devices perform intraepistemic work and let humans focus on the interepistemic hermeneutic challenges that our devices cannot envisage and pursue; artificial 'intellects' cannot perhaps think that in creating our own cognitive centres we may forget that our epistemic foci ultimately displace other theories into a periphery of our own making. It is in fact risky to call something nonsense because it aims at a sense different from the sense that a certain vocabulary is trying to make.

It is questionable whether epistemologies ought to be regarded as immune from the influences of our disparate ways of coping with life. This purported immunity ultimately entails the duty of artificial narrowness and compartmentalization. The autonomy of each epistemic area is thus supposed to require of itself high standards of cognitive insulation and a dread of 'contamination'; moves outside of its encompassing logic are not even contemplated. While insisting on the merits of 'sound knowledge', the more reasonable members of a rational community often recognize the need to compare their own interests with different interests which they are supposed to ignore – thus becoming seriously tempted to develop metaphoric links. Although convinced of their adherence to the sounder way of doing philosophy they regard its claim to prevail as a debatable question and thus escape the constraints of group loyalty. However productive, a refined epistemology cannot be seen as entitled to prevail epistemologically. 'Monomania, even when it produces Nobel prizes, is not really the ideal scientific condition',[37] concisely remarks Midgley, probably herself inclining toward an interepistemic approach.

What is significant with regard to maturation is the depth at which world perspectives, whether actual or imaginary, are transformed. The deadening congealment which is 'imposed' for long periods of time in a given culture is tightly interwoven with the literalization of certain metaphors and with the latent prohibition to disrupt them. Live metaphoric expressions, in fact, constitute a call to surpass the habitual limits of a culture which may be presented as if it were some ultimate, changeless structure. Discouraging our metaphoric potential thus functions as a preliminary measure for averting transformational attempts. Metaphoric links, moreover, may not only operate in a synchronic, ahistorical dimension, but can be utilized to think and metabolize our own philosophical history which might otherwise appear as a sequence of unrelated epistemic systems. The question of changes in philosophical fashions is not only distressing because it frustrates our unconscious desire for stable and reassuring paradigms; it is also a puzzling phenomenon because we are not equipped for reconnecting the sequence of theoretical stances which characterize our intellectual history: if they are hardly connected how are we to use this heritage? This disquieting condition is dramatically inconspicuous especially with regard to our recent or contemporary cognitive efforts whose reciprocal links we often fail to see. The wider intellectual community largely ignores the brilliant logical elucidations which compose much of our philosophical literature; in fact they often appear to contain unsituated discussions produced in response to comparable antecedent enterprises.

As is known, the ideas that one generation of scholars regarded as essential and indubitable are subsequently exposed as vague and unproductive by their successors. And yet, however common the turnover in intellectual fashions, we somehow tend to believe that it will not happen again. One of the reasons for this unwitting disbelief is that we have never sufficiently cared about developing metaphoric links which may reconnect different epistemic conglomerations. Our intellectual heritage thus becomes more the concern of the *history* of philosophy than of live *philosophy*: yet another one of our innumerable dichotomies.

4   The oppositional metaphor

ON BEING RIGHT IN ARGUMENTS

'Socrates keeps reducing the sophist to silence, but does he have *right* on his side when he does this?' asks Wittgenstein. 'Well, it is true that the sophist does not know what he thinks he knows; but that is no triumph for Socrates.'[1] In fact to criticize the arguments of our interlocutors we customarily abstract the features to which they attach the utmost importance and produce counter-examples in which those same features appear, but in which the conclusion they claim does not quite follow. In this way we repeatedly try to defeat our 'sophists' and demonstrate that they do not really know what they think they know. And the reason why we generally fail to see in the Socratic method a maieutics of thought and perceive instead the paradigm of an ironic style of debate[2] is that we are not (yet) able to conceive of philosophical discussion being conducted in any other way: we hesitate to effect an epistemic shift from the reassuring frame of 'right' on to the challenging domain of 'responsibility'. We are still triumph-dependent and care-avoidant thinkers.

It is possible that some of our language games are derivatives of phylogenetic territorial behaviour transferred on to the level of symbolic interactions, a level where humans can admirably theorize about and justify what they do. Nozick points out that once the deductive connections are recognized, and we see where a premiss leads, we may either accept the conclusion or else reject one of the premisses we previously accepted.[3] But in arguments we customarily look for premisses that the interlocutor could not possibly abandon. It is not then a question of merely pointing out deductive connections among statements but of forcing someone to *change his mind*, reshape his thinking in accordance with our own. In fact, the underlying assumption which structures most linguistic expressions of our argumentative culture is a latent oppositional metaphor whereby we strive to gain approving allies, extend our epistemic ground, export research models, and obtain intellectual tributes. The problem to be discerned is that not only do we perform according to territorial paradigms but also we commonly believe that it is the way we 'should' go about – as if it were a 'conviction'.[4] In Moulton's view, since we make use of adversarial patterns in our ways of doing philosophy we also claim that these are the best available and most illuminating procedures.[5]

Lakoff and Johnson significantly conflate the concept of 'argument' with the conceptual metaphor 'argument is war'.[6] A wide variety of expressions reflecting such a powerful epistemic metaphor become evident when we observe our talk of *defending* claims, *attacking* points, *winning* arguments, etc.[7] And they insist that we 'don't just *talk* about arguments in terms of war. We actually win or lose arguments. We see the person we are arguing with as an opponent. We attack his positions and we defend our own. We gain and lose ground. We plan and use strategies.'[8] The philosophic enterprise could thus be seen as a 'debate between *adversaries* who try to defend their own views against counterexamples and produce counterexamples to opposing views'.[9]

And yet, perhaps, the oppositional metaphor of (philosophical) argumentation is objectionable primarily because it imperceptibly permeates our culture at large, thus ultimately soaring to the epistemic status of dominant paradigm.[10] One of the best ways to monitor the scope and influence of a ruling metaphor is then to *show* that there is some such metaphor at work, that it *is* 'just' a metaphor, and that *other* ways of arguing and reasoning also exist; these emanate from different, 'lesser' metaphors such as, for instance, 'Argument is agriculture', 'Argument is therapy', or 'Argument is development'. Such 'marginal' paradigms might be hospitable to questions of this kind: 'Which alternative premises would make this argument a better one?', 'Is this argument innovative and fruitful?' or 'How would it inter-digitate with other theses?'. If allowed to work themselves out to their logical conclusions, such alternative paradigms might significantly influence our practices and enhance the search for greater scope in exhibiting the reasons for accepting or refusing an argument. A thesis may in fact be determined as much by the implicit philosophical antecedents as by the way in which humans handle their mental life.

Much of what we attempt in our arguments still appears in great part structured by the concept of conflict. 'The normal way for us to talk about attacking a position is to use the words "attack a position". Our conventional ways of talking about arguments presuppose a metaphor we are hardly ever conscious of. The metaphor is not merely in the words we use, it is in our very concept of an argument. *The language of argument is not poetic, fanciful, or rhetorical; it is literal.*' [11] At least in this limited sense there is a significant convergence with Davidson's insistence that the meaning of metaphoric expressions is their literal meaning and that their force derives from what the words, in their most literal interpretation, mean, and nothing more.[12]

The problem with our epistemic predicament is the deceptive assumption that all genuine philosophical disagreements can be resolved through the use of strate-gically strict argumentative language. Such an imperceptible but constraining belief is eminently suitable for oppositional paradigms: isolated adversarial arguments, in fact, would be superfluous or inappropriate if it were recognized that it is an interwoven synergy of life *and* arguments that determines philosophical persua-sions. The exclusive adherence to the oppositional method in the evaluation of a line of reasoning thus appears more applicable to secure the right to 'be right' than to develop any sort of appreciative responsibility for whatever arguments are offered in dialogic situations. It almost seems that in the human interactions called 'philosophy' we ultimately seek to produce arguments so powerful that they just cannot be refused, so cogent that they reverberate into the very *life* of the inter-locutor and cause an 'illness' unless they are accepted; a 'good' argument must be such that anyone who wants to safeguard the coherence of his own cognitive and affectual organization must eventually accept it.

The language of academic philosophy can be a rather coercive one, for argu-ments are best when they 'force' us to a conclusion, and are not so good when not so cogent. A philosophical argument is an attempt to get someone to believe something whether he wants to believe it or not: a successful philosophical argument *forces* someone to a belief. Ultimately, the ideal argument would be the one that leaves no possible answer to the interlocutor, reducing him to impotent silence. Nozick remarks that 'Perhaps philosophers need arguments so powerful that they set up reverberations in the brain: if the person refuses to accept the conclusion, he *dies*. How is that for a powerful argument? . . . A "perfect" philosophical argument would leave no choice.'[13]

The problem with alternative forms of discussion is that they are strikingly inconspicuous in our culture because they deviate from an immemorial way of reasoning, constantly addressed to an antagonist, and because they are by far more complex, profound and ultimately more demanding and much less appealing than the exhilaration of 'being right'. And although we may succeed in defeating our adversaries by proving their theses wrong, they often do not change their convic-tions or abandon their enterprises. This may be an indication that they pursue an undertaking or ulterior path of rationality that is just not captured by our customary oppositional paradigm. There is a great deal of residual rationality which is left out of the stringent adversarial tests and which is none the less essential to structure the complex reasoning which we try to scrutinize. Proving an argument wrong, in fact, may be as cogent an enterprise as it is ultimately unconvincing. This dialectic style probably expresses the best cognitive 'justice' that we can achieve even though it may be the case that by combating a conviction, we persistently miss the point that determines conviction. Significantly, Wittgenstein remarks, 'One says, e.g., "One *feels* conviction, one does not infer it from one's own words or tone of voice". But what does it mean to say one *feels* conviction? What is *true* is: *one does not make an inference from one's own words to one's own conviction*; nor yet to the actions arising from the conviction.'[14]

The oppositional metaphor, moreover, requires that we systematically eradicate language from life inasmuch as criticism works at its best when objections can be addressed to isolated parts of whatever position we intend to oppose.[15] A polemic attention to argumentative segments demands that we ignore that claims on any topic hardly ever exist in isolation and that they are aspects of an integrated system of ideas – of a form of life. Self-contained claims though they may seem, arguments are upthrusts of an underlying culture which is at once local, and for all that, a part of a life pattern. And so, while they inevitably convey a specifiable meaning, they are part of a more general intellectual context. The antagonistic method of con-ducting philosophical work risks obscuring the cohesion needed to assure the internal exchange that might logically justify a division of an argument between its parts. In our limiting adversarial outlook we may tacitly give up the right to attempt the comparisons that may enliven our philosophical work such as, for instance, the confrontation between the logic of different cultures, between our current epistemology and that of our evolutionary forebears, between our live thinking and that of the devices constructed to simulate it.[16]

So deeply ingrained is our oppositional metaphor that we tend to regard arguments which are structured and conducted differently as no arguments at all.[17] As an 'acceptable' alternative, parts of these unacceptable presentations are extracted, translated into proper oppositional style and utilized within standard antagonistic procedures. Such translation is necessary not only because we use belligerent strategies in our 'serious' arguments but also because we basically understand in terms of conflicts whatever we are doing when we engage in argumentative discussion.

That we are not entirely satisfied with the oppositional paradigm – even though we tend to praise winners – may be revealed by the inexpressible admiration we occasionally experience for those thinkers who contend in a playful way, who transform a battle into an encounter, or who do not seem to take the argument too seriously. And even though we may know how and why a controversial argument is initiated, we do not quite know how to stop or how to transform it into a different sort of symbolic interaction.[18] We may perceive the sterility of an endless extended argument and wish for an inversion of the adversarial trend before it 'naturally' goes out of fashion. The belated extinction of a philosophical problem may indeed be the result of an immemorial combative style, ultimately tending to perpetuate itself even when the thinkers involved are no longer genuinely interested in the original controversy; as if the litigation had to go on for 'logical' reasons whose validity is no longer recognized.

As innumerable books have criticized the derivatives of classical metaphysics and as the trend is so pervasive, one may be tempted to conceive of our much criticized classicity as a beneficial asset which may salvage us from the risks of philosophical sterility. What could we philosophize about if we had no 'antagonist' implicitly to criticize, uproot and devalue? Whereas the habitual critical perspective seems to insinuate that we cannot be creative because of the constraints of our classicity, we could also hypothesize that being insufficiently *philo*-sophical we can do no more than inveigh against the purported constraining dictates of classical metaphysics – or even of contemporary science.[19]

The fashionable games of our intellectual subcultures may encourage us to avoid vital issues by litigating over marginal ones. A compulsion to abide by the oppositional metaphor may thus, unnoticed, impoverish our approach to inquiries. This detrimental metaphoric spell even induces thinkers to subdivide into ever smaller groups, which are characterized by a decreasing understanding of each other's projects. But this is neither a necessary aspect of inquiry nor, of course, an advantage to it.[20] Such an involution of our natural love of knowledge may ultimately be due to a lack of concern for life itself. Should we be more appreciative of life we would more easily notice that our hidden, divisive, splitting procedures tend to induce a 'culture' of lifeless artefacts. And the illusory 'alternative' that comes to mind, that of an encompassing, all-embracing ideology, is once again the outcome of an oppositional compulsion. Unless we are vigilantly aware of these constraining epistemic dictates we will be tacitly controlled by them in such a way that our thinking cannot properly engage with life itself.

Perhaps our disputatiousness serves the occult purpose of relieving the stressful coexistence with major unresolved problems and of rendering them inconspicuous. In a perspective attempting to reconnect life and thinking it is essential to consider the *motives* for philosophizing as profoundly interwoven with its actual *structure*. Extensively used to the point of semantic saturation, the notion of 'reality' might then profitably be substituted by expressions indicating our embodied, living condition. Bearing in mind our condition as finite and differentiated living creatures, the question re-emerges of the applicability of our thinking to interactions with world and persons. Disputatious attention to a few chosen problems contrasts with a dramatic neglect of other questions usually related to our survival, coexistence, and appreciation of our entire life cycle.

But there is yet another consideration which indicates that the epistemic exclusion of our situation as creatures is an undesirable project; a variety of affects which we may subsume under the general idea of pugnacity are in fact endemic emotions in research and even play a role in shaping its internal organization. And while we concede that some aspects of this belligerent method may produce valuable insights and a refinement of theses, we must also recognize that in our culture we frequently incline to opposition for its own sake. The sensible person looking at cultural events past and present often remarks that what was occupying the minds of an epoch and what prevented the people from seeing the problems they might have been tackling was a constant unprofitable warfare among intellectual factions. Similarly the reasonable person reflecting upon current world vicissitudes often remarks that if only the immense investments in 'defence' enterprises were avoided, major impending problems could be profitably confronted. In view of the unprecedented amount and organization of knowledge we could probably perform much better in both practical and theoretical questions[21] if we could control the proliferation of disputes inducing a style of chronic 'philosophical' waste.

AGREEMENT AND DISAGREEMENT

An attempt to theorize a non-oppositional, innovative approach to argumentative procedures clearly emerges from Davidson's writings. In his view, in fact, the 'principle of charity' generally counsels us to prefer theories of interpretation that minimize disagreement.[22] Indeed, the sort of theoretical preference which turns out to be advocated in an inhospitable cultural background, as the tendency to disagree seems all too deeply rooted in our intellectual heritage.

Significantly, Ogden remarks that Aristotelian philosophy was '*obsessed* with the problem of oppositions'.[23] In the *Metaphysics* we read, for instance, that 'since science is potency which depends upon the possession of a rational formula, it follows that whereas the "salutary" can only produce health, and the "calefactory" only heat, and the "frigorific" only cold, the scientific man can produce both contrary results'.[24] And the rigidity induced by the oppositional style 'scientific man' is so pervasive that a 'principle of charity' almost appear excessively innovative, and ultimately too 'risky'.

And yet, Davidson insists:

> Since charity is not an option but a condition of having a workable theory, it is meaningless to suggest that we might fall into massive error by endorsing it . . . Charity is forced on us; whether we like it or not, if we want to understand others, we must count them right in most matters. If we can produce a theory that reconciles charity and the formal conditions for a theory, we have done all that could be done to ensure communication. Nothing more is possible, and nothing more is needed.[25]

And although in his view no single principle of optimum charity emerges, charity in interpreting the words and thoughts of others remains unavoidable: 'Just as we must maximize agreement, or risk not making sense of what the alien is talking about, so we must maximize the self-consistency we attribute to him, on pain of not understanding *him*.'[26]

By our resonances of alikeness we try in fact to grasp our interlocutors' experience while, of course, in the doing we do not conflate identities. It is our mutuality which allows us to further discover our individuality; the more we can appreciate echoes of agreement, the more we enhance the possibility of locating and symbolizing differences. Similarly a measure of detachment from the oppositional style does not endorse the absurd aim of rendering disagreement and error unnoticeable; it rather strives to point out that 'widespread agreement is the only possible background against which disputes and mistakes can be interpreted. Making sense of the utterances and behaviour of others, even their most aberrant behaviour, requires us to find a great deal of reason and truth in them. To see too much unreason on the part of others is simply to undermine our ability to understand what it is they are unreasonable about.'[27]

And one of the hidden difficulties in further developing a principle of charity possibly derives from a fear of being constrained by colonizing views.

The tremendous danger that the oppositional method purports to avert is that other 'charitable' methods may ultimately give preferential treatment to certain theses by sparing them the strict tests of adverse criticism. In the 'argument is war' culture[28] which we inhabit, the belief prevails that the risks of being forced into an epistemic constraint (which we may reasonably want to challenge) are somehow monitored; and, in fact, the art of producing dissentient attacks is at a premium in contemporary philosophy. But we cannot safeguard our oppositional styles as if we still had to defend our creative thinking from the pressure of mythologies, ideologies or metaphysical world-views. The overestimation of dangers may link us to a family of bellicose metaphors which we do not really need. The oppositional metaphor which guides much philosophical practice might even become obsolete and out of taste; indeed it would be more justifiable if philosophy had to break free from mythologic beliefs, oppressive ideologies, or from some encompassing theodicy – as if it were deeply convinced of a terrible impending imposition. A mature philosophy looking to the future may perhaps attempt to develop links, meet challenges, rather than fight obscuring forces. And yet, because of the 'old-fashioned' (and dominant) oppositional method, contributions which are not modelled through it are still likely to be regarded as philosophically marginal.

There is, moreover, one unacknowledged but serious danger which the oppositional paradigm does not confront: the risk that certain propensities remain totally exempt from any criticism just because they are not sufficiently identified and thus remain either unrefuted or unused. To the extent that the facets and details of certain philosophical positions remain obscure, they are immune from any form of criticism and development – thus stubbornly surviving beneath the skirmishes of our argumentative philosophy. As long as we focus on criticizing distinguishable claims and well-identified theses, the underlying principles will remain unnoticed and undisturbed even though they may be as influential as they are invisible. It is possible, for instance, that the latent and persistent need to resist some hypothetical obscurantism has led us significantly to privilege problems of semantic meaning over questions of pragmatic meaning. And it is this kind of programming that may escape being judged for what it is. In this connection Moulton remarks that in philosophy of language the questions investigated 'are analyzed when possible in terms of properties that can be subjected to deductive reasoning. Semantic theory has detoured questions of meaning into questions of truth. Meaning is discussed in terms of the deductive consequences of sentences. We ask not what a sentence says, but what it guarantees, what we can deduce from it. Relations among ideas that affect the meaning are either assimilated to the deductive model or ignored.'[29]

A culture pervaded by an oppositional epistemology prevents us from duly appreciating systems of ideas that are *not* directed to a hypothetical opponent.[30] As a further example of a programmatic scheme that may elude criticism, we should point out that in such a 'culture' the incorrectness of using oppositional reasoning in a non-oppositional context may remain sadly unnoticed. But at the same time developments of the 'principle of charity' might prove greatly illuminating.

It is possible that, with humans, expressions of competitive aggressiveness have been gradually transferred from a physical basis to the symbolic domain. Moulton points out that even though such 'positive' concepts as activity, authority, ambition, competence, success are not demonstrably related to aggressiveness, it is frequently believed that aggressive behaviour is a sign of these generally acclaimed human characteristics.[31] And although it is possible that expressions of competitive aggressiveness have been gradually transposed from a biological basis to the 'logical' level, the 'argument is war' metaphor need not be the best structure, or best validating criterion, for arguments. It is perhaps only classical and stable, not necessarily permanent or superior. Although 'charitable' discourse (in a Davidsonian sense) can be more effective than belligerent language, the conceptual conflation of aggressiveness with positive concepts such as force and competence has made this circumstance difficult to appreciate.

If we consider the metaphor 'argument is war' and if we also acknowledge that most of the philosophical enterprise is indeed constituted by argument, discussion, 'dialogue', dialectics, we could infer that such a metaphor does not only indicate *one* of the paradigms of philosophy but also that it is hierarchized as *the* dominant paradigm. Produced by the conflation of dominance and competence, such a pervasive yet unperceived model may tacitly constrain all of our work. Under these circumstances, it is not so much a problem of breaking free from it as of simply coming to regard it as frequently superfluous. And further attempts to explain such seminal metaphors may ultimately contribute to our cognitive evolution in the sense of enhancing the possibility of shifts from, for instance, disputatious paradigms to agricultural models.

CONTROVERSIAL ZEAL

In the perspective of the oppositional metaphor it is generally believed that *the* rational way of dealing with our thinking is to subject it to the most severe forms of adversarial criticism. Moulton suggests that through this same oppositional metaphor it is tacitly stipulated that the most appropriate way of producing valid contributions is to prefigure as many contesting objections as one can possibly think of and, at the same time, develop counter-arguments which can confront such adverse criticism.[32] The justification of this generalized approach is that arguments which can sustain a strict search for internal incongruences are superior to those which succumb to equally sharp forms of challenge. The scope, fertility and linking force of an argument thus tend to remain unappreciated in such a perspective. Possibly pointing into this same 'psychological' direction, Wittgenstein remarks: 'Why shouldn't it be that one excludes mutually contradictory conclusions: not because they are contradictory but because they are useless?' Or put it like this: one need not shy away from them as from something unclean, because they are contradictory: let them be excluded because they are no use for anything.[33] Or 'charitably' include them, if they *can* be of use.

If we ask whether the purpose of intellectual inquiry is to obtain 'right' answers or to avoid 'wrong' ones, we would *prima facie* suggest that these two enterprises are quite comparable and even complementary; and yet, however imperceptibly, the two programmes actually diverge. Dominant features of our culture seem to confine us in the sheer avoidance of the wrong answers with a consequent devaluation of striving for the creative ones; and what restrains us from 'striving for' usually springs from a boundless admiration for the parsimony, lucidity and consistency commonly admired in our western tradition. We are trained to fear vagueness to the point that we almost think of philosophical probity as of the production of unassailable defensive arguments. We almost come to think of inquiry as consolidating a well-defended position rather than – for instance – as developing and enriching a piece of our intellectual heritage. But of course the latter attitude would fall outside of the belligerent outlook and would thrive instead in the domain of some sort of 'agricultural' metaphor. The idea of the quest for knowledge is thus transformed into a quest for intellectual 'safety' and for the sort of epistemology that can function as a deterrent. Research is subconsciously conceived of not so much as the effort to understand something that is of vital importance but rather as the accumulation of discussion that is unquestionably correct, almost regardless of its content and prospects.

Reflecting on a few citations reported by Peters one could be inclined to think that the Roman Law tradition seems to connect the attainment of truth to the idea of torture. In Ulpian we read that 'By torture we are to understand the torment and suffering of the body in order to elicit the truth', while from Bocer we learn that 'Torture is interrogation by torment of the body . . . for the purpose of eliciting the truth.' And in the thirteenth century Azo writes that 'Torture is the inquiry after truth by means of torment.' As these excerpts appear to suggest, abominable practices seemed acceptable to the juridical determination of the truth.[34]

In our current procedural style the worst thing that could happen would be to make a mistake, as locally defined, and to have it exposed in one's intellectual milieu – with no consideration for the different, but sad, prospect of investing whole lives in just saying nothing wrong. In this intellectual climate we almost grow addicted to seeking security from error and potential deterrents of criticism. And, of course, one of the safest positions is criticism of the errors of others, by means of a progressive refinement of the adversarial techniques generated within the oppositional metaphor. It is possible that part of the 'attraction' for clarity arises from a profound revulsion at being exposed as wrong; and, indeed, this is not an irrelevant feeling but a pervasive attitude which shapes the style of our discussions to the point where we are saturated with extenuating logomachies and induced to ask whether it is still *philo*-sophy that we are after or a compulsive quest for 'being right' – as if it were equivalent to being well and, thus, surviving. And the deceptive alternative that clarity might then be unjustly sacrificed for the sake of peace is yet another instantiation of our immemorial adversarial mentality.

The adversarial habit, moreover, seems to flow from a convention that the negative approach always wins in prestige. Scholars who cogently reject a position are always at an advantage with respect to those who propose something, and those who can successfully criticize perhaps soar to a higher intellectual status than those who can produce germinative ideas. But controversial zeal leads to divisions, and divisions induce us to either exile the adversary or secede ourselves, with the prospect that a different milieu will be a more purified area of knowledge. As is well known, the emblematic style for this endemic attempt to purify philosophy through adversarial procedures rather than cultivate it by means of some sort of (agri)cultural 'logic' is usually traced back to the Cartesian approach: 'I thought that . . . I ought to reject as absolutely false all opinions in regard to which I could suppose the least grounds for doubt.'[35] And yet, in a perspective whereby we regard language and philosophy as expressions of human life, the illusion of finality and transparency, together with the concurrent inclination to abhor 'the least grounds for doubt' might instead be regarded as no more than a form of idealization to be tolerated, monitored and lived by. As has been suggested, the need for philosophy arose in the first place out of Socratic attempts to collate some very different ways of practical thinking and, subsequently, out of Plato's far more ambitious effort to relate all these ways of thinking to the emerging certainties of mathematics[36] – the abstract domain of undisputable connections which so fascinated Descartes.

Midgley points out in this connection that if we start to disagree with members of our own intellectual community, the easiest way of coping with the stressful situation is to adhere to an opposing group: 'This ensures that our intellect never has more than two alternatives to consider, and that it usually knows in advance which of them to reject.'[37] This looks as if single 'right' or 'positive' alternatives dominated our cognitive culture. Some simple rules of logic which we have chosen to inherit, in fact, have so imbued our thinking that they ultimately function as principles of order – ever widening the gap between logic and life. To create order, the oppositional metaphor tends to divide the world into irremediable opposites; as we cannot, yet, think in a connubial or commensal way, we must think in a bi-polar style. Basically in accord with the principles of identity (ruling that A must be equal to A), of contradiction (stipulating that nothing can be A and not-A), and of the excluded middle (establishing that anything must be either A or not-A), the oppositional metaphor tends to stress the presence of only *one* 'positive' term which stands out against its 'negative' contrary. This is indeed a powerful basis for all forms of onto-valuational dualism, or hierarchization.

Adversarial intellectual orientations actually *share* one important assumption: the delusive conviction that only one of their positions can survive. This means that they 'have' to attack the other and thus they differ only about which front it should be on. The idea of a spectrum, of a connecting ground, on which diversified stances can coexist is hardly conceivable and thus, philosophically, non-existent. The Wittgensteinian suggestion of 'seeing connections' and 'inventing intermediate cases'[38] could only be sustained by a sufficiently developed metaphoric capacity to generate linkages.

In the perspective of our ontogeny, we could even conjecture that the adversarial method is as widespread and appealing as it is as a direct continuation of our inchoate developmental experiences, which may have been felt as rejecting and unreliable ways of structuring interactions. In fact, under the compulsion to be adversarial in order to 'critically evaluate' the presentation of a thesis, we are induced to challenge a lively cluster of ideas by taking each claim separately, while at the same time accepting premises which we only use in order to beat our antagonists on their own terms. In a phylogenetic perspective, the adversarial pattern has little connection with the *philo*-sophy we generally advocate inasmuch as it almost appears to be a successful translation of archaic territorial attitudes into a symbolic cultural domain:[39] paradoxically, while it is highly formalized and detached from life it is comfortably similar to the immemorial patterns of our hominization experiences.

5   The maturation of knowledge

PROBLEMS OF LITERALITY

From a synoptic view of our Greek heritage we could surmise that by devaluing metaphoricity and upgrading epistemic literality, a rationalist claim prevails in which knowledge can be assessed without reference to tradition, culture and human finitude. The 'essential' way of thinking is then to be described in terms of stable principles and general ideas which transcend the dynamics of everyday events. The value – and fascination – of our nascent western thought consists, in fact, in its revolutionary claim to supplant preceding theories of decision-making, which were primarily dependent upon myths, tradition and institutional power; this is our celebrated transition from mythology to rationality. A new form of adjudicating knowledge claims is propagated which is only linked to logical principles, whereby anyone lucidly examining the propositions will be led to a comparable conclusion. At this level of cognitive abstraction the unique individuality of the person no longer enters into a process of rational thinking uninfluenced by the metaphors of tradition. But the belief that thinking should be construed as a thinker-independent process does not coincide with the devaluation of the sophist's tendency to deal with argumentative sequences so as to serve his self-interests. In fact, the interests of the pure philosophers and those of the opportunistic sophists may primarily differ in the sort of power to which they aspire: *cognitive* control as differentiated from *social* control. From our classical background we thus tacitly derive a literalist view of language which often occurs in our philosophical debates. The literality of meanings is here generally regarded as primary and proper, while any propensity for metaphoric usage is deemed parasitic and deviant, alien to 'normal'[1] communication and only acceptable to the extent that it can be paraphrased into the standard vocabulary of the dominant context.

Since the deeper and earliest semantic levels in our ontogeny may not entail a clear distinction between literal and metaphoric language, the reason why literal meanings are regarded as primary with respect to metaphoric meanings is probably a pragmatic one. Literal uses in fact establish the official meaning within any epistemological conglomeration, the use that most *facilitates* the network of internal commensurable communications – and 'easy communication has survival value', remarks Davidson in 'Thought and talk'.[2] Literal use is the more easily manageable in the sense that it is the one least open to misunderstanding and equivocations within a viable epistemic frame. Such practical advantages seem sufficiently to account for the customary hierarchization of meanings whereby the authoritative – because authorial – status of literality is tacitly established.

If we were more in touch with our origins and mortality, we would not automatically privilege arguments about knowledge claims, and would perhaps give new and higher value to the ways in which our language models interactive contexts. In this perspective, terms which we regard as metaphysical hypotheses could be interpreted as the derivatives of our relative blindness to the biological nature of our linguisticity: as living creatures, in fact, we would gladly barter our *relatively stable* rights for *permanent* ones and thus extend the same exchange on to our cognitive and symbolic behaviour.

Of course linguistic performance is typically, although not necessarily, a conduit which is sufficiently regular among a 'large' number of persons to provide for that community the general notions of rule, correctness and standards. And yet the utility of such notions within any phatic community appears to be independent of the utility of an ultimate meta-epistemology which might guide the translation of one language into another. We thus unwittingly pay tribute to the assumption of the primacy of literalness. When Black asks 'How does a metaphor work?', he too may be silently agreeing with a rather mechanistic view of language in which one has already placed irregular and unpredictable uses of language within the orbit of notions such as 'mastery of the language'.[3] It is precisely this 'mastery' that systematically fails to account for metaphoric processes. The idea of a mastery of language seems coextensive to the notion of meaning and thus implies that we may 'find out' and explain how a metaphor actually works. Certain domains of normal science and literality usually display a (*façade* of) linguistic parsimony which undoubtedly increases their prestige. And yet the very same modesty employed for external relations is transformed into complacent self-legitimating attitudes in domestic affairs; and when appreciative recognition is somehow delayed, a suppressed irritation may result. And then we go to some lengths to re-assess the central issues of our speciality in order to make those who do not pay tribute seem necessarily ignorant or primitive. Once the homage has been received, we hasten to decline it in order to display exemplary scientific parsimony.[4]

Parsimony and coherence, at their worst, may unduly encourage lucidity at the price of adequacy, and simply reflect our preference for the clarity of language rather than for the complexity we do not wish to confront. And yet, paradoxically, the issue of literal parsimony as a caution against the proliferation of redundancies in theorizing may also conceal an excessive valuation of certain verbal constructions; unrelated abstractions may not only accompany effusive discussion but strict linguistic parsimony as well. And whenever we attempt to link abstractions emerging from closed system experimentation to the domain of application, a reimmersion into more complex systems of interpretation is inevitably demanded. The more public uses of language which are the object of much contemporary analysis tacitly upgrade a sort of detachment from the daily life of humans. It is the wider context of a living language as the place of experience that may ultimately rest unacknowledged in our philosophies. If we would collect samples of the dense verbal clamour that can be heard during the breaks of congresses, or in the corridors of courts, and if we could seriously listen to that intricacy of voices we might perhaps confront inventive humans trying laboriously to negotiate with the literality of ruling languages.

If we describe a developing person as inclining to speak at all metaphorically, we also 'think' that he must know that he does; and this he can know only if he has some proto-theory of meaning establishing that non-metaphorical expressions are the (literal) norm. In this sense, then, we would say that the construction of metaphorical utterances requires the antecedent presence of literal language. And yet this belief can only be regarded as the inevitable conclusion of typical arguments of our classicity; in isolation, the statement that metaphors necessarily require an established background of literality would be nothing like a self-evident axiom. The primacy of literality could only be established in closely circumscribed contexts: as soon as a system is opened or extended such primacy would dissolve into obsolescence. A clearer awareness of the interaction between literality and metaphoricity may thus entail an opportunity for greater freedom in 'playing' with figure and background structures. An 'excessive' propensity for literal meanings may ultimately be detrimental to the life of language inasmuch as it becomes increasingly detached from the immense complexity of human interactions. The univocity of literal meanings is in fact directly dependent upon the degree to which contexts are circumscribed; the more the domain is clearly defined the more literality is to be found and utilized.

By not appreciating the characteristic of being relatively stable, as distinct from definitely permanent, we confer upon the vocabulary of any cultural context (or standard epistemology) the power to make us blind to the increasing complexity of nature and culture.[5] And yet humans seem constantly eager to see beyond, and in spite of, the canonical differences and similarities induced by a local (or temporal) domain of literality constraining the phatic community. An excessive regard for literal meanings constantly intimates that established differences and similarities are 'good enough' for us and that we should restrict our understanding to whatever the standard vocabulary allows us to construe.

A hypothetical domain of literalness in which the mind manipulates abstract and translucid elements of language would entail an epistemic position of absolute independence from the underlying travails of construction and construal. This independence would dispense with affects and contingencies, with the evolution and involution of traditions – indeed an elitist and lifeless view of independence. And once an 'independent' culture has a certain structure, then a certain mode of doing philosophy gets locked into place, such as, for instance, a primary concern for theories of meaning and a lesser attention to the interactive aspects of language.

In a 'juvenile' approach to any given epistemology we may think that the construal of reality involves the application of literal procedures or algorithms capable of automatically generating reliable solutions; and once our thinking is well ingrained with theories and concepts we may even incline toward being text-dependent readers of the world. An attitude of devaluational hierarchization of inner life and language and a tribute to literality do of course perform a relevant function in an ontogenetic perspective, since the developing mind can thus begin to categorize experience in a stable and consensual manner. And yet, in the process of constructing a consensual reality the person in the making internalizes an epistemic structure which downgrades the more personal aspects of inner life. This results in an increasing negation of the sort of life emanating from one's own depths – all the way to the utmost tolerable atrophy. Inner messages are thus given up in favour of the literal language proposed by the epistemic community. More generally, the higher levels of language development can be accompanied by a decline of metaphoric constructs so that self and reality come to be increasingly defined in terms of the vocabulary of dominant epistemologies and disembodied languages. Labouvie-Vief points out, for instance, that 'adolescents' seem to operate within a deductive structure in which problems are seen as unambiguous and not requiring interpretation: 'These individuals are highly text-dependent, believing that conclusions are immanent in the text rather than emerging from the active thinking process of thinkers.' Hence for adolescents of all ages ambiguity is attributed to faulty thinking rather than to rationally justifiable qualitative differences between different readers of the text.[6]

If metaphor is regarded as an essential aspect of linguistic life, this entails an expectation of constant evolution in meanings. And yet the commensurable, literalist background of any standard epistemology cannot possibly allow for a 'physiological' transformation of meanings inasmuch as a literal meaning which is not constant and univocal automatically comes to be regarded as equivocal, and thus only suitable for exclusion. As equivocation is incompatible with deductive logic because, of course, a deductive argument is invalid unless its terms retain their sense from premises to conclusion, Arbib and Hesse maintain that 'language cannot . . . be assimilated to an ideal logic *except as a limiting case in special circumstances*'. Hierarchizing whatever literal language there is as if it were the language for adjudicating not only 'truth claims' but, correlatively, all sorts of conflicts would ultimately sustain a split-inducing language causing indefinite sequences of fragmentation.

THE PATHOLOGY OF LITERALNESS

Offering advantages such as sparing the tensions of inner life, the systematic adherence to literalness may ultimately incline the individual to identify with external situations and objects to the point of avoiding contact with expressions of his own self. In this perspective we are quite distant from a view of metaphoric language as an intriguing topic of scholarly concern: use of metaphoric language appears instead profoundly interwoven with the actual development of our inner life. As the style of ratiocination operating through univocal literal language is oriented towards facts and action, events involving anxiety and inner pain may come to appear as perplexingly non-mental, or perhaps as physiological pauses in the regular course of successfully using the world by means of codified knowledge. For an emblematic assessment of literalness we could invoke the Cartesian contention that 'clear and distinct ideas are commonly associated with names',[9] in conjunction with the claim that 'we can scarcely conceive of anything so distinctly as to be able to separate . . . that which we conceive from the words chosen to express the same'.[10] This contention implies a truncated understanding of events, frozen at synchronic cross-sections in time.[11]

Even recreational activities may ultimately come to lack playfulness and to be performed with the same demanding attitude as any other productive activity. These literalistic styles, moreover, tend to shape the quality of life in ways which are difficult to identify because our usual methods of observation largely depend upon the literal vocabulary of our dominant epistemologies. The prevalence of a literalist inclination could thus be viewed as a life-damaging compulsion to be 'normal'. We can perceive this inclination whenever there is a tendency to paraphrase or translate our metaphoric attempts into objective utterances even at the cost of annulling original meanings and de-symbolizing our own linguisticity. Should this tendency become dominant to the point of discarding our emergent thoughts, we would then become permanently constrained into the boundaries of literalness. And whenever forced to confront complex life situations, or 'foreign' areas of literalness, the atrophy of our metaphoric capacities would inevitably be betrayed.

In the potential dominance of conventions and literalness we can discern a novel method for somehow assessing an inconspicuous form of human pathology which we could name the 'literalist distortion', for lack of a better term. As we know, we commonly regard as mentally ill those who do not have a sufficiently good sense of reality and of interpersonal transactions. But then, this generalized approach could be integrated, by converse, with a concern for those who are so firmly in contact with standard reality that they ultimately forsake a contact with the deeper sources of their subjectivity, and thus with a more creative participation in reality. The domain of literalness gravitates in fact towards a sign-type of language characterized by a one-to-one correspondence to events and for a tightly defined equivalence to such events;[12] a less literal language would allow for a one-to-many relationship, for a surplus of meanings, as Ricoeur puts it,[13] which are not exact equivalents but rather *suggest* the nature of that which is expressed in language. As is maintained in psychoanalytic culture, there are subjects who may even develop a vicarious personality only intent upon being 'objective', and primarily engaged with standard representationalist concerns to the detriment of any awareness of messages originating from within.

The self-propagating power of languages which have been crystallized into epistemologies induces a cultural climate which, in extreme cases, makes it impossible for us to advance to the level of being speaking individuals, and confines us instead in 'spoken subjects' – in the sense that language actually speaks through us. The unquestioned literalness of language seems to possess a robotic autonomy of its own, such that it expands with no regard for the subject's efforts of self-creation. In this sort of linguistic life 'acting' appears as preferable to any form of elaboration and creativity; substitution of situations, persons, and things thus becomes preferable to any form of laborious repair and transformation. Broken relations are replaced with fresh relations, discarded objects with new objects in a general style derived from the consumption of standard goods and world-views, rather than from a personalized generation of culture. And indeed, a literal language would hardly allow us to fathom our own depths and recover resources for responsibly coping with the world. Once a more personal language is discredited in favour of a more literal one, whose power is guaranteed by a background of epistemological commensurability, the instruments for dealing with our own selves are still more endangered.

It is possible that new forms of pathology are now emerging, or else that we are now gaining an awareness of painful styles of life which have always existed. Life-damaging inclinations may be detected in a tendency to gravitate towards literalness in such a way that the more personal non-literal expressions are increasingly atrophied.[14] What is left is a mute distress due to the annulment of one's inner life, or the need to search for ways of symbolizing such inner void in response to the rare occasions when someone may try to construe our irrepressible metaphoric attempts. In some cases it is almost as if a literalistic vicarious personality were at work, capable only of objective transactions and virtually incapable of authentic relations – almost an inclination to be an object among objects. Experiences are privileged to the extent that they are amenable to expression through the literal language which prevails, at the cost of inducing an even greater discrepancy from the experiences emanating from a 'silenced', concealed part of the self. At the level of verbalization a situation is created whereby language may be recruited to endorse a potentially increasing gap between a private 'true' self and a social 'false' self; and because a false self can be reinforced by means of dialogic responses, it will increasingly establish its dominance.[15] Literal language might even become the almost exclusive means for being with others and sharing life's vicissitudes: it may sadly be the case that whenever a more personal language is used, the environment tends not to respond, as if the individual were non-existent. To adhere to a literalist language is perhaps to try desperately to be normal. And we can envisage a common literalist danger in the form of a massive transfer of inner conditions upon standard expressions so as to increasingly de-symbolize inner events. If this attitude predominates and is used to get rid of unbearable inner states, we inevitably move in the direction of a literalist pathology. And by depending upon such literalness we can also increasingly entrust our inner functions to concrete objects and tangible situations. However well we use and coordinate these externalized inner functions, we may in fact construct for ourselves a life space of meaningless abundance.

Literal language may illusively 'function' as a mechanism for purifying interactions from residues of unbearable meanings, and for rendering everything 'normal'. By means of conventional language we can deal with meanings in such a way as to cancel their fullness and devitalize them at the same time.[16] The dominance of these procedures may be so familiar that it is found acceptable: indeed we may be constantly depriving of significance the expressions we cannot accommodate in whatever context of literality we inhabit. And yet, the salient question does not so much pertain to the damage inflicted by the non-construal of metaphoric efforts but rather to the *acceptance* of an interactive paradigm of non-construal; should this permeate the general style of our language games we would embark in a silent collusion with the unmonitorable degradation of human linguisticity. In our subservience to the domination of literalness we may become mainly interested in facts. And yet, our inclination toward facticity is not an emanation of curiosity aiming to enrich the complexity of experience in the modes of scientific creativity; adhering to factual conditions would be more like a reassuring closeness in which we tend to be impersonal and thing-like. When this propensity dominates, it can be accompanied by an active interest in being part of an organizational structure in which pseudo-intimacy is enhanced in place of a challenging personal closeness.[17] It is interesting to note that expressions of rage and hatred may even come to constitute rare opportunities for the experience of depth and intimacy; the literalist cultural atmosphere may thus suddenly be shat-tered with a paradoxical 'relief' for the interlocutors engaged in it. To obtain a stronger contact, recourse is made to metaphors triggering hostility which in turn can elicit signals of personalized intentions otherwise concealed. In this perspective even such disruptive ways of breaking through literalness may ultimately be a way to 'remedy' the estrangement of an individual from the inner life of another. Similarly, in the course of rebellion against the suffocating language of literalness one may be tempted to evade 'mental' contexts of any kind and to seek refuge in the most disparate action contexts.

The pragmatic reward for the addiction to literal language and quasi-extinct metaphoric expressions is a guarantee of normality and a reassurance of belonging to the mainstream of culture; it is a valuational reassurance offered by a visible behaviour constantly in keeping with whatever standard epistemology is in force. Bruner remarks that because we feel insecure, we do not like to admit our humanity; and even our scientific products 'have about them an aseptic quality designed to proclaim the intellectual purity of our enterprise'.[18] Through a stable concern for objective behavioural actions, individuals may even tend to become more 'objects' them 'subjects'. In such a potential general tendency we might perceive the inconspicuous conviction that one's profound roots of the mind – what we call the 'unconscious' – are something quite obsolete, in fact useless and only worth discarding in view of 'serious' progress. 'Education' at times almost seems to favour a subtle, yet massive, atrophy of our curiosity as if the intention were to impart a 'substantial' education with the proviso that it be of no use for purposes of personal creativity. In the educational act of instilling knowledge what is offered is something which the recipient cannot – or should not – learn to produce on his own.[19] Bombarded by information, one has to pretend to develop while probably feeling impoverished by a tangle of linguistic games in which one is hooked, and which one is unable to stop playing because they tend to perpetuate the epistemol-ogy from which they emanate.

Deconstructive metaphors could thus be regarded as successful articulations of profound desires to break free from ossified personal or intersubjective structures that tend to exclude from life; they may in fact serve the salutary function of neutralizing the 'poisonous' influence of an excessively conventional language. If not in practice, at least in theory or in hypothetical terms, alternative ways of conceptualizing ourselves and the world can be attained through deconstructive metaphors providing logical escapes from unlivable world-views. And whenever circumstances compel one to re-enter a subjective life for which the standard vocabulary is not sufficient, one may opt for whatever cultural forms of psychic anaesthesia seem to be available.

In an evolutionary perspective, metaphors tend to represent the relatively more cultural features of our life in terms of its more natural aspects. One of the unacknowledged effects of this tendency is to regard as fixed and natural even conditions which are historically contingent and for which changing human agents are responsible. Thus, even endemic metaphors which hinder self-creation projects may become fixated in character structures generating correlative world-views.[20] There is perhaps a need for therapeutic metaphors to exorcise the effects of the unpleasant ones which tend, deceptively, to solidify into our so-called human nature. Major transformations need in fact to be expressed in an extraliteral language capable of indicating potential structures other than those which have become so stable as to appear 'logical' or 'natural'. The salient question is what could be the nature of interactive relations depending upon epistemic literality. Such relations could be described as generally imitative and virtually non-metabolic, as if our saturation with literal language could only induce imitative acquisitions which exclude all forms of personal metabolic effort; world-views can be thus developed which resemble a sequence of detached beliefs operating in a vacuum.

Developing individuals confined within the unidentifiable boundaries of a widely literal linguisticity may laboriously seek construals of their metaphoric attempts in either relatively distant interactions or, conversely, may strive to develop the 'art' of a secret intrapsychic dialogue as an alternative to impossible interpersonal exchanges. An awareness of abandonment and isolation may come to dominate one's inner world whenever absence of appropriate construals is persistent enough. At this critical point of vulnerability, the evolving person is prepared for what could be termed bonding with whatever culture is available and for locking into it without reservations. And to disrespect the rules of whatever cultural context one may need to integrate with will mean banishment and loss of links – even with the refuge community. To avert such danger, individuals tend to accept without question the strictures the system imposes, with further detriment to authentic languaging. In whichever contexts literalness is at a premium there are positive reinforcements for adaptation to a standard vocabulary and the lack of interest in metaphoric construal may be so widespread that whatever cannot be heard ultimately becomes non-existent – unheard of. To the extent that we are unwittingly absorbed into the pathology of literalness we are inhibited in the symbolization of inner life; 'intimacy' is thus attained not through metaphor but through destructive relations which may never erupt into overt violence inasmuch as they are not implemented in the attack on psychic life but in the *prevention* of it. The worst of dangers is thus the one most likely to be unnoticed. Not only may there be an inability for metaphoric construal but also a fear of creative expressions, which threaten cohesive normality; an interest in 'metaphoric' language is only acceptable for the purpose of paying tributes to the literalness of the phatic community – to 'reality' itself. To be really good is to be superior in being normal. Silently threatening the life of culture, may be an endemic tendency to participate in disparate plausible activities that are ultimately detached from deeper personal concerns. The hierarchization of official languages as the highest forms of linguisticity almost seems to incline our lives to gravitate toward external objects or canonized structures in such a way as to achieve a painless atrophy of inner resources. And yet the emptying out of our personal minds may turn out to be unbearable. But to make the predicament worse whenever distress is so intense as to be voiced, we may be faced with the horror of not being able to articulate the inner condition, as if we had constantly to be indifferent to our own selves: almost as if there were nothing to disapprove just because we have no *way* to complain or no-*thing* to complain about.

The present concern is not with the analysis of why some metaphors can express what Black calls the sense of the 'rich correspondences and analogies of domains conventionally separated',[21] but rather with the accompanying claim that this role sustains our life-enhancing engagement in metaphoric talk. Cooper, for instance, remarks that 'metaphor is an essential tool at the embryonic stage of theory, and is therefore sustained by whatever sustains theorizing about the world and ourselves.'[22] But then we should ask what life would be like if we could not even minimally contribute to theories about the world and ourselves, and if this potential were not developed at all. In the case of individuals whose languaging is excessively literal (or 'normal' to the point of being pathological), there is hardly any theorizing about the world and the self. The individual excludes himself from creative life by passively adhering to whatever theories are there to be utilized. Such outright normality may in fact conceal a benumbing pathology – a nameless one – which is so perfectly camouflaged as to remain unnoticed and thus not amenable to any form of articulation.

The sort of literal language which is appropriate within certain areas of human culture can easily tend towards territorial expansion inasmuch as it comes to be seen as the most valuable of languages – the only one linked with objectivity and thus rightfully entitled to be exported. Such honorary extensions may be fatal to the inner lives of humans as they can result in a form of literalistic control so severe as to damage the joint evolution of affects and cognition. Ontogenetically, stereotyped ways of literal discourse may become ossified into categories which claim to define life itself even though they only embody remote caricatures of life; the result is a mental apparatus which only serves the purpose of excluding the individual from life or else of producing a lifeless imitation of it. Attempts at introspective life are blocked inasmuch as the metaphoric resources of the subject have been repeatedly 'corrected' and reduced to a literal language which 'denies' the innumerable subtleties of the individual's personal existence. The continued prevalence of literal language may then stabilize in a sort of behaviour more suited to the simple discharge of affects than to the communication and use of inner events.

To the extent that we can appreciate the metaphorical features of psychic life, we recognize that they also have implications for the epistemology of psychological studies. In this perspective, then, psychological research cannot discount endeavours to recover what lies forgotten beneath the literalizing attitudes of whatever epistemologies are in force. The effort to reconnect literalness and metaphoricity is not a question of generating revolutionary ideas but of recovering a culture's neglected but not quite forgotten stories.[23]

COGNITION AND MATURITY

The theme of integration which seems to characterize later life developments is reflected in myths and literature: stories featuring young protagonists highlight conquests of the outer world and a heroic mastery of the 'unconscious', whereas narratives about 'adults' basically present a quest for maturity rather than adventure, coexistence rather than victory. And, indeed, the inward journey after mid-life seems to be the theme of mythical writings. The general idea of this transformation appears to relate to profound processes aiming to cope with, and integrate, heterogeneous bits of reality and to attenuate denials, divisions and projections. That the central task of adulthood is the reorganization of affectual life is a salient aspect of most theories of the self. Jung anticipates this view in his claim that a major goal of maturation is to go beyond exclusive identifications with the conscious ego and to re-link one's inner world with archetypal structures from which the ego originally emerged.

Our initial cultural maturation is probably aided by the concurrent development of a notion of the mind as an enlightening agency of individual ratiocination and volition, as something not only distinct but almost opposed to organismic processes, which are themselves not subject to rational and volitional control.[24] The life cycle of our intellectual evolution could perhaps be described in terms of a way 'out' of organismic conditions and traditional thinking, and then as a recovery through creative integration of these same dimensions.

From our laboriously acquired capacity to see the ego as a mental and idealized agent of ratiocination we may then attempt to re-link our intellectuality to its affectual and finite roots. It is worth noting, incidentally, that most theories of self-development have primarily emphasized juvenile, or heroic, ego functions which could perhaps be exemplified with the territorial Freudian slogan 'Where id was, there ego shall be.'[25] In the earlier part of a mind's life cycle we may generally 'perceive' a propensity for transformational projects, almost a passion for change for its own sake – whether obtained by our own resources or caused by external agents. In what we might call the maturity of our development, integration and adaptation seem gradually to prevail over an inclination towards 'changing the world'.

The relevance of human metaphoricity may also be highlighted in connection with our enduring hopes for transformational changes. And yet it is not always clear whether we seek authentic changes or the continuation of an archaic relation with something or someone, which signifies for us the experience of transformations coming to us from an external source. As we know, our whole advertising system thrives on a powerful ambiguity whereby anything such as goods or theories are presented as capable of producing changes that will significantly transform our inner world. Bollas suggests that these metaphorically advertised items are not so much noteworthy as genuine instruments of transformation but rather for their evocative force: they somehow re-link us with experiences that we may have never properly thought about, but which we have nevertheless 'known' by living through them.[26] The captivating promises in areas ranging from commodities to ideals may resonate with those phases in our development in which major life-enhancing transformations were vividly expected from external figures. The intense quality of these experiences and expectations, which we somehow 'know' but cannot clearly think about and articulate, is what renders the call effective. Promotional calls of any kind thus seem to rely on promises which connect with early episodes in our itinerary, rather than upon thoughts or even fantasies emanating from our maturing selves.

Any anticipation of being transformed *by* a 'superior' epistemology may be connected to significant experiences in our lives and may consequently inspire an otherwise inexplicable awe toward any theoretical context emitting – indeed, radiating – transformational promises. But then, 'Intelligent practice is not a step-child of theory', objects Ryle. 'On the contrary, theorizing is one practice amongst others and is itself intelligently or stupidly conducted.'[27] Thus metaphors work their wonders in our adult life partly as a consequence of original expectations of transformational events. This linkage does not so much emerge in explicit cognitive terms but rather through reverberations of extreme vicissitudes in our self-formation itinerary. The force of certain metaphoric presentations may be seen as the correlate of our active search for symbolic equivalents of inchoate transformational agents, and for the intensity of such experiences. For indeed, in our early experiences parents *can* transform our inner world through their behaviour. 'Idealization' of theories, persons, or possessions, may function as attempts to somehow verify and confirm that something or someone is endowed with sure transformational powers.[28] And the converse of these expectations is the endemic urge to change the world or to conflate with agents to which this capacity is 'justifiably' attributed. The persistent search for 'perfect' cognitive theories not only represents a longing for ideal mutative objects but can also be an indication of deficiencies in the experience of one's capacities in world assessment. The question also arises whether an insatiable demand for more clarity and stability than can ever be obtained from the intellectual side of life could derive from a sense of insufficient visibility of primal interactive rules. The weaker the salvational power of early interlocutors the greater the disposition to adhere to implicit or explicit transformational promises emanating from prestigious theories. Under extreme circumstances of narcissistic weakness, parental figures may even tend to use their offspring as their own transformational agents by demanding the fulfilment of their own life expectations; the unformed human beings may thus be emptied of their own projects and only function as containers of alien expectations which they cannot possibly satisfy.

Kept intact by the frequent tributes we pay to any dominant epistemology, our semantic reality is constantly and eloquently voiced to the point that we grow fearful of silence as if it might appear hopelessly empty. We may have to re-learn to seek the advantages of our innermost language; a language which differs from the propositional logic chattering in our heads. But then, the evidence that makes any proposition certain is seldom, if ever, supplied by one single more certain item; the evidence rather consists in a great variety of connections which can be made on every side, between it and the profound remainder of our experience. Our perspective, in some sense, departs from the Ockamist policy – *Entia non sunt multiplicanda propter necessitatem* – of preferring the method of cancellation and parsimony to the method of spontaneous multiplication. In our exclusive pursuit of clarity we may in fact fail to see that familiar, accepted ideas seem clearer than unfamiliar ones. In this connection we may invoke Rorty's argument to the effect that the line between the domains of epistemology and hermeneutics is not a matter of the difference between theoretical and practical endeavours, nor yet between understanding and explaining: 'The difference is purely one of familiarity', he concludes.[29]

As we know, the clarity of an argument depends on its relation to the relevant premisses. But in life-dependent circumstances, as distinct from purely formal enclaves, most of the premisses of an argument are never fully stated, and many of them have never been made explicit. Midgley suggests that the real need is somehow to gain an awareness of the variety of concealed premisses which prompt our arguments and to select the ones that are more directly relevant,[30] which would indeed be a challenging enterprise. But then, whenever clarity is the sole aim, it can be conveniently attained by 'failing' to appreciate any premisses except those known as the more likely to lead to one's own conclusions.[31] The complexity of life is thus easily sacrificed to clarity.

And, indeed, even our theories of knowledge are basically guided by underlying metaphors of human interaction. To try to understand them properly, that is, in conjunction with their practical effects, one ought to consider the underlying variety of antecedents. Theories generated by different metaphors may actually deal with different aspects of knowledge so that our laborious comparisons attempted for the sake of 'perfecting' norm-setting standards of knowledge may turn out to be fruitless, much as would happen if comparing answers to different questions.[32] Recent developments in diverse fields indicate that intellectual maturity could be the major result of balancing operations allowing for a metaphorical conversation between diverse epistemologies and real life events. Rooted in a defensive idealization of pure thinking, the classical distinction and valuational dualism separating formal thought from the rest of our intelligence may finally come across as a limiting condition interfering with maturation and creativity.

6 The relationship between digital and analogic styles

NOTES ON THE DIFFERENCE BETWEEN DIGITAL AND ANALOGIC STYLES

In the great developments of western culture emphasis has been shifting from the search for meaning to the management of information; there has been an overall move away from the elaboration of integrative goals towards the processing of discrete elements.[1] Computation has silently come to be regarded as one of the ruling paradigms, and epistemic commensurability has soared to the highest criterion for the evaluation of a wide variety of issues emerging in our age. Once the ideas of computation, algorithms and commensurability permeate culture at large, a message is only 'meaningful' if it reduces alternative choices and minimizes polysemous, connotative or metaphoric components. And this general understanding of meaning may be regarded as one of the main factors enhancing the qualities of incisive lucidity and predictive power of western logic. If we observe a structure through a digital outlook it does in fact appear to us as made up of discrete elements capable of coming together at the highest level of organization. Unequivocal and denotative features are singled out so that messages can be channelled through antecedently established logical sequences approximating the exactitude of a digital language. Such symbolic structures are eminently suited to satisfy our unending search for clarity and univocity even though they often imply a dismissal of deeper connecting dimensions. However limiting, this procedural style is essential to safeguard the consistency of formal and cognitive structures. Highlighting digital ways of operating we can in fact appreciate how distinct elements can indefinitely interact with other elements.

In a dialogic perspective, the use of such terms as 'discrete' and 'continuous' (as interactive variants of digital and analogic processes), may aid in the identification of contexts which point to a unified interaction, on the one hand, and of different contexts which involve separate selves operating as closed systems, on the other. Each of these contexts may represent one of the aspects of the living structure of our linguisticity. And yet what is striking is that both of these communicative modes seem primarily bent on maintaining their own specific style, with hardly any interest in the other form of communication or in the maturational evolution of the global context itself.

Highlighting analogical functions, we can instead perceive structures that are really quite cohesive and not indistinct from one another. If we look at a structure as if it were a continuity we may recognize in it a rich potential of internal 'communication' inasmuch as its parts may function as open systems with regard to each other. Any such structure may only define itself in terms of what belongs to it and only grows by incorporating elements which become unrecognizable as separate elements. Such communicative potential of an analogically organized structure does not provide for specific internal roles nor for boundaries with external areas of input and output. In this sense, then, it almost prevents innovative contacts with external elements. In such structures no part may function as a point of observation for other parts, and since there is no sufficient distance between any of its parts we cannot properly think of an interaction *between* them. This level could be thought of as the area of unconscious communications and of the overlapping of meanings in stabilized collusions; and yet this is also the matrix of empathetic productions, and of perceptions which can be germinal and illuminating.

At the analogic level there prevails a mode of thinking that is a matter of more evocation and personal usage, while the digital level is ideally suited to deal with classes, relations, and structures. At the analogic level our thoughts appear as 'dynamic' and 'exciting' – constantly transcending linguistic norms. And transformations deriving from the conjunction of what should be kept separate, according to any standard logic, may cause both disturbances and excitement, for these thoughts are in fact open and may overextend reality, as in fantasy. The digital level, in contrast, appears as relatively peaceful and well regulated inasmuch as our literalness tends semantically to circumscribe thoughts so that they stay in place and do not disturb the balance of structures. And the reason why our cognitive theories frequently run into trouble could be due to the fact that we are inexorably embedded in a primal cognitive basis in which experiences escape from the limits imposed by words.

As linguistic variants of digital and analogic processes, literality and metaphor may be caught in a secret rivalry as each attempts to absorb each other's task. In our integrative outlook, though, we can opt for striving toward a renovating logic of coexistence rather than toward a 'territorial' behaviour – however transposed in the discursive domain.[2] We may not have a culture equal to the challenges of survival and evolution until we can both distinguish, and closely compare with each other, the central attitudes of philosophy, science and art in order constantly to revise them.

Although the modes of digital and analogic thinking cannot be exclusively related to literal and metaphoric interactions, even Bruner[3] has recently recast an awareness of such non-integrated duality in terms of a distinction between 'narrative' and 'paradigmatic' modes of knowing, which construe and verify reality in rather different ways. The 'narrative' orientation to reality may be exemplified by stories in which a 'truthful', meaningful account is based on figurative language and psychological causality of human experiences, whereas the 'paradigmatic' way depends upon exact rules and deductive reasoning. Although affects and deductions are frequently interwined, they never fuse, or combine, to form one inclusive type of experience, or a super-logic, which would comprise both modes as components of a more general logic. In Matte Blanco's view it is not impossible to conceive of a higher-dimensional logic which would have the logic of deductions and the logic of affects as substructures of it.[4] Should such a logical frame ever be available, instead of defining the analogic symmetrical structure of affects in terms of the violations of the classical logic of asymmetries, we could define it in terms of this much wider conception of our mental functions. Perhaps this 'new' logic would not be obvious in an intuitive way to our intelligence as the familiar logic underlying our ratiocination; it might require a noteworthy evolutionary advancement for us to regard it as familiar and hence intuitively logical. In Matte Blanco's perspective, however, it is a question of a *higher* number of dimensions which makes our lower-dimensional thinking incapable of grasping the unconscious 'just as a painted tray cannot be a recipient for real apples';[5] and this is the reason why we cannot be aware of them and why they are unconscious in us. Thus if we had a consciousness capable of a higher number of dimensions than that required to think in terms of classical logic, then we would be aware not only of our propositional thinking but also of our symmetrical, unconscious thinking. In Matte Blanco's view our every-day thoughts and feelings about persons, things and their interactions mean different things to us at what may be called *deeper* levels in our minds.[6] Such differences in 'depth' may be conceptually differentiated according to the degree of symmetrization routinely present at that level. In these terms, experience can be viewed as typified by the interwoven proportion of symmetrical and asymmetrical logic. Differing qualities, or phases, of experience can be characterized by the prevailing combination of the two modes of logic.[7] As remote derivatives of the principle of non-contradiction, requirements for a temporal succession of distinct events and for a location of separate objects seem to be tacitly propagated in our culture. In our current forms of communication, the analogic elements may be internal to them, while the digital components utilize previously selected signals which somehow constrain the communicative event.[8] While a 'digital' language can be isomorphically translated into another equivalent, the underlying 'analogic' modes only allow for a greater local resonance between different elements; and yet, even when it carries a truth claim and an objective referent, a statement at times includes enigmatic and contradictory features. Our complete experiences, and our ways of conceptualizing them, are thus only partially separate and somehow influence one another.

Computation has been also developing into a model of the mind, and the concept of computability has inexorably eroded the general notion of ratiocination. In Bruner's view,[9] cognitive processes are increasingly equated with programs that could be performed by computational algorithms, and the success of efforts to account for human capacities such as, for instance, memory or concept attainment, is ultimately deemed to coincide with the ability to simulate such capacities through computerized programs. In Rorty's synoptic view, the distinction between 'rationality' and something else has traditionally been drawn so as to coincide roughly with a distinction between inference and imagination: we are being rational, 'so the story goes', in so far as we adhere to the logical structure given at the beginning of the inquiry and so long as we can offer an argument for the belief developed at the end of the inquiry by referring back to the beliefs held at the beginning.[10] And with regard to the genesis of 'rationality', we could say that the epistemology of Piaget is prevalently Apollonian in that it is written in the framework of reasonableness in human life; in methodology it accordingly tends towards the timeless security of exact science. In contrast, Freudian 'rationality' tends to be Dionysian in that it emphasizes the emotional and the instinctual human factors. Differently incorporating digital and analogic processes, the two approaches are themselves demonstrations of two different 'styles' of knowledge.

Rorty also remarks that 'the scientists' may have been erroneously thought of as 'going up or down flow-charts labeled "the logic of confirmation" or "the logic of explanation" and as operating within a logical space in which, magically, all possible descriptions of everything were already at hand.[11] Insofar as this logical structure is unavailable or not clearly perceived, it is the 'responsibility' of conceptual analysis to make it visible, that is, to translate every nuclear locution into a clear one, where 'clear' means something like 'accessible to every rational inquirer'. And yet 'scientists' and scholars probably do not regard rational inquiry as a matter of gathering knowledge into a unifiable, consensual context, by translating – or forcing – one's passion for research into the vocabulary of a set of sentences which any rational inquirer would regard as truth-value bearers.

The outstanding benefits of a univocal and 'digital' language can thus be attained by ignoring affectual resonances and marginal languages. The structure of this approach can be seen as summed up in a remark in Hartmann's *Philosophy of the Unconscious*: 'Mankind very naturally began its research in Philosophy with the examination of what was immediately given in consciousness.'[12] To this statement we could juxtapose Bruner's remark that 'reaching for knowledge with the right hand is science. Yet to say only that much of science is to overlook one of its excitements, for the great hypotheses of science are gifts carried in the left . . . And should we say that reaching for knowledge with the left hand is art? Again it is not enough, for . . . there is a barrier between undisciplined fantasy and art.'[13]

CONNECTIONS BETWEEN DIGITAL AND ANALOGIC PROCESSES

Human beings insist on attempting to make apparently useless exchanges between the digital and analogic styles: while the digital and analogic ways of our linguisticity can exhibit more readily appreciable products, the laborious shifts from one to the other may even seem particularly arduous and fruitless. Such changes of perspective encourage enough flexibility of mind for an 'encounter', or confrontation, of the two styles to take place in such a way that the digital qualities of our reasoning are not endangered and the cohesive tendency of our analogic thinking is not threatened.[14] We could even say that perhaps these two modes of knowledge resemble the planes of a Moebius strip, which locally appear as separate enterprises in different domains, but while following each plane around the strip we come to recognize that it is in fact the same unified path that we are exploring. Metaphoric language thus seems particularly suited to moving epistemically between any of the mobile logical poles which can be envisaged on any segment of the strip. The distinction between the hermeneutical and the epistemological approach would consequently appear as a relative one, indicating a polarity which comprises a continuum of diversified outlooks.[15] The opposition between the participatory and the detached approach can arise on any stretch of the spectrum where one 'objective' point of view claims dominance over another, more 'subjective' one, and that claim is resisted.[16] We thus have digital processes and analogic processes, asymmetrical relations in what we call conscious thinking and symmetrical relations in our so-called unconscious life, organismic experiences and mental experiences. Problems arise when we seek to identify *relationships between* the two, and (metaphoric) links connecting such basic modes of our being. Already Freud in his exploration of the manifest content of dreams, as distinct from a hidden content, frequently resorts to ambiguous terms which are described as 'verbal bridges' (*Wortbrücken*) connecting hidden and manifest meanings. In a note he 'explains' that polisemous terms function as mechanisms of connection and exchange: when these points of conjunction are displaced we find ourselves on a different track; and it is precisely on this latter track that we find the thoughts hidden behind the narrative of a dream.[17]

Johnson, for instance, is among those who repeatedly argue that image schemata supporting our thought processes derive from what happens to us as organisms and are non-propositional in nature. 'They exist rather, in a continuous *analog* fashion in our understanding.'[18] Once again we are confronted with the oppositional juxtaposition of *analog* functions, such as image schemata, and *digital* processes such as the calculus of propositions, which we employ for purposes of argumentation and understanding. A 'convenient' attitude would be to opt for one or other of the functions and to elaborate our view of linguisticity (rationality, understanding, humanness . . .) through either of these two basic polarities without 'excessive' concern for the *relation* between our biological existence and our dialogic life, between life and rational life. But then, as our formal languages have by now reached a formidable development – indeed, a maturity – we may be safe in seriously considering their links with organic, affectual and individual life. Epistemic and linguistic maturity could in fact dispense with the 'conviction' that propositional and affectual modes of operating constitute incommensurable domains of cultural functioning, separated by inviolable boundaries. Usually attempted by means of metaphoric expressions, the crossing of such boundaries often entails a thorough recontextualization of problems and thus new, relatively stable, conglomerations of literality. And yet, to the extent that epistemic literalness 'refuses' to integrate elements deriving from the affectual pole of life it silently becomes prone to the self-defeating irrationality of obsolescence and isolation.[19] An awareness of such potential irrationality deriving from a divisive approach, and the irrepressible quest for integrated forms of ratiocination, seem imperceptibly to reaffirm the germinal strength of what we call a humanistic culture.

As metaphors create links which overcome categorical distinctions such as animate/inanimate, cosmic/biological, human/animal, they constitute a fascinating domain in which we may closely observe the procedures we actually use to move from one way of reasoning to another. There is much talk about the vivacity of metaphors probably because they make it possible for the mind to move from the use of abstract and circumscribed principles operating at the propositional level, to the 'concrete', holistic images which thrive in the analogic domain. Metaphors provide a mediation between these levels and thus appear 'alive' because they *enliven* the mind through the creation of contacts between separate domains.

Johnson remarks that most discussions imply a distinction between a meaning (regarded as conceptual, propositional and representational) and a background (regarded as pre-intentional and non-representational) against which meaning emerges.[20] This entails that there are non-propositional structures in our living background that play a more relevant role in the elaboration of meaning than is usually allowed by objectivist outlooks. And if we take this generally accepted view seriously enough, we will need to confront the question of the relationship (interaction, rapport, exchanges) between meaning and background. As the two domains usually make a joint presentation, it should be illuminating to explore the possible interactions of the two. There is no question, therefore, of either focusing on understanding (as a variant of background), or explaining (as a variant of meaning), inasmuch as the currently devalued understanding may actually come across as the generative basis of explanatory knowledge. In this perspective, then, it is not surprising that our official languages do relate to the world and link with events – which have been previously 'understood' through our participatory life experience.

Even our more refined and normal products could be seen as providing a 'disguise' for deeper motives silently claiming expression. In a diachronic perspective, mental events can be recognized in which we gain correct and subtle intuitions of our interactive condition – even though we are hardly aware of them.[21] Wonderful or frightening truths can be developed regarding our interpersonal predicament, and our subsequent standard knowledge may actually encode our subliminal perceptions in such a way as to render our intuitions consensually usable and to defend the mind from unbearable impressions. Univocal, digital language could thus be seen as the successful newcomer; and although it can be distinguishable in descriptive terms, it cannot be separated in our lived knowledge or culture if it is not to be at risk of suffering extensive deterioration. And such potential deteriorations cannot be properly monitored, or even articulated, because the literality of any relatively stable epistemology cannot, *per se*, appreciate the necessity or plausibility of exploring links with analogic or affectual dimensions. The unnoticed devaluation of connecting metaphors may thus collude with a sort of philosophical fiction whereby we could split ourselves into distinct knowers of true sentences, on the one hand, and choosers of attitudes on the other. Our irrepressible metaphoricity contributes nevertheless to an epistemic perspective whereby we understand something of the object *and* of the cognitive attitude of the subject, thus enhancing a two-way relationship which reconnects the intellectual style of speakers with the thing we speak about.

Unless we constantly seek connecting mediations with deeper levels of the mind, our objectifying analytic behaviour can be both overrated and underrated. A succession of analytic advances may be conducive to a conception of reality that leaves our personal perspective further and further behind, possibly sacrificing our 'natural' propensity for completeness and integration. We cannot accept forgetting about our subjective starting-point indefinitely for, indeed, our early experiences belong to the complex reality we seek to understand. Connecting difficulties are in fact likely to obtrude whenever the analytical approach confronts the life of the mind and tries to encompass subjectivity in its cognitive scope. This linkage between available knowledge and the activities of the mind is frequently attempted outside philosophical scholasticism since it finds the material intractable and usually opts for more conceptually homogeneous issues. Nagel suggests that the content of an objective view and its claims to completeness are inevitably affected by the attempt to combine them with the view from where we are; similarly, the subjective standpoint and its claims are modified in the attempt to coexist with the objective.[22] And yet whenever the two outlooks cannot be satisfactorily integrated it is philosophically honest to recognize their incompatibility and to refrain from putting the whole problem out of sight by cognitively suppressing one of the two sides. Indeed, issues belonging to a no man's land between different faculties are confusing and thereby threatening to the executive powers of the mind. In Nagel's view there is no way of telling how much of reality lies beyond the reach of present or future objectivity or any other conceivable form of human understanding.[23] But then, while the concept of an unconscious dimension is intricate, it is not quite 'mysterious'; taking one's total capacity for granted and regarding it as unsurprising is in fact the rule, rather than the exception, among human beings.

Perhaps with the exception of thinkers such as Vico,[24] it is inherent in classic philosophical projects to define intellectual advance as a 'powerful' source of decision-making which can rightfully disregard the force of both unconscious and traditional sources of authority. To some extent it is plausible to agree with classic philosophy in the sense that genuine rational choice is only possible in a context of potential equals capable of rational confrontations. Indeed, it is typical of a more juvenile vein of thinking to strive to transcend traditional authority and to seek outer, impersonal structures of meaning, entirely distinct from one's intertwined history of affects and thoughts. And yet, in a hypothetical intellectual maturity we might even become hospitable to subjective and traditional factors in a growing appreciation of their utility in our endeavours to be more thoroughly 'objective'. The sort of objectivity which is intended is not of the 'God's eye view' type, but one which is provisional and embodied. We cannot simply regard affects as a mere appendage to our minds and thus adhere to the naïve view that the computational aspects of the mind are in principle quite separable from our emotional life. It is precisely this dichotomy that some philosophers intend to question through the exploration of a metaphoric life, attempting to create links between such differing domains as digital and affectual ways of functioning. Just think of the passion that even the most cerebral research workers bring to the study of deductive or empirical problems.[25] And perhaps, whenever there is a discussion of 'truth conditions' and general hypotheses, it would be more profitable to try to include rather than exclude what could be called person-reality: our immensely complex and inescapable condition as living creatures.

The digital style may thus gain in creativity while in the analogic area gaps and hiatuses may be opened in such a way that temporary sight-lines are created which render one part visible to the other in an asymmetrical fashion. The implication is that in the passage from the domain of analogic dynamics to the domain of digital ratiocination, and vice versa, a 'logical' space is generated which could be indicated as a space for metaphorical processes. This is an area of creativity which is limited on one side by the survival functions of our affectual life, and on the other side, by highly regulated ways of consensual logic, these being the necessary margins for an intermediate area of creative innovations. As distinct from the more linear and literal ways of describing experience, metaphoricity uses one thing to understand another entirely different one, yielding an affectual as well as a cognitive understanding; couched in imagery, metaphor is as much a purely rational process.

It may be appropriate to invoke Sperry's contention to the effect that we have came round to thinking of the two hemispheres as normally functioning together as an integral unit and to accepting a revised and upgraded picture of the right hemisphere's functional capacities.[26] The classic neurologic doctrine of one-sided dominance, with a major and minor hemisphere, is replaced by the idea of a bilateral complementary specialization. As research in general is more than hospitable to those voices of the social order which support its existence, it is no wonder that the theoretical contexts focusing on exploration of 'meaning' have been rewoven into contexts concerned with the processing of information. But it is noteworthy that a growing interest in metaphoric language is none the less contemporary with the occurrence of the information revolution permeating the post-industrial world.[27] In Sperry's view advances in research on the right hemisphere seem to tell us, among other things, that our educational system basically discriminates against one whole half of the brain; he refers, of course, to the non-verbal, non-mathematical hemisphere, which has its own perceptual and spatial mode of reasoning. In our present school system – he insists – the 'minor' hemisphere of the brain gets only the barest minimum of formal training, almost nothing compared with the things that we do to train the left, or 'major', hemisphere.[28] And we would resolve to educate the 'minor' only if our complex predicament resulted in an unlivable condition. Equally necessary as the practice of exactitude, human metaphoricity provides the language for seeking ever more relational precision; it creates a realm for fruitful borrowing and mutual enrichment – a level of abstraction where discourses with separate content and incommensurable vocabularies can make attempts at interactive synergies.

INQUIRIES INTO DISCRETENESS AND CONTINUITY

Derivatives of Cartesian 'categories' of mind and body, our rational-versus-instinctual distinctions seem tacitly to influence our culture in such a way that they segregate modes of experience which are in fact constantly interacting. Activities in which our biological life is less conspicuous can be temporarily relegated to the outer margins of experience in such a way that the focus of attention is on a linguistic event, and this is the sort of language with which 'philosophy' is primarily concerned; experiences in which our embodied life necessarily comes into focus are either neglected or else regarded as an aspect of nature which our cognitive language should accurately represent. And yet, in a heuristic perspective, we could more fruitfully think in terms of fluctuations in an ongoing process of contextualizations and recontextualizations along a continuum of experience in which segments and polarities can in fact be emphasized for purposes of local discussion.

Through a metaphoric appreciation of language, knowledge is seen not so much as the task of 'getting reality right' but rather as the enterprise of developing linguistic habits for coping with whatever reality-in-the-making we may have to confront. My work is in line with those who welcome the standard distinction between explaining exact phenomena and interpreting elusive occurrences but do not conceptually use distinctions as irreducible dichotomies. Discreteness and continuity can thus be viewed as complementary concepts emerging against a background of linguistic evolution in which there could be no sharp division between metaphorical and literal language. It is common knowledge that at the 'opposite' ends of a continuum, relatively clear instances of canonical and of creative expressions are fairly easy to recognize, even though it is usually accepted that there are continual interactions between these two poles whenever metaphorical constructs become more popular or literal concepts are used in innovative ways. In a joint perspective of continuity *and* discreteness we can of course appreciate that once a metaphor is refined into an accepted theory, it becomes easy to regard it as an isolated, clearly identifiable, static entity which 'exudes' meaning independently of human elaborations. The distinction between innovation and normality is, however, best understood when terms are sufficiently 'canonized' and when the emergent language is viewed as differing not so much in kind but in degree. Canonical language may be conceived of, roughly, as a limit towards which language tends while its connotative fullness and force diminish. There is new language constantly coming forth, of course, but its triumph is brief at best.[29]

Hoffman, for instance, argues that even 'proposition' is no less a metaphor for thought than 'picture' is a metaphor for imagery; advocates of the proposition metaphor claim that the picture metaphor requires the presence of a homunculus that can interpret picture images, while their own propositional metaphor also seems to demand a comparable homunculus that can *call up* rules and *produce* inferences; Hoffman concludes that the fallacy at work is the assumption that any theory suspected of being metaphorical is necessarily inadequate and in need of being replaced by some better and literal theory, even though what is usually substituted is yet another metaphor.[30] In a metaphoric approach rooted in serious listening we may then work on the assumption that categorical distinctions typically invoked by professional philosophers are useful as long they appreciably enhance discussion and research, and that conceptual terms should be abandoned as soon as they are no longer productive. 'Unfortunately' in this approach there is no exciting victory since there is no way to identify wrong philosophical approaches to blame and ban, and no way to create something which will once and for all abolish binary oppositions in philosophy. It is hard work, none the less, inasmuch as it requires the creation of new abilities to cope with the emerging events that a listening approach allows us to heed. The more honestly we listen, the less we can regard the central beliefs of our doctrines as necessary and natural and consider peripheral ones as contingent or cultural.

Rorty is among those who are inclined to describe human knowledge through the metaphor of a continual reweaving of a web of beliefs and desires. And in so far as we adopt this metaphor we will tend to regard the web as seamless, in the sense that we shall no longer use epistemological distinctions to divide it: 'So we shall no longer think of ourselves as having reliable "sources" of knowledge called "reason" or "sensation", nor unreliable ones called "tradition" or "common opinion".'[31] In this prevailing climate no binding distinction can be revived between notions which have functioned as the conceptual hinges of our western tradition: *nous* versus *doxa*, that is 'reason' versus 'opinion' – in a long series of comparable oppositional dichotomies. While the classic approach insists on the separation of such realms as cognition and empathy, thinking and feeling, a maturational approach emerging from an awareness of metaphorical processes proposes instead that those realms constitute but complementary and reciprocally indispensable polarities to be instrumentally identified within our evolving rationality. Indeed, we may subconsciously be on the lookout for a logic that can even re-link us to the organismic texture of life.

Arbib and Hesse are also among those who suggest that 'the notion of an *essentially embodied subject* aspires to break the dualism of mind/body, mind/brain, subject/object, materialism/idealism, self/other, and fact/value: it holds these dualisms to be untenable'.[32] Operating within the cultural area of psycho-analysis, Muratori attempts to go beyond divisive dualisms by utilizing the two concepts of 'discreteness' and 'continuity' as paradigms suitable to capture different levels of the *same* interactive structure: one pertaining to the profound undistinguishable features of the relation and the other encompassing distinct items possibly amenable to digital processing.[33]

Speaking from disparate persuasions and distant cultural premises, authors such as Parker, Derrida and Quine somehow converge in highlighting an essential reciprocity between continuity and discreteness. Significantly, Parker talks about metaphor as a 'plot' in both senses, as 'space' *and* 'story': a space of discovery *and* a myth of transformation.[34] In her outlook the description of metaphor in terms of 'impertinence' and 'ungrammaticality' or predicative 'deviance' which after a process of transposition becomes 'pertinence', 'grammaticality', or acceptability at another level, begins to sound like the 'plot of a Shakespearean comedy: an initial challenge to the existing order by a misfit or young impertinent, a retreat into a transformative "green space", and the emergence of a "new" order with the former misfit now its ruler (a plot which accounts for both the "rule" of metaphor and its "freshness").'[35] The 'plot' of metaphor as creative *space* is subsumed within the plot of a *process* of reintegration at new levels, thus implying a necessary conjunction of discreteness and continuity.

As a piece of written language lacks the 'detrimental' or 'comforting' presence of both the author of the language and of the thing to which it refers, for Derrida a text, or a context, in fact induces a sequence of translations.[36] Once a text is detached from the authorial intention behind it, its readers no longer have the necessity, or the capacity, to adhere to such an absent intention. It is thus possible for a written piece of language to enter into a chain of meaning associations inasmuch as the text cannot incorporate any univocal or absolute meaning. Significants thus behave as correlates of other significants and nothing emerges which is entirely outside of an indefinite sequence of diverse significants. He writes, in fact, that what inaugurates the dynamics of meaningfulness is precisely what makes it impossible to terminate it.

In his afterthoughts on metaphor Quine almost seems to re-link human ontogeny and scientific theorizing as an unbroken continuum: 'Besides serving us at the growing edge of science and beyond, metaphor figures even in our first learning of language; or, if not quite metaphor, something akin to it.'[37] Here a logician propagates a comparative, relational mode of understanding that I assume to be fundamental to human cognition. He in fact remarks that by means of 'creative extensions through analogy' we may even forge a metaphor at each succeeding application of an earlier word or phrase:[38] 'It is a mistake, then, to think of linguistic usage as literalistic in its main body and metaphorical in its trimming. Metaphor (or something like it) governs both the growth of language and our acquisition of it.'[39]

THE INTERACTION BETWEEN METAPHORICITY AND LITERALNESS

If we can conceive of an interaction between 'representatives' of literal and metaphoric languages we may realize that narratives and constructs which relate to matters largely external to a normal vocabulary in fact do function as 'coded', secret channels of communication for the undiscerned interactions between normal and metaphoric discourse. And whenever a talented emissary of literal language actually perceives that the message expressed in coded language refers in fact to the behaviour of normal language, the subsequent construction of the metaphoric speaker may be characterized by further advancements in the illuminating line contributed by the sensitive response from the emissary of normal discourse. The attempt to develop ourselves, or educate others, may at least in part consist in the metaphoric activity of creating connections between a standard epistemology and some 'alien' frame of reference, between an original discipline and another discipline which seems to pursue incommensurable aims in an incommensurable vocabulary.[40] The attempt may also consist in an inverse movement of our metaphoric processes whereby we reinterpret our familiar world in the unfamiliar terminology of our newer inventions. The trick could be something comparable to what adults do with children, namely an exchange of the same word or thought: a commitment at once serious and playful to respond from one's own premises so that the concept bounces back in such a way that it can be retrieved by the other's inner domain and become gradually improved. In this very real 'language game' the winner is not the one who can defeat the interlocutor, or the alien threatening stranger – as is the case in ancient mythologies or contemporary scholastic writing; the real winner is the extraordinary player, the one who can create some kind of a (linguistic) game with an epistemic frame which 'lesser' players have to regard as totally alien, not amenable to any sort of exchange. It is a game implying risk, effort and discipline – indeed genius – in the attempt to link increasingly different world views. The winner is not an endogamous player who can powerfully control from the inside a homogeneous epistemic area, but the exogamous and talented thinker whose vital metaphors do successfully link his own area of literality with a domain previously regarded as totally useless for cross-fertilization. And no courteous response is to be expected from an alien frame of mind because the inner world of 'aliens' such as, for instance, infants and dying people, hermits and business managers, simply will not respond unless the metaphoric attempt is such that it creates a very relevant link.

Thus, if we allow for an interaction between the emissaries of normal discourse and the proponents of metaphoric constructs, we can suggest that there actually is some form of 'dialogue' and that normal language is to some extent responsible for what the metaphor is ceaselessly trying to say. The generation of metaphoric utterances could thus be a reaction both to the standard messages of normal language and to its implications. The responses of metaphoric speakers may contain in disguise, in a codified manner, the 'unconscious' perception of the meanings expressed or implied by the utterances of normal discourse. But the full significances of these meanings is only dimly grasped by normal language and its destabilizing effect is thus attenuated. In this way the reciprocal attitudes of metaphoricity and literalness are somehow known even though they are not thought out propositionally – thus keeping under control the risks of an excessive mobility. In fact the emissaries of literal language might even interpret the perception and message of the metaphoric speaker on condition that he is prepared to recognize and appreciate the assumptions which functionally support the normal position.

Whenever standard epistemologies demand that their relative stability should receive as homage the attribute of permanence, that their regularity be upgraded to a norm-setting normality, then much of the metaphoric talk may be seen as a reaction to such unjustifiable amplification of certain regular terms in our vocabulary. Cultural expressions which we regard as incongruous may simply be a response to those equally incongruous attributes which 'must' be conferred upon standard epistemologies. The oddness of the unorthodox may be a response to the absurd behaviour of the orthodox, expressing their presumptions through the channels of literal discourse. It may in fact seem absurd, to the unorthodox, that the orthodox actually rate all their projects in terms of an advancing cognitive project, that is in terms of an ultimate dependence upon truth claims from which they derive a 'rightful' disdain for all 'subrational' outlooks. Paradoxically, we may subconsciously perceive the folly of a normal discourse which presents itself as utterly timeless and logical. In this very limited sense, then, the timelessness of our unconscious dynamics seems to coincide with the sort of timelessness often attributed to logical constructs while they are in force.[41]

A listening dialogue between the emissaries of diversity and the guardians of regular language could in principle exist, and an opportunity could be created to recontextualize our cultural scenario so that the representatives may share responsibility for eliciting reactions in the other group. We may otherwise have to be content with the sterile and monotonous exchange of disparaging attributions. A listening approach would, on the contrary, be hospitable to both the explorers of diversity and to the inhabitants of regular language. Insisting that there are germinal linguistic expressions that culture fails to use to the full, the former strive to make these candidates for the official language; the guardians of whatever is the current scholasticism strive, on their part, to make sure that the coherent development of their theses is not degraded or contaminated. The specialists in particularity, as Rorty says, fear the dangers of stillness while the specialists in normality take precautions against the dangers of deterioration. But then, as we attempt to transform ourselves by internalizing further self-descriptions, such personal changes may make inroads on the confidence induced by all variants of realism – linguistic, epistemological, political. Seriously entertaining the possibility of alternative self-descriptions we undermine our own reliance on the knowledge gained through normal discourses. The reassuring function of a standard vocabulary is thus maintained at the cost of the flow of dialogue from one epistemology to the other, that is, across different disciplines, premises and purposes.

THE HEURISTIC USE OF METAPHORS

Hinting at possibly inaccessible terrain and at a choice of perspective in interpreting reality, metaphors are customarily suspect in any normal discipline. However elusive, they are rightly suspected because they either shape or deconstruct the framework of what is claimed as real. Significantly, metaphors and models are often the last to be perceived by those who use them, so deeply embedded are they in the system they hold together. We are not therefore concerned with the elucidation of any particular structure but rather in exploring the pervasive circulation of metaphors in our cognitive and interactive activities. In a culture whose speciality is specialization, the search for a sense of interconnecting integration is highly problematic. And yet the fact that we are rooted in an intricately interwoven structure of relations has become the inescapable heritage of our time. Our 'intellectual' products are in fact assessed not only by their appropriateness within their own field but by their capacity to connect and reach further.[42] Putnam, for instance, is among those who hold that the *real* problem has to do with the evolution of culture. 'We are world- makers', he says, 'in the sense that we are constantly making new worlds out of old ones.'[43]

Speech is probably literal or conventional within its own domain; only when it crosses conceptual borders in order to be interpreted elsewhere does it appear richly metaphoric. Because, of course, it is the language that we receive, rather than the one which we transmit, that appears more strongly figurative. In the mainstream of contemporary philosophy the sort of language which serves as a repertoire of metaphors is invariably the language of 'successful' adults. The language which is spoken, and forcefully spoken, at the margins of social life by those who are trying to enter and by those who are walking out of the scene, is generally ignored; or else it is considered 'simply metaphorical', since the only proper language is thought to be the vocabulary of whatever dominant world-view is in force. Young children and moribunds may be making 'literal' statements, although not from the point of view of those occupying the centre of cultural life, the locus from which authorial, and thus authoritative, statements emanate. A statement, then, can be metaphorical just because it is peripheral, almost as if biological conditions could actually determine the way we establish epistemic distinctions; the next step should be a long overdue research into empirical logic.[44]

Parker invokes Cicero's *De Oratore* to illustrate precisely the laborious emigration and immigration of metaphors.[45] She suggests that a metaphor can be imported to supply a local need, but if a word already exists to occupy the place, the 'alien' or 'translated' term must justify its displacement of the rightful occupant not only by its 'resemblance' to it but by its superiority. Even then, however, the immigrant must be as civil as possible – an outsider on his best behaviour. This interactive approach best emerges in Cicero's language: 'If one is afraid of the metaphor's appearing a little too harsh, it should be softened down with a word of introduction (*mollienda est praepositio saepe verbo*). . . . In fact the metaphor ought to have an apologetic air, so as to look as if it had entered a place that does not belong to it (*ut deducta esse in alienum locum*), . . . and as if it had come with permission, without forcing its way in (*non vi venisse videatur*)'.[46] Interactive life, by converse, has very often figured as the *explanandum* of analogy, the puzzling field to be illuminated in the borrowed light of different domains such as navigation, medicine or agriculture; indeed the very notions of 'evolution' and 'revolution' may be seen as cases of this tendency since they emerge from biological and cosmological concerns. And yet significant texts sometimes reverse the direction of metaphorization and thus revert to the argument that social life itself supplies a metaphor for life in general. This can be seen whenever arguments very largely rest upon a common base of social imagery.[47]

In Leary's outlook

> To say that the mind is a living thing or that a living thing is a machine – as also to say that emotions are forces, or that the senses are signal detection devices, or that behavioral problems are illnesses – is to suggest a set of resemblances between the members of each of these pairs of terms.[48]

In fact, even the celebrated computer metaphor, with its related vocabulary of information processing, feature analysis, and software programs, has not only filtered into scientific models and popular speech but also has become quite compatible with the paradigms of cognitive psychology.[49] Several contributions have given impetus to this movement and recent reformulations of mind–brain–self controversies are often couched in computer analogies and models. The computer metaphor has proved to be highly heuristic, stimulating not only empirical research but considerable theorizing and debate regarding the nature of the self and mind–brain issues.[50] But, once again, it is not our purpose to illustrate the cognitive value of a specific family of metaphors; we rather try to explore the circulation of metaphoric constructs, an interdisciplinary circularity which enlivens the advance of our culture. As a challenge, Hoffman proposes that it would be impossible to give a generally acceptable description of *either* computers or minds without using metaphorical language. People in fact speak about computers as if they do what brains do, and they speak about heads as if they do what computers do; but this raises an interesting possibility in Hoffman's view:

> If an intelligent computer were able to communicate effectively about its representations, it would need the language that people use to create, manipulate, and talk about representations – the cognitive metaphors that we mortals use to understand representations, language, memory, perception, meaning and other cognitive phenomena.[51]

Far from being merely illustrative, certain metaphors constitute the very foundation of a theory. In Darwin's case, the celebrated metaphor of natural selection functions as the basis of the whole speculative enterprise. But then Leary discerningly asks whether 'Nature' – with a capital N, as he typically had it – does actually select. Not really, because Darwin's articulation of evolutionary theory was a derivative of his analogical (and rhetorical) comparison between the so-called artificial selection of animals as performed by humans, on the one hand, and the putatively natural selection of variants carried out by 'Nature', on the other.[52] Leary also demonstrates that in the history of science metaphors have been borrowed back and forth from society to science; Newton, for instance, drew on the idea of social solidarity, or 'sociability', in devising his concept of gravity.[53] In a synoptic view of Freud's use of metaphors, Leary remarks that indeed a taxonomist would have to work extensively to classify his many metaphoric expressions derived from social and political life, from the field of physical dynamics and hydraulics, anthropology and mythology. In his use of such metaphors as energy and force, flow and resistance, repression and conversion, defence and aggression, he probably followed his own research policy of changing analogies and comparisons as often as necessary.[54] As is well known, somatic similarities have been used in developing scientific concepts while, more recently, computer science is in return employed to metaphorize physiological processes. There is, then, a two-way flow of metaphorization which is not free of 'risk': we could believe that since 'science is power', by converse anything that is sufficiently powerful could even be regarded as 'scientific'.

The previous examples may indicate that in scientific enterprises metaphors perform just as they should. They can assist in generating theoretical classification systems and ideas for experiments, and they can also suggest the ways in which the phenomena under consideration demand further description or theorizing. But it is no fault of a metaphor that it sometimes seems 'wrong', as in fact that can be one of its virtues. It is just not proper to say that a metaphor is wrong, because metaphoricity is essentially with us to enhance a *process*.[55] In this approach, then, it becomes natural to direct attention to constructs that involve isomorphic analogies moving across different domains. In fact what we have are research practices which are right or wrong depending on how they square with local standards; and standards are right or wrong depending on how they correspond to our regular priorities. Metaphoric constructs thus can be instrumentally lent and borrowed.[56] Just as we generally seek to make sense of puzzling circumstances in terms of familiar ones, so we look to well-known phenomena of other sorts, whether natural or artificial, for analogs of situations that we wish to comprehend; and conversely we ponder over our own experience for analogs of other natural and artificial phenomena. Science texbooks of physics and chemistry are often short on prose and long on mathematical or formulaic expressions; such texts, in fact, do not attempt to convey a sense of the historical synthesis of the concepts they use and of the reasons for selecting a given methodology. A 'symbolic' game is proposed, leaving in the background the multiple reasons for playing it.

Although theory is a rigorous intellectual exercise involving a highly disciplined type of critical thinking, it none the less embodies a perspective and a 'tone'. Theory at its best is heuristic, in Olds's view, serving to generate new hypotheses and new inquiries into the relationship between concepts; and it is equally to be valued for its integrative function, that is, for its capacity to enhance the circulation of principles.[57]

THE QUEST FOR ACCURACY

Thinkers often appear to have to choose between consistency and credibility; and a propensity to opt for consistency seems to prevail as a precaution against the danger of being regarded as incoherent. In our pursuit of rigorous intellectual products we may in fact tend to discard a number of features which do not fit our discourse and thus produce lucid work which is primarily remarkable for consistency – possibly to the detriment of accuracy and depth. The fact that such a selected and treasured language rarely occurs outside the pages of books is no serious deterrent to our scholarly enterprises.

Opening enormous possibilities for world control, the acquisition of proper language also provides a powerful instrument to move about successfully in a phatic community. In an individual perspective, however, there are difficulties attached to our growing mastery of language: although our words are ideal instruments to establish clear categories, they seem inadequate to describe either the profound sense of a total experience, or the innumerable subtleties which derive from the conceptual differences emerging from our lived life. With the successful mastery of language we run the twofold risk of separating affects and thoughts and of breaking up a total experience into a description of its putative component elements thus producing an impoverished and 'false' experience.[58] The moment efficient, descriptive language enters our life, an increasing separation is established between our world of personal experience and a world of cognitive language. We are then forced to confront at least two different versions of events: a complex one, and a rather schematic one. In our contemporary culture we are often confronted with situations which seem to exacerbate the difficulties of enduring a separation which almost turns into a sort of schism.[59] We should be aware, in fact, that to envisage sharp lines is a productive strategy in abstract thought, as it frequently tries to veer off along tangents of its own making. And some of these intellectual demarcations become respectable by repetition, as they serve a practical purpose in marking off areas of univocity and agreement.[60]

But then, if a measure of ambiguity allows for a constant search for ever greater accuracy, we should also ask why ambiguity is so unbearable. The difficulties of ambiguity probably derive from an insufficiently clear line of demarcation separating what is appropriate from what is unacceptable, almost as if we had to cope with an obsession intellectually to subdivide what is frequently indivisible in life; and to cope with this 'necessity' we even try to postulate the existence of atemporal and acultural structures from which to deduce criteria for separating what is clear from what is ambiguous. We actively try to avoid ambiguity in both our behaviour and in our thinking as if our basic epistemology regarded ambiguous expressions as something sordid and repulsive. And if we invoke the metaphor of our eating functions to describe these rejecting tendencies, we could say that ambiguities are difficult to swallow, not appetizing, and nauseating.[61] The deep need we have to reject any degree of ambivalence induces the 'healthy' as well as the 'ill' to resort to various forms of purification, separation and exorcism in order to render mixtures cleaner and clearer – so that we do not have to 'vomit' them. If we could attain a better awareness of these profound difficulties and of our inadequacy in coping with individual and cultural ambivalence, we might then endure and even utilize them. If we could hypothesize a common origin of the pervasive tendency to distinguish, separate and isolate ourselves from generally 'contaminated' conditions, we should become able to think and reason explicity about our common fears of having to 'vomit' something unacceptable; and whatever is to be rejected may be unacceptable because it is insufficiently pure or homogeneous in logical, affectual or aesthetical terms. This tendency, however, could also indicate an insufficient capacity to endure even a minimum of ambiguity, and to confront it logically. The evidence for this human predicament is a propensity intellectually to 'vomit' ambivalences and confusions through the use of verbal expressions such as 'distasteful' and 'unpresentable'. We almost come to see an equivalence between the affectual and cognitive perception of ambiguity as something intoxicating which cannot possibly be metabolized. It is as if we were confronted with the incapacity to absorb something which is unacceptable because too ambivalent – and yet indivisible. Our search for accuracy and precision is perhaps a derivative of our capacity to generate and tolerate the ambiguity of our connecting metaphors, that is, of our efforts to somehow reconnect the terms of our situations of ambivalence, ambiguity and incongruity. And whenever we cannot tolerate any mixture or contamination we also cannot profit from those areas in which things do not have an immiscible single meaning but possibly a number of further meanings;[62] unfortunately, such domains may ultimately seem too sordid to cope with and utilize.

Some scholars treat metaphoric usage as entirely inconsequential for thinking and only usable for communication. In this view metaphorization can only help to name the interactive experiences for which a standard vocabulary provides no ready terminology; its use is thought to expand the resources of communicative language and to facilitate the transmission of personal resonances by consigning to speech the evanescent, the apparently insubstantial and the unconventional aspects of the interaction. And yet, human thought unfolds through an irrepressible concern for specificity and precision, which is what constantly accompanies our serious interest in whatever exceeds official language. Metaphor cannot be reduced to the change of meaning of a term with respect to its literal meaning; this change is in fact instrumental to a more complex process whose ultimate purpose is to show some hidden feature, or subtlety, which could not previously be identified or evidenced. Thus for the sake of accuracy and subtlety a transition can be advocated from the study of sentences *per se* to the study of utterances as pertaining to the living complexity of cultural contexts. In Rorty's view there is nothing in existence, prior to the metaphor's occurrence, that is sufficient to understand such metaphorical use; and if 'understanding' or 'interpreting' means 'bringing under an antecedent scheme', then metaphors cannot be understood or interpreted.

> But if we extend these two notions to mean something like 'making use of' or 'coping with', then we can say that we come to understand metaphors in the same way that we come to understand anomalous natural phenomena. We do so by revising our theories so as to fit them around the new material. We interpret metaphors in the same sense in which we interpret anomalies – by casting around for possible revisions in our theories which may help to handle the surprises.[63]

And whenever we are not inspired by enough intellectual curiosity to see new contexts for our words, we may simply ignore the 'surprise' and thus forestall any quest for accuracy.

A tendency to dwell on a disquieting thought rather than hasten to elucidate its propositional status effectively transposes us onto a different level and perhaps creates a sense of disclosure to hidden features. Wider knowledge might derive precisely from those anomalies which only become conspicuous when we are prepared to revise our own discourse. The intensity which metaphors engender enhances the life of the focused and uninhibited exploring mind, and even prepares it to be surprised by anomalies. A metaphoric ability is a needed element in the intellectual *life* of individuals and communities; only when subtle questioning begins, one must deal with the proposed answers not by outright acceptance or rejection but with limited and qualified consideration – repeating with the sages of the Upanishads, *Neti, neti,* 'Not quite that, not quite that.' In this sense, then, the deconstructive use of metaphors can be just as relevant as the more favoured accounts articulated in world- modelling terms. Cooper remarks that it would be wrong to regard 'disintegrative' metaphors as parasitic on those better suited for constructive purposes. In fact he sees no reason why it should not be a main purpose of metaphor to convey, for instance, a sense of a 'troubled and trembling world', in comparison with which their use in providing models or filters would always have been a minor one.[64]

We can now invoke Wittgenstein's provocative question: 'What is important about depicting anomalies precisely? If you cannot do it, that shows you do not know your way around concepts.'[65] If we do not know our way around concepts when failing to depict anomalies accurately, either we have not sufficiently mastered the vocabulary of the epistemology we inhabit, or else we may be dealing with concepts which are not sufficient to capture the anomalies, or subtleties, that we may be honest enough to recognize. Cultural anthropologists, such as Douglas, have suggested that all anomalies in conceptual systems are in fact inherently threatening.[66] And yet, if we sufficiently repress our intellectual curiosity and disregard our aspiration for precision and subtlety, we may continue to 'describe' anomalies in a defensive fashion and thus wrongly think that we 'find our way around concepts'. The question at issue is one of opting for a greater or lesser interest in anomalies and, as a consequence, for a greater or lesser measure of accuracy.

Whatever else can be said about psychoanalytic culture, we can easily grant that, at least in theory, it implies a demand for the utmost attention for all kinds of anomalies. And what we call psychic anomalies can be described not so much by representational means but rather through attentive participation to the linguistic behaviour of the interlocutor. Psychoanalytic culture could be characterized by a fascination with anomalies and by a determination to seek connections with deeper contexts. The demand for this approach is nowhere better reflected than in Wittgenstein's remark that 'One doesn't put the question marks deep enough down.'[67] But then, the deeper the question marks, the less adequate our literality. With an inclination to be fascinated by anomalies of all kinds, to be intrigued not so much by the mechanisms of memory but by the fact of forgetting, not so much by the process of perception but by our capacity to create perceptual blind spots, and even by our ability not to listen, we may learn to appreciate the language of illness, silence, confusion – a language that we can hardly approach and cope with, a language which may even induce a sense of silliness. 'Never stay up on the barren heights of cleverness, but come down into the green valley of silliness', urges Wittgenstein.[68] The practice and enduring of our silliness is perhaps advocated by Wittgenstein as a strenuous philosophical methodology enabling us to confront something for which we are unprepared, and for which we run the risk of not knowing what to say – of making fools of ourselves. 'For a philosopher there is more grass growing down in the valleys of silliness than up on the barren heights of cleverness', he insists.[69]

The concern for anomalies is not related to a humane attitude or an exhortation to tolerate exceptions and 'heresies'. I believe that Wittgenstein, instead, is basically urging us to cultivate a taste for precision; he is not interested in anomalies *per se*, but in the *effort* to depict them with ever greater attention. Everything functions correctly within any powerful epistemology, and there is nothing wrong with its success except that it leaves out a great deal of the specificity of human expressiveness.[70] From within a standard vocabulary certain features of an interactive field can, in fact, be seen with extreme clarity only at the cost of ignoring other potential aspects of that same domain of interaction. And such aspects can all too easily be ignored or dismissed as sheer anomalies. In our constant concern for qualitative accuracy and for the complexity of individual variations, the differentiative approach to research could be seen as complementary to rule-conscious outlooks based on statistical averaging, and the current return to the study of narratives could be viewed as the starting-point for further endeavours.

7   Detachment and participation

EMBODIED PHILOSOPHY

Theories of rationality do not usually provide sufficient accounts of the possible metaphorical aspects of our thinking. Even major theoretical writings significantly depending upon metaphoric passages in their attempt to explore the logic of discovery hardly ever regard metaphoricity as essential to the structure of rationality. They *use* rather than explain metaphor. The question probably concerns an entire philosophical orientation which fails to grant our metaphoric potential its proper role in the development of cognitive theories. In such a reduced perspective rational thought could then be considered as an algorithmic management of propositions. The incarnate condition and life cycle of humans engaged in enhancing their own rationality would thus have no significant bearing on the structure of thinking, which is ultimately viewed as transcending the nature of our bodily experiences.[1] And even if it is tacitly acknowledged that our lived life influences philosophy, such a vital factor is often deemed unworthy of philosophical scrutiny.

To approach the 'important questions of everyday life',[2] when we have been persistently ignoring them, may then pose special problems. Our philosophical thinking tends in fact to abide by our customary 'detached' concerns and quietly to shift away from the *more* disquieting problems of coexistence with persons and nature. Of course our patterns of thought 'naturally' contain certain mechanisms of defence against alarming inner turmoil, but we also somehow aspire to an awareness of these mechanisms.

In Johnson's view, this current approach derives from the prevalence of objectivist outlooks whereby understanding consists in performing with propositional states: 'Even if image schemata were to be acknowledged, they would only be allowed to influence meaning and understanding in so far as they could be translated into, or reduced to, finitary propositional representations.'[3] And yet research into the propositional and sentential structure of our thinking might be more enlightening if we could link it with those areas of meaning which are rendered operative by a network of metaphoric projections emerging from the complexity of human development.

If we try to look at inquiry in terms of cultural transformation, it is difficult to adhere to the idea that some propositional context is intrinsically privileged – as being different from simply useful for some particular human purpose.[4] By escaping the exclusivist notion that there are radically diverse methods, specific to the 'nature' of different objects of inquiry, one may turn attention from the domain of detached objects and direct it to the more practical question of the purposes which a particular inquiry is actually seeking to pursue.[5] The effect of relinquishing this constraint may be an increased capacity to modulate our philosophical language in a way which inclines more towards cultural and societal purposes rather than towards exclusively methodological-ontological targets. With this viewpoint we reappreciate the burden of knowingly *choosing* which purposes are more inspiring than others: the 'intrinsic nature' of reality or language, in fact, no longer indicates which concerns we are to pursue.

And even if we manage to achieve an impersonal perspective, whatever insights result from this detachment need to be made part of a personal view before they can significantly influence research. The pursuit of what seems – 'impersonally' – the best cognitive approach may be an important aspect of research, but its place in the project is to be determined from a personal standpoint, because the mind's life is always the life of a particular person which cannot be enhanced in abstract detachment. And if we consider the phatic community of the individual, it is possible that the diversity of the guiding metaphors may derive from the different purposes for engaging in research.

Arbib and Hesse invoke apt examples of specific extended metaphors generating different types of discourses.[6] From the extended metaphor discussed by Lakoff and Johnson – 'Argument is war'[7] – a rich variety of phrases can be derived such as 'Your claims are *indefensible*', 'He *attacked* every weak point in my argument', and 'His criticisms were *right on target*'. Arbib and Hesse then hypothesize that this extended metaphor may come to be substituted in our 'dialectic' culture by 'Argument is logic', with the consequence of generating expressions such as: 'Your conclusion does not follow', 'You must make your premises explicit', and 'That assumption is obviously true'.[8] To some philosophers this may seem the only correct way of conducting arguments, but Arbib and Hesse also point out that this way of talking about argument is especially dependent on a basic metaphor: 'Argument is logic'. They subsequently invoke a further metaphor equally familiar in our argumentative contexts – 'Argument is negotiation' – with its ensuing derivatives such as 'Can we meet each other on common ground?', 'What compromises are possible?', and 'I cannot sacrifice my most basic assumptions'.[9]

Such clusters of derivatives are equally revealing of certain sets of value judgements regarding the nature of argument. Whether it be combat, logic or negotiation does not depend on the argument itself but upon some deep-seated metaphoric properties; these are so profoundly interwoven with our affectual life that they ultimately influence our so-called intellectual behaviour. To make explicit the ramifications of our dominant metaphors is to engage in a practice which brings us inexorably close to our inner life and which thus enhances unforeseen shifts in our axes of culture. The general picture changes: from clusters of changeless talking heads to a historical community of living creatures.

In a sufficiently circumscribed area, an awareness of the metaphors we generate and live by would possibly tend to render us more responsible with regard to our beliefs and desires as well as to the sort of interactive world induced by the multitude of our self-fulfilling prophecies. Reaching out for a philosophy of participation one can easily adhere to the Wittgensteinian interrogative: 'What is the use of studying philosophy if all that it does for you is to enable you to talk with some plausibility about some abstruse questions of logic etc., and if it does not improve your thinking about the important questions of everyday life?' [10]

Humans, in fact, are both a natural part of the world and the creators of the sciences through which they try to cope with it. Our interactive life, of which the pursuit of scientific knowledge is an aspect, is then to be regarded as inevitably interwoven with everyday questions of personal meaning and value; pursuing the Baconian dream of mastery over nature, humans may come to think of themselves as much too distinct from nature and thus legitimately empowered to an absolute domination of it. [11] Domination, moreover, cannot be all too simply equated with detachment in the sense of a lack of participation; the dominant control of an object involves, in fact, an archaic, predatory mode of relation which is profoundly passionate and intrusive, however detached it may appear.

Of course scientific theory provides models that are distinguishable from other types of social and poetic constructions inasmuch as they are constrained by formal regulations and feedback loops involving experimentation in the natural world; [12] scientific theory thus largely transcends societal and biological conditions. And yet, its 'meta-cultural' features can be erroneously extended in the sense of an excessive transcendence of the cultural vicissitudes and life cycles of humans. This question may also be revealed by a sense of incredulity that one can be an individual living being even while engaged in scientific pursuits. [13] There seems to be a pattern in the different requests for detachment which justifies us in suspecting a common philosophical difficulty behind all of them, a difficulty which is often liable to be obscured. Detachment, in fact, is not detached at all and may reflect instead a 'cold' passion for control and domination which is rendered unnoticeable by being part of the pre-emptive requirements of the generalized epistemic programme.

The difficulty of locating some sufficiently detached point of departure also resonates in Putnam's suggestion that to ask a human being in a time-bound culture to include in his philosophical survey those modes of linguistic existence that will transcend his own 'is to ask for an impossible Archimedean point'. [14] Within theoretical frameworks influenced by the notion of a thinker-free rationality, intellectual processes are described primarily in terms of their orientation toward outer, verifiable thinking. In doing so, however, the life cycle of intellectual processes tends to be ignored together with the idea of the 'maturation' of thinking in the sense of a possible combination of functions. An onto-valuational dualism seems to be implied whereby we deal with more personalized modes of adaptive functioning as if they were sub-rational. In the language of one of Langer's original remarks, 'Everything that falls outside the domain of analytical, propositional, and formal thought is merely classified as emotive, irrational, and animalian' [15] – thus unworthy of philosophical scrutiny.

The detached approach presents itself as the *right* way for the individual to look at the world and at his place in it. We seem to develop this kind of detachment 'naturally', in order to monitor the subjective distortions of a purely internal view, and to correct the parochialism engendered by the contingencies of [one's] over-specific nature and circumstances.[16] But detachment is not merely a rectifying approach: it claims a position of exclusive 'rightness' as the most accurate account of how to get at things as they really are. And this epistemic dominance is not imposed upon us from external constraints, but derives from the intrinsic appeal of impersonal detachment to individual reflection.[17]

An over-estimation of the successes in the natural sciences may have, unnoticed, influenced contemporary philosophy in its sustained concern for truth-conditions, meaning and representation. In this cultural climate we naturally tend to regard 'cognition' as the most prestigious term in our professional vocabulary and the 'cognitive function' of any discourse as the most enlightening role that we can attribute to our cultural activities. In this same climate we may even extend notions of truth, meaning and reference in such a way that they can be used to upgrade the philosophical quality of our recent concern with our metaphoric function.[18] Similarly we may be tempted to discuss the metaphors we live by as if they simply were distinct but largely equivalent figures of human language and as if there were no question of relevance, efficacy, scope, quality or even of their occult pathogenic nature.

If we accept the premiss that as living beings we can only operate within the limits given by our resources, the world-view with which we deal is the one that we can experience by means of the beliefs and desires of our biological species. Whatever the central principles of a cultural era, we thus operate within a cognitive sphere whose origins and modes we cannot properly establish. To the extent that we think of ourselves as living beings we can possibly admit that we cannot trace the ultimate origins of an experience; and whenever we try to obtain the source of an idea or principle we would inevitably confront a receding background of biological interdependencies.

The distinction between the domains of meaning and cognition on the one side and the realm of affects and experience on the other, is perhaps more practical and provisional than we are prepared to admit.[19] It is a demarcation between events whose occurrences are largely predictable on the basis of some antecedent theory, and events which are less predictable; it is moreover a discrimination which changes just as culture evolves. And even knowledge, of course, could not evolve if language were only used for the purposes of making appropriate moves *within* the best-accredited of language games; the evolution of knowledge, I believe, is more likely to result from the metaphoric linkage of diverse epistemic cultures.

Our enthusiasm for those rational ways of life which can be more public and legal than archaic modes of communication may even be used to serve an obscuring function. Although we constantly proclaim our desire for rational standards of culture we are none the less constantly seeking profound attachment bonds. Unless this co-presence of motivations is sufficiently recognized, the human search for attachments may become obscured and thus subject to perverse distortions, while our advancements in rationality tend to become detached from our ineliminable physical condition.[20]

Possibly arguing to a similar effect, Bruner suggests that plausible interpretations are preferable to causal explanations especially when the achievement of a causal explanation 'forces us to *artificialize* what we are studying to a point almost beyond recognition as representative of human life.'[21] And indeed, this is the tricky fate of the language that is the object of linguistic philosophy. In a historical perspective, however, we could say that there was once a move away from the inscrutable privacy of our mental life and towards the public availability and analysability of language. But as soon as the study of language has become sufficiently mature finally to be hospitable to such figures as metaphor we are once again open to a renewed awareness of our mental life.

A SCRUTINY OF DETACHMENT

A hierarchy of values separating a 'logical' language from our naturally human linguisticity may be used to validate modes of control largely cut off from human kinds of interdependency and solidarity. Certain creatures, or conditions, are associated with 'body' and 'nature', both inherently mindless and in need of control. In this time-honoured view, subjugation of the everyday events of languaging becomes a necessity and a natural prerogative of abstract language. And this 'logical' necessity for mastery and control over sub-rational domains (of language) may turn out to be as compelling as the activity which it constantly strives to regulate.

In a densely allusive style Aristotle remarks, 'For that which can foresee by the exercise of the mind is by nature lord and master, and that which can with its body give effect to such foresight is a subject, and by nature a slave; hence master and slave have the same interest.'[22] It is also interesting to note that Aristotle's treatment of metaphor is significantly open to its societal implications. He seems to suggest in a variety of ways that slaves must speak plainly before their masters and thus abstain from the 'genius' of metaphoricity.[23] Imaginative linguistic efforts may serve in fact to transform the world-view of interlocutors and, obviously, slaves are not supposed to compete with their masters, not even in 'metaphoric' terms. Detachment, thus, is to be statutory and epistemologically legislative.[24]

An intellectual avoidance of biological existence is one of the disquieting features of our western history. There seems to be a tendency to reach out for lucid abstract symbolizations and to eschew the opaque interactive conditions with which we repeatedly collide. Much like the daring courage of expeditions, the initial genius of innovative theorizing can be misinterpreted with regard to its motivations. It could be that we simply strive to avoid what is too close to us as we are not sufficiently prepared to confront it. We subconsciously *know* the dangers of the concatenation of the events which surround us and thus just cannot incline to *think* them properly. As we somehow 'know' of difficulties which we cannot reason about, we develop refined intellectual inclinations for detached challenges of an unknown nature; we thus come even to privilege the detachment of our 'abstract' philosophy.[25] When we confront the difficulties of our formalized relations we clearly recognize their glittering quality and the potentially gratifying outcome of proving our formal ratiocinations to be just *right*. And yet, our western tradition is perhaps now sufficiently mature to seek links between our formal achievements and ordinary human activities.

Significantly, Leder points out that 'The minimal materiality of linguistic signs demands only a minimal though intricate use of the body: small gestures of the writing hand, a swift scanning by the eyes, subtle movements of the lips and tongue. This serves an important function in the body economy, allowing for maximal speed and combinatory number in exchange for little expenditure of energy. The result is that language use is compatible with relegating most of the body in a merely supportive role.'[26] It is similarly recognized that as long as we are 'healthy' nothing strikes us about our being alive; it is only when our well-being is disturbed that we necessarily notice our condition as living organisms. In human speech, however, our *spoken* language remains sufficiently associated with its organic origin and commonly takes place in the interactive context of a living speaker and his listener; but when the abstract terms of a culture are absorbed into propositional thinking, the living creatures seem to come close to disembodiment. It is almost as if a speaker were detached from his bodily life. 'Thinking simply seems to come, involving no material substructure', remarks Leder.[27]

The freedom to create metaphors seems to depend upon the awareness that it may be useless to hint that some clusters of words bear a special relation – that of accurate representation – to something that is what it is apart from cultural discourses, apart from any prevailing human description. We can only be free enough to 'think' metaphorically if we can appreciate that a distinction between 'reality' and 'appearance' is ultimately a way of suggesting that some formulations become privileged for some plausible reason. And the participating style in which we approach our metaphoric expressions closely resembles the language we use to discuss the *enhancement* of our life concerns; metaphors can be good or bad, useful or useless whereas the calculus of propositions conducted within the literalness of an epistemic enclosure may only be valued in terms of being either correct or incorrect. This same participating inclination, which is not satisfied by the tasks imposed by the literalness of an epistemological culture, may also support our metaphoric efforts to connect diverse realms of literalness – thus developing links between domains which would otherwise be alien to each other.

As long as rationality is viewed as consisting of abstract logical connections among homogeneous concepts and propositions, no reference can be made to organic dynamics or to metaphorical projections of these relations on to the level of abstract reasoning. To explore such links might be perceived as detrimental to the lucidity of logics because contacts are envisaged with developmental structures and ultimately with 'fearsome' affectual dynamics.

The problem with our culture is that the generation of concepts and terms is followed by their relegation into a level of irreducible abstractness and detachment from life. Possibly pointing in this same direction Derrida remarks that 'The signifier seems to fade away at the very moment it is produced; it seems already to belong to the element of ideality. It phenomenologically reduces itself, trans-forming the worldly opacity of its body into pure diaphaneity'.[28]

And of course the detachment of our visual culture, as distinct from the more involving process of listening, significantly prevails in a tradition dominated by a view of knowledge, or mind, as capable of accurately mirroring persons and world. As Rorty repeatedly points out,[29] the visual metaphor of mind has played a determinative role in our intellectual history. Plato describes the intellect as the 'eye of the soul'[30] gazing upon the *eidos*, a term that, while generally understood as immaterial form or idea, retains its etymological sense of 'visible' image. Similarly, Descartes refers to the intellect as the 'eye of the mind'.[31] Thus for Descartes, as for Plato before him, the true self is often (though not always) identified primarily with the mind or soul. And moreover 'This me, that is to say the soul by which I am what I am, is entirely distinct from body'.[32] Participation can thus hardly derive from an outlook which precludes relating with entire human beings. And no 'stories' become available to re-link segregated domains.

As developing humans absorb narratives they get ideas about how they may create links within potentially chaotic situations.[33] Meaningful stories contribute to maturing persons' attempts to engage with interactive life and to perceive some order in the disparate attachments they create. And the developing subject who is deprived of narratives is apt to have to adopt strategies to avoid a reality which he cannot interpret and cope with. An avoidant outlook may easily interdigitate with adult forms of epistemic detachment and increase its rigidity because an 'absence' of attachment bonds is especially difficult to think out and articulate.

WAYS OF COGNITIVE PARTICIPATION

To the extent that we put ourselves at a distance from the 'scheme and content' paradigms which influence our culture, we may be inclined to welcome among our philosophical concerns an appreciation of the linguistic spectrum which extends, without interruption, from inchoate 'biological' expressions on to the more soph-isticated of formal games. Segments of the language spectrum taken in isolation, for purposes of local research, may ultimately conceal basic functions of our linguisticity. Conversely, broader philosophical concerns may come to include, for instance, the language of the dying – an ignored language – as well as the language of the 'victims' of what may have been the injurious custom of generally referring to children as the 'in-fants' – the non-speakers. The conceptual coarseness of these demarcations and the magnitude of their blind spots are not frequently confronted in philosophical inquiry. Once language becomes excessively disembodied in the history of hominization, it may well become indifferent to life and death, destruc-tion and construction, inasmuch as the representationalist preoccupations associated with objectivity of meaning absorb most of our 'philosophical' concerns.

We seem to be involved in a circular situation in which sufficient pre-linguistic interaction is effective enough to create a capacity to project life patterns into our more abstract concerns. In this perspective adult rationality interdigitates with developing mental life by construing and thus enhancing metaphoric projections which in turn foster our 'abstract' ways of reasoning. While we begin to recognize this productive circle we inevitably break the putatively impassable barrier between domains which our intellectual heritage presented to us as entirely distinct and heterogeneous. For centuries we have been taught cognitive symbolizations which could be grouped in either one of reciprocally alien modes of describing the world. Whatever philosophy talked about was either matter or form, synthetic or a priori, extended or mental; it was either an idea or its tangible copy, empirical or logical, experiential or formal, non- propositional or propositional, instinctual or rational, in a monotonous sequence of subtle and comparable variants. And what is remarkable about these dichotomies is that they determine alien 'worlds', ultimately inducing a cognitive condition of excessive detachment and insufficient participation. It is a condition which we are perhaps mature enough to monitor and remedy.[34]

One of the ways of surpassing the epistemic structures of the mind–body dualism – for instance – would be to start out conceptually from inchoate or conclusive life situations; focusing on these parts of the life cycle it would not be so natural to think of distinctions between mind and body. Conversely, the general idea of dualism may be uncritically enhanced through the conceptual exclusion of such common situations. Indeed, the quasi-obsolete mind–body problem is perhaps an example of one of the largely *academic* problems with which we are preoccupied.

Whenever we perceive the world as we do, we easily overlook that we *behave* in a way to perceive it as such and that the world is part of the loop created by our language, beliefs and desires. Through our philosophical traditionalism, however, we divisively think of knowledge as either an objective or a subjective experience: there is a 'world', of course, and we can perceive it either as it 'really' is or through our unique subjectivity. And yet, if we also accept the complexity of listening, of metaphoric language, and of human reciprocity, we can also think of transforming our dualistic approach: in an interactive outlook, in fact, the ideas of a knowing 'subject' pursuing truth, and of an 'objective' reality being described are constantly rewoven and recontextualized.

We 'inhabit' a living organism rich with its phylogenetic history and its constant state of experience from within as well as from without. This highly personal network which we usually call the self has a coherence which is also capable of reflecting on its own life. It does seem, in fact, that our full concept of understanding 'requires a rich pattern of interaction with the world rather than the hermetically closed loops of the dictionary or the semantic network'.[35]

By suggesting that a theory of intellectual processes be extended so as to include profound, non-propositional dynamics, one is of course not advising that it be made dependent upon those behaviours. There is no question of dominance of dependent elements but rather of re-linking segregated domains. It is generally held that ratiocination arises out of a process of detachment from the way organisms interact, of reaching out beyond it in search of a logic that surpasses local applicability. In a similar way, the idea of maturity cannot imply a return to the rule of affects and myths: intellectual maturation seriously demands, instead, that we confront the paradoxical tension of our being both rational and affectual and of relinquishing artificial segregations – an interactive tension from which novelty and progress are more likely to derive. And although there is a suggestion that our logic must be integrated or, at least, reconnected with our affectual life, a discussion of maturity is, of course, to maintain the utmost logical rigour in its processes, criticism and comparative evaluations. Indeed such an emphasis on public lucidity is mandatory if we are to differentiate integrative inclusions from regressive temptations to renounce rationality. We can only talk about philosophical maturity if we are lucid enough to monitor both regressive dangers as well as the inner splittings that segregate affectual areas of our rational life.

In a metaphoric perspective we can appreciate that the absence of a secure starting-point can create the occasion for seeing that even a progressive elimination of errors does not guarantee any permanent objectivity and any vantage point which is more suited than others for a potentially 'universal' sort of understanding. In this outlook we should try to close the loop of possible starting-points which are dynamically interwoven. And terms we have tried to keep sharply distinct such as scheme and content, law and society, form and matter, may then be recontextualized so as to appear increasingly interwoven. In the work which I try to pursue there is no way of 'breaking' vicious circles but rather of expanding the circularity of our recurrent experiences in such a way as to reverse the ancient insult of calling it 'vicious'. My aspiration is to argue in favour of a devout and lucid attention to the virtuous circularity of our life and language. And yet our legitimate distaste for vicious circles probably stems from an archaic desire to stand out and on top of knowledge in such a way as to locate self-subsistent starting points from which to develop truthful representations and cogent arguments.

There is an aspect of human metaphoricity which is independent of the question of its cognitive function and which is not related to its aesthetic character, an aspect which derives from the question of the specific use we make of any metaphor. This particular function could be viewed as the capacity to generate relatedness.[36] There is in fact a unique way in which the persons engaged in construction and construal of metaphors are drawn closer to one another. For a distinctively social animal, from his early experiences to any form of epistemic enterprise, the instruments which enhance closeness must be at a premium for both affectual and cognitive survival.

There is a variety of human expressions which are largely dependent upon construction and construal, just as metaphors are. We begin freely to cross lines of demarcation between sense and nonsense whenever certain 'unfamiliar' sounds of the immature person such as, for instance, a cry or a burp acquire their own specific familiarity and become instruments of communication. As 'sounds' become adopted and increasingly used, they tend to make more and more sense until gradually what was just an 'exclamation' becomes a message and properly starts to convey the information that creates intimacy. And of course the acceptance and serious usage of early 'metaphors' implies that they be cited in arguments, used to justify beliefs, treated correctly or incorrectly. The process of creating familiarity is coextensive to the evolution whereby an expression is transformed from a simple cause of belief into a shareable reason of belief,[37] the sort of shareability which creates bondedness.

If closeness and metaphor sustain one another, then we might expect that metaphorical talk will be dominant in situations where closeness is at a premium. The critical metaphors will be those whose interpretation requires a significant capacity for intimacy in the form of being able to appreciate the derivatives of profound personal experiences. According to Cooper these metaphors will be 'recondite' ones, to which access is privileged.[38] There is indeed a rich variety of non-literal articulations which enhance, allude to and nourish the especially deep ties between interlocutors.

If we think of dialogue, at least two different and complementary approaches are discernible. One considers the dyad as composed of distinct persons reacting to one another in terms of a stimulus–response model or in terms of closed systems producing interactions. The other approach is rooted in a 'communicational *continuum*' deriving from metaphoric links which turn out to be dominant with respect to single bits of standard communication of meanings.[39] This outlook may facilitate the appreciation of the language spectrum which extends beneath the more conspicuous segments of our symbolic behaviour.

In Rorty's view, for a stimulus to become part of language is for it to assume a place in an interactive web, in a dynamics of communication – ultimately to meet with a sufficient process of construal. 'It is pointless to ask what there is about the noise which brings about this double describability, as noise and as language. Whether it occurs is a matter of what is going on in the rest of the universe, not of something which lay deep within the noise itself. This double describability is brought about not by the unfolding of latent content . . . but by . . . shifts in causal relations to other noises.'[40]

This is perhaps an extreme statement, advanced to argue further that there is no clear demarcation between stimulus and message just as there is no clearly identifiable point of transition indicating where our early metaphors become constitutive of our literal language.

8 The awareness of metaphoric projections

METAPHORIC PROJECTIONS

Gesturing philosophers engaged in argument are portrayed in Raphael's painting known as *The School of Athens:* Plato pointing his index finger in the direction of the heavenly spheres, and Aristotle moving his hand down toward the natural grounding of things. Of course these gestures are pictorially suggestive of what would be the main trajectories of our nascent western philosophy – ultimately idealism and realism. And yet these bodily attitudes are only an ostensive indication of our main philosophical orientations: they could be interpreted, in fact, as a presentation of our coexistence with a pre-philosophical life, with the bodily 'unconscious' movements which concur to structure and shape intellectual developments.

Although not belonging to language proper, bodily behaviour is a way of expressing inclinations which cannot (yet) be articulated in argumentative language and which none the less influence subsequent epistemic developments. And the transition between 'behavioural' expressions and rational constructions might be regarded as the result of laborious metaphoric projections capable of linking seemingly alien domains, or levels of expression. Although less biologically endowed than other living creatures, it is our specifically human genius for creating symbolic connections between life and language which significantly enhances our capacities for survival and development.

More physiologically inclined than Plato, Aristotle resolutely affirms that our capacity to think metaphorically 'is a sign of genius since a good metaphor implies an *intuitive* perception of similarity of dissimilars'.[1] And no domains are commonly regarded as more dissimilar than physical and mental life, than affects and cognition, intuition and analysis.

Emanating from the most disparate sources, concepts such as 'belief', 'desire', 'tendency', and 'imagination' are becoming increasingly popular in the vocabulary of contemporary philosophy and are thus prompting unavoidable questions on the nature of the relations between propositional and non-propositional factors in our linguistic life. It is almost as if our human 'genius' could generate ever new grappling instruments that we can throw upwards and forward so that we can laboriously direct our cognitive potential to further domains. Each step forward requires us, in fact, to relinquish some familiar element and to connect with something that is as yet unknown, in a way somehow approximating our general idea of metabolic processes. More biologically oriented than other thinkers, Aristotle not only suggests that metaphoricity is 'by far the greatest thing in language'[2] but also that 'it is the one thing that cannot be learnt from others.'[3] To the extent that we circumscribe the notion of learning within the confines of an intellectual and propositional enterprise, our metaphoric inclination is indeed one thing that can not be taught by others or learned. At least some aspects of our linguisticity are then not entirely propositional but intensely vital, profoundly relational and apt to provoke perceptual transformations within the self.

In Strawson's view, even the actual perception of an object 'is, as it were, soaked with or animated by, or infused with – the metaphors are *à la choix* – the thought of other past *or possible* perceptions' thus including self-awareness and unconscious perceptions. In this perspective, then, imagination is the faculty of producing actual representatives of non-actual perceptions; and 'an actual perception . . . owes its character essentially to that *internal link, of which we find it so difficult to give but a metaphorical description*, with other . . . non-actual perceptions. Non-actual perceptions are in a sense represented in, *alive in*, the present perception.'[4] The thematization of such perceptual problems reverberates into the realm of affects, inner propensities and life-styles – a domain presumably linked to physical functions differing in structure from language proper and none the less influencing it. Although the two realms of 'affects' and 'thoughts' operate by a different (and possibly incompatible) 'logic', yet they are being revealed as indispensable to one another in the cultural interactions we live by. Human metaphoricity may then be regarded as a central topic inasmuch as metaphor frequently turns out to be one of the instruments whereby we attempt transitions, projections, links between mutually 'alien' – and reciprocally necessary – aspects of our living condition. 'Metaphor consists in giving the thing a name that belongs to something else', succinctly affirms Aristotle.[5]

Purely intellectual accounts only cover a small range of possibilities and do not sufficiently explain our cognitive grasp of the central features of any theory or contingent situation; such main structures could not be adequately understood independently of a metaphoric connection with our 'profound' life or cultural roots. The details of an argument can be grasped in a purely intellectual way but not the guideline of it; similarly, the more local algorithms of an epistemology can be mastered in a purely rational manner but not the general profile of the epistemology to which they belong, nor its shifts, evolution and reciprocities.[6]

In what might be regarded as a synoptic assessment of the enigmas of human perception, Goodman remarks that 'The eye comes always ancient to its work, obsessed by its own past and by old and new insinuations of the ear, nose and tongue, fingers, heart and brain. It functions not as an instrument self-powered and alone, but as a dutiful member of a complex and capricious organism.'[7]

COGNITIVE PROPENSITIES

As Wittgenstein insists that we are 'most strongly tempted' or 'strongly inclined' to use projections of behavioural propensities in articulating assertions regarding the state of our minds, we could surmise that in his perspective such attitudes ultimately function as determinative factors of knowledge – or even as constraints:

> There are various reasons which incline us to look at the fact of something being possible, someone being able to do something . . . as the fact that he (or it) is in a particular state. Roughly speaking, this comes to saying that 'A is in the state of being able to do something' is the form of representation we are most strongly tempted to adopt; or, as one could also put it, we are strongly inclined to use the metaphor of something being in a peculiar state for saying that something can behave in a particular way. And this way of representation, or this metaphor, is embodied in the expression 'He is capable of . . .'.[8]

Behavioural dispositions thus come to be seen as profoundly interwoven with the notion of our various capacities, extending from the more practical to the more 'intellectual' ones. Developed in a variety of highly technical and logically cogent argumentations, our western scholasticism becomes ever more elaborate and yet increasingly detached from the complex experiences of our embodied condition.[9] The question of connections and reciprocities thus comes across as one of the central problems in the evolution of our rationality.

Philosophy may have been drawn to interdigitate with societal life to the extent that it could be used to sustain the world-views which direct coexistence and produce the indispensable identities that humans live by. In this sense, 'philosophy' has been vastly appreciated and invoked. Conversely, it would be enlightening to try to approach philosophy as connected with the less societal aspects of human life, that is with those efforts which are not intended to provide further forms of control but rather to explore synergies and reciprocities between cultural and biological aspects of the human condition.[10]

For if we inconspicuously ignore the will to control which is covertly at work in the production of language theories as well as in other 'neutral' aspects of culture, we are being too respectful of the beliefs which are collectively concealed in our epistemologies.

Indeed, our condition of living creatures is often looked upon as an unfortunate negative contingency, comparable to a hindrance in our reaching out for knowledge and truth. And the reason why this is not *always* the case is that for major philosophical attempts to establish the rule of 'pure reason' there often emerges a cultural reaction disposed to utilize features of our embodied condition in the way of an adversarial argument to be directed against antecedent philosophical constructions. Think of Aristotle responding to the 'divine' Plato, Feuerbach reacting to the masterful Hegel, or Hume putting himself at a distance from the enlightened Descartes.

We may thus perceive a recurrence of compensatory replies to those epistemologies which hierarchize a primacy of the pure mind entailing a tacit devaluation of our creative pursuits.

Our language is commonly regarded as transparent, and we usually see through it rather than being aware of it.[11] But even when philosophical attention thematizes linguistic problems, emphasis gravitates towards its representational functions with a tendency to ignore the biological origins and constraints of our linguisticity. Even the term 'mortals', so often used in the vocabulary of early philosophers as a synonym for human creatures, appears as a way of minimally acknowledging our condition of living beings and of preserving a safe distance from the conceptual problems of relating to the complexity of life. The only absolute challenge to the executive powers of the mind, the inevitability of death, somehow threatens the ego and thus tends to be excluded from awareness. The obscured inevitability of a life-end creates an epistemic atmosphere of timelessness as it removes with unarguable authority the dimension of ignorance which characterizes the future. Our linguistic games, then, can only be articulated within a cognitive area which is placed at a sufficiently safe distance from the ignorance of both our origin and termination. By pointing to the extreme margin of our condition and by labelling us 'mortals', a good measure of abstraction and detachment is instilled; our predicament is thus connected with the inclusive and 'unthinkable' concept of death in such a way that we should be satisfied with the pre-emptive proformal admission that – of course – 'all men are mortal.' This much being granted, 'philosophy' may, illusorily, be free from questions of its links with the innumerable complexities of our actual life cycle.

And yet, our lucid and detached reasoning instantly succumbs when confronted with the slightest pressure from the vestiges of our immemorial 'territorial brain' which operates alongside our cognitive structures. Even the most prestigious theatres of our western rationality are periodically shaken by destructive dynamics which unfold with a total indifference toward our best ratiocination, incapable of resisting the archaic mechanisms of human nature. When faced by the incursions of such mechanisms, our lucid thinking tends instantly to become defenceless, however powerful and cogent it may be; this sort of thinking, nevertheless, resumes its usual logomachies as soon as the period of terror has come to an end.[12]

A philosophical 'education' may come to prevail which imperceptibly induces us to regard primal curiosity as a condition which obscures the intellect and only inclines us to erroneous language. We might thus regard our immature condition as one which persists until the ruling epistemic language is sufficiently powerful to counterbalance the 'regressive' influences of our affectual and biological roots. Unless our scholasticisms become sufficiently mature to develop links with our ineradicable embodied condition, an outlook of separation and tacit disparagement of life may continue indefinitely to prevail.[13] If the ruling conglomerations of our culture cannot negotiate with our personal language it becomes necessary to keep it at a distance by means of secret and effective schisms. And yet the rule of reason may have been once as necessary as is now the development of links with whatever it is that it rules.

In no way might a cultural reappropriation of life be regarded as a hidden attempt to naturalize our humanity or contaminate our logic; it is rather a way of further using our philosophical potential to raise our standards of precision while mitigating the gross arrogance of our intellectuality and the idea of our mind as an autonomous 'agent'. This approach seems to follow in the tradition of Wittgenstein's therapeutic efforts to free ourselves from a variety of intellectual bewitchments.[14] The tone and subtlety of certain Wittgensteinian remarks might be interpreted as an effort to mitigate the purported autarchy of the mind: 'It is misleading then to talk of thinking as of a "mental activity", he resolutely affirms. And he adds:

> We may say that thinking is essentially the activity of operating with signs. This activity is performed by the hand, when we think by writing, by the mouth and larynx, when we think by speaking; and if we think by imagining signs or pictures, I can give you no agent that thinks. If then you say that in such cases the mind thinks, I would only draw your attention to the fact the you are using a metaphor, that here the mind is an agent in a different sense from that in which the hand can be said to be the agent in writing.[15]

A less direct and mitigated sense of 'agency' clearly emerges from these remarks.

EMBODIED EXPERIENCE

There is an increasing interest in scrutinizing an often neglected area of cognition in which features which are typically regarded as 'organismic', affectual or unconscious are extrapolated on to the conceptual and rational levels of human life by means of metaphoric projections.[16] I am concerned with how plausible it is to construe our rationality in other ways, for instance, as a network of projections that extend from our immature behaviour to our abstract reasoning and that in turn influence the quality of our life experiences. Metaphoricity is a basic mode of functioning whereby we project patterns from one domain of experience in order to structure another domain of a different kind. So conceived, metaphor is not merely a linguistic mode of expression since it is one of the main cognitive and relational factors by which we develop a sense of coherence among our innumerable experiences. Through our metaphoric capacity we make use of patterns which evolve out of our affectual experience in order to organize our more abstract understanding. Metaphorical projections connecting biological life to dialogic existence seem to utilize our early interactions to regulate transitions to a sequence of abstract enterprises. Johnson confronts the long-overdue task of discussing in detail the ways in which embodied schemata are linked with cognitive processes, showing that such basic concepts as balance, scale, force and cycles emerge from our biological experiences.[17]

It is, in fact, by virtue of our metaphorically applied structures that we can manage to reason *about* concepts. Creativity is deployed in our inclination to extend inchoate structures since it is by means of this transference of models that we shape a more comprehensible world in which we can reflect upon the concepts we use.[18] Some relevant patterns in our rationality are metaphorically related to our life as organisms in the sense that structures emanating from our life experiences are attached to domains which become intelligible precisely on account of these projections. This is the distinctively human play of projecting a schema generated in our experience of being alive on to a non-biological and potentially organizable domain. As the specific genius of human language, metaphoricity is thus seen to rest on the capacity to transpose the patterns derived from experience of our own life – to the extent that such experience is not denied, obscured or atrophied by an excess of literalness. And the imagination through which we organize a coherent experience of our daily vicissitudes can in turn be instrumental exploring our profound, inchoate domains by means of an appropriate interpretation of our unconscious expressions. In a sense, our metaphoric genius may consist in the disposition to be hospitable to and to make links with the primal gestures of our living condition,[19] and to create a circulation of interdependencies. This enterprise is both is both serious and playful, but certainly not automatic.

An awareness of biological events can be figuratively developed as a schema for producing meanings which can be organized at more abstract levels of cognition. As Johnson often indicates,[20] this expansion and elaboration may take the form of metaphorical projections from the realm of primary physical and affectual interactions to rational processes such as conscious self-reflection and the dialectics of inferences. Exemplifying his theory by means of the concept of 'balance', Johnson claims that we could not begin to understand its various meanings without invoking preconceptual bodily structures within our global network of significance. 'The view of metaphor that emerges goes beyond the purview of traditional theories in so far as it treats metaphor as a matter of projections and mappings across different domains in the actual structuring of our experience (and not just in our reflection on already existing structures).'[21] He insists that the experience of balance is so essential to a coherent experience of the world and to our survival in it that we are seldom ever aware of its presence. Our experience of bodily balance is in fact metaphorized in our 'understanding of balanced personalities, balanced views, balanced systems, balanced equations, the balance of power, the balance of justice, and so on'.[22] In his analysis of the various senses of 'balance' he shows that there are possible connections between putatively very different uses of the term 'balance'. We use this same word in disparate domains 'for the reason that they are structurally related by the same set of underlying schemata, metaphorically elaborated'.[23] In Johnson's view,[24] human reasoning could be considered metaphorical throughout its entire unfolding inasmuch as it involves image-schematic structures that can be translated from physical on to more abstract domains of understanding; this is a capacity for ordering mental life into unified, meaningful wholes that we can understand and reason about. And yet it must be emphasized that there is nothing automatic or conflict-free in these projections; for indeed we may risk absurdities unless we are constantly concerned with the biological background from which we evolve, *and* with the symbolic world in which we live, in the light of the *laborious* activities which bring such powerful forces together.[25]

Considered as the capacity to generate eminently rigorous scientific contributions or highly significant artistic expressions, the notion of genius is frequently associated with the idea of a profound and enlightening rationality. This outlook is at variance with the equally widespread notion that creativity is 'irrational'. And one of the reasons why creative imagination is not considered rational is that we do not (yet) have a 'logic of creativity, that is a definite pattern, algorithm, or inferential structure for creative reasoning'[26] while we do have more far-reaching insights into our current rationality. Johnson remarks that it is a commonly held idea that there is nothing that can be said to explain the 'mystery' of creativity and that in spite of its indispensability it is still regarded as a non-rational process; furthermore, if we think of 'creativity as a process of generating new connections among *ideas*, then it does seem inexplicable, for we cannot figure out where the connections come from, if not from rule-governed relations among the concepts or ideas themselves.'[27]

Indeed, bridging the enduring gulf between life and philosophy is a project of cultural significance. And yet it may be ineffective to point out the creative prospects which may derive from re-linking our initial gestures with our philosophy. In fact an epistemic picture which separates thinking from life may still continue to exert a powerful influence which we ought to appreciate. We cannot escape from a picture until we understand the mechanisms of convenience whereby it maintains its hold.[28] And of course if it did not represent a way of thinking with a powerful intellectual appeal, it would not be worth struggling against. There is little point in refuting 'errors' which no one is inclined to make.[29] Indeed, splitting mechanisms are essential for purposes of control and for a control-dependent knowledge – a sort of epistemic *divide et impera*. The conviction inspiring the present work is that it is no longer productive to rely on dissociative practices. Our traditional idea of an immaterial reason shapes a variety of cultural assumptions, such as our belief in the schism of mind and body, which in turn induces an increase in dissociative practices. It is then ultimately a question of self-fulfilling prophecies originating from the belief in a disembodied pure mind.[30]

In fact, even though metaphorical projections are usually considered components of human understanding they are not regarded as essential to a 'proper', philosophical sense of understanding. It is just this previously peripheral factor which is now regarded as being one of the central issues. Language becomes part of a synergy only when one is conscious of language itself, or when there is a simultaneous awareness of both the language and its origin.[31] For this to occur, language must become 'alive', that is, capable of drawing attention to the function it plays in our cognitive ontogeny.

THE CIRCULATION OF METAPHORS

No philosopher has ever given expression to the full content of his mind [remarks Wolfson]. Some of them tell us only part of it . . . some of them philosophize as birds sing, without being aware that they are repeating ancient tunes . . . And the uttered words of philosophers . . . are nothing but floating buoys which signal the presence of submerged, unuttered thoughts. The purpose of . . . philosophy, therefore, is to uncover these unuttered thoughts, to reconstruct the latent processes of reasoning that always lie behind uttered words.[32]

To pursue this philosophical project of revealing unuttered thoughts, we should confront the issue of being able to gain a measure of greater intellectual mobility, such as the freedom to make reversals of background and figure: on nearly every approach metaphor is appraised within a framework that takes literalness for granted; and yet even this frame owes its existence to the historical sedimentations of our metaphoric potential. There is a latent epistemic constraint whereby we must adhere to the stipulation of what is to be regarded as standard background and what we may appreciate as metaphoric figure; this is the sort of intellectual immobility from which there is little to gain.

In the general domain of social criticism, for instance, there has been a profusion of studies aiming to reveal the conflicts of interests which are tenaciously concealed by a prevalent rhetoric. Such works try to uncover the illusionistic language whereby a non-existent identity of purposes is attributed to certain individuals by the authors of a standard epistemology. Taking some synoptic and succinct examples we may note that in the Aristotelian view of society 'that which can foresee by the exercise of the mind is by nature lord and master, and that which can with its body give effect to such foresight is a subject, and by nature a slave; hence master and slave have the same interest.'[33] Or else: 'For where there is nothing in common to ruler and ruled . . . there is no justice; e.g. between . . . master and slave; the latter in each case is benefited by that which uses it'.[34]

'Truth' itself, in fact, repeatedly turns out to be relative to an accepted system of beliefs that reflect the relations that a phatic community has with the world it occupies. What language expresses at once shapes our accepted system of concepts and in turn is influenced by it. We cannot escape this circularity but instead can strive attentively to inhabit it. That literalness and metaphoricity are profoundly interwoven and that this vital condition inevitably creates problems has already been indicated by Aristotle remarking that 'if one should not argue in metaphors, it is clear that one should not define either by metaphor . . . ; for then one necessarily argues in metaphors.'[35] And if we regard metaphor as generally emblematic of non-literal language and analogies, we may come to regard this frequently necessary and interwoven approach as particularly fruitful. Even though occupied with considerations remote from our present concerns, Kepler makes a significant revelation: 'And I cherish more than anything else the analogies, my most trustworthy masters. They know all the secrets of nature, and they ought to be least neglected.'[36] In a broad sense, he points in the direction of an ongoing circulation of metaphoric connections.

There appears to be a vast 'circularity' in the way we generate metaphors. From somatic images we come to produce complex artefacts, all the way to the superb combinations of hardware and software. And once the use of these products is thoroughly absorbed by our culture, it becomes 'natural' for us to use it as the basis for generating further metaphoric constructs such as for instance the very popular ones indicating that the mind can be interpreted as a computing device. As is well known, cognitive approaches give an account of the relation of mind and world which may in principle be adequate to describe a variety of human competences. We learn to cope with the world by representing, or misrepresenting it, in terms of mental schemata which are tested and modified by feed-back mechanisms. In view of this highly complex set of relations, the concept of reduction to the computer model is also quite complex. As Arbib and Hesse point out 'it is possible that the complete mechanism may never be knowable in practice or even in principle.' They further claim that, in any case, there is no immediate prospect of our being able to translate our usual talk about language into talk simply about hardware and software.[37] But then, whether or not it is possible to 'reduce' or 'translate' minds into computers, there is an increasing trend in our culture to metaphorize minds into machines, thus encouraging philosophy to focus on the as yet neglected background of a pervasive circulation of metaphors. In this connection Arbib and Hesse express the conviction that the concurrent advancement of computer technology and cognitive science requires a significant effort of philosophical imagination if they are not to influence human self-understanding in a detrimental way. In view of the immense plasticity of our minds, it is not impossible that we might come to view ourselves as certain theories of intelligence model us, with the concomitant atrophy of whatever potentials we persistently ignore.

A deep-seated circulation of metaphors whose concentration causes them to interfere with one another, seems occasionally to surface in Wittgenstein's work: although he appears to repudiate mentalist criteria of meaning in favour of the consensual basis offered by the notion of language games, the 'dualist' metaphors persist even though they are questioned – but by no means exorcised. He remarks, for instance, that 'Silent "*internal*" speech is not a half-hidden phenomenon which is as it were seen through a veil. It is not hidden *at all*, but the concept may easily confuse us, for it runs over a long stretch cheek by jowl with the concept of an "outward" process, and yet does not coincide with it.'[38] We are somehow warned against accepting certain problematic metaphors such as those of 'hiddenness'; but then his remark uses the idea of silent 'internal' speech and at the same time by the use of those typical quotation marks, he indicates that the phrase is not to be taken literally. He is in fact attempting to articulate a distinction which can only be presented in figurative guise; and yet it seems to be undetermined by the very choice of metaphorical terms. The fact is that sometimes – or often, perhaps – we try to say new things with old metaphors which seem to contradict what we are trying to say. And yet, while drawing upon our 'classics', we generally do not perceive the problems generated by those essential links provided by figurative language in the sense that we instead choose to neglect them in favour of some much needed overall consistency.

'Human' sciences, as somehow distinguishable from the more 'natural' sciences, constantly confront a pre-interpreted world where the construction of meaning-frames is a condition for focusing on whatever it is that they seek to analyse. This is the reason why it is appropriate to be aware of a double hermeneutic dimension in the social sciences, creating a circuit between a frequently ignored preliminary structure of experience *and* the theory-dependent elaboration of that same experience: basically, two different and interacting metaphors at work. As Habermas points out, our problems of interpretative understanding do not come into play only through the theory-dependency of data description and the para-digm-dependency of our theoretical languages: 'There is already a problem of understanding below the threshold of theory construction, namely in *obtaining* data and not first in theoretically describing them; for the everyday experience that can be *transformed* into scientific operations is, for its part, *already* symbolically structured and inaccessible to mere observation.'[39] In the domain of human inter-actions as well as in research we tend to neglect that 'antecedent' ways of communication – or metaphors – coexist with later ways and that the two modes profoundly and imperceptibly influence one another. As living beings, we are to confront a linguistic history which tends to include rather than to exclude those developmental steps of which we try to gain some awareness.

9   The metaphoric function

THE DEVELOPMENT OF IDENTITY

Metaphoric expressions break from predetermined meanings in a way that invites interlocutors to participate in the creation of language; this invitation is eminently suited to facilitate development and which renders human linguisticity an exemplary open system of constructions. So it is unaccountable that this open sort of language tends to be ignored in our scholarly inquiries. One may for instance wonder what the infancy, parenting, and ultimate senescence of humans would be like in the absence of just that non-literal language that metaphorical concerns try to explore.[1] Paradoxically, birth, reproduction and death in the human species would not be truly human with the sole aid of the sort of language focused upon by the majority of linguistic studies; continually confronted with *that* sort of language a human infant would hardly develop, or else might 'evolve' into a sad imitation of a human.

With respect to the initial parent–infant dialogue, we could not, technically, speak of metaphoric language as such, since for one of the two interlocutors there is virtually no literal language to rely on.[2] Indeed a convergence in attitude, or viewpoint, between parent and infant is not something that could easily figure in a literal paraphrase of their 'metaphoric' interactions: these are perhaps suggestive of a germinative context in which a use of language prevails which is more 'biological' than 'logical'. As is common knowledge, there is a comparatively high degree of closeness among those who can share ordinary interpretive competence. This is the relatedness engaged in by those who can rely on being understood whenever they use their 'ordinary' language. Although the familiarity enjoyed by competent speakers of the same phatic micro- or macro-community is a precondition for innumerable co-operative activities, there are special maturational phases where intimacy of a much closer kind is required. And some special metaphorical language needs to be created and shared for the purpose of attempting the very special project of personal growth.

Granted that metaphorical talk is used to produce familiarity with fellow speakers, there can still be varying answers to the question *why* creatures talk metaphorically. And even if we approach the problem in a developmental perspective, claiming that inchoate language is constitutive of parent–infant dyads, we still have no cogent reason to think that what may originate a practice must be what maintains it. Pursuing the question why humans talk metaphorically Cooper asks, 'What sustains our engagement in metaphorical talk?', and also, 'What function does metaphorical talk serve, and in the absence of which it would not be the pervasive phenomenon that it is?'.[3] In Cooper's view, the suggestion that these interrogatives have no answers – on the grounds that talking metaphorically is something we 'just do' – is not quite satisfactory; it is in fact difficult to believe that using metaphors is something we 'just do', irrespective of any sustaining function.[4] Whatever the answer, the ineluctable human predicament which clearly emerges in connection with these questions is that it is not true at all that we 'just do that': metaphoricity, in fact, is just not an automatic human process. Some developing individuals simply cannot manage to speak metaphorically and imitatively restrict themselves to the paths of whatever available literal language there is; it is possible that they may simply not succeed in developing the 'genius'[5] for the construction and construal of metaphors. If this unfortunate condition is not sufficiently recognized, then we may enter domains of discussion which tend to become increasingly detached from the inner lives of speakers, where development is a challenging process more than an automatic one.

The more vital sort of closeness induced by metaphoric sharing derives from the beliefs that a speaker must take his partner (or interlocutor) to share – if his use of metaphor is to be appropriate. And there is often serious risk in deciding whether or not a belief is sufficiently well grounded. This is the case especially when there cannot be an ordinary language in which a metaphoric utterance could possibly be translated or which could approximate to its efficacy. Thus the central concern is not so much the generation of the sort of language required to belong into any sub-community or dyad, however special and restricted. The concern refers to the basic paradigm of the situation. Indeed, beneath the links of a shared vocabulary and propensities, which metaphors so often presuppose for their construal, there is also a sharing of values, which must also become presupposed if the use of metaphor is to be attempted. Responsive appreciation of certain very special linguistic efforts does in fact reinforce a profound value system – which is something that could never figure in the paraphrase of such language. In our pre-literal intimacy we 'learn' with intensity and immediacy whether danger comes from inside or outside, whether the individual exists or only the group does; such very early interactions even 'teach' us whether words themselves are tools or weapons, precious or worthless.

If we hypothesize that infants are endowed with some innate logic which may interact with the logic of their human environment and that these exchanges are at work well before mental (logical, rational, intellectual, cognitive) operations can be identified, then we could suppose that the developing individual gets to know a great deal about human ways of life. And yet what he knows has not been learned in terms of what we normally regard as a conscious learning experience. In our mature languages we have no simple way to express a capacity for knowing something even though we cannot properly think and speak about what we know.[6] Oedipus, Hamlet, and Smerdyakov can be thought of as having an exact knowledge of experiences that they cannot propositionally enunciate. An early metaphoric life is thus also a way of attempting to represent what we know but cannot yet think. In early life we are 'taught' how to interact with persons and things even though the instruction takes place through a variety of interactions primarily conducted outside of the proper linguistic domain. Such an evolving bi-personal field of experience could not be properly conceptualized in terms of the vocabulary through which we assess canonized relations. And perhaps a developing interactive field cannot be entirely representable even though a variety of fantasies may 'represent' our inner experience of what is going on in the meaningful exchanges of what we already 'know'.

In the development of identity, personal pronouns acquire their full significance through the attributions of innumerable metaphoric images. 'You are a . . . ', followed by a vast variety of terms is, for instance, a common way of addressing infants. As a precondition for becoming real subjects of their actions, pronouns seem to function as objects of observation for themselves by participating into the point of view of others.[7] It is a question of an interpersonal attribution of qualities drawn from the most disparate domains of cultural and natural life. The central issue thus concerns the attribution of predicates to pronouns. As a conceptual background there is of course the basic assumption that the immature self is forever intent upon enhancing personal growth by absorbing appropriate 'descriptions'. Our primal understanding of metaphorical processes derives from a familiarity with the dynamics whereby attributions are performed and from a cognitive mastery of these activities.[8] It is a question of being able to focus on a specific predicate and of reversing the itinerary through the connecting verb and towards the pronoun coming into being for an increasing appreciation of the subject and of its features.

Whenever it is possible to create consensual metaphors between two interlocutors, then one of the two may choose to respond *within* the same metaphoric agreement, *outside* of it, or else within an *intermediate* area extending between the metaphor which creates intimacy for the two partners, and the surrounding epistemology.[9] Although we have a cultural bias towards the visual paradigm whereby the mind is regarded as a mirroring apparatus and knowledge as the pursuit of accurate representation,[10] we can none the less envisage a continuum in our quest for personhood: it ultimately reconnects the extremities of sight and insight. 'Sight' might refer to the classical cognitive tasks, and 'insight' could indicate the less obvious efforts to appreciate and develop features of the inner world. But then, intuitions of one's inner life appearing to oppose the standards of canonized culture can be seriously threatening as the subject may obscurely fear the dangers of falling outside a realm of consensual rationality and acceptability. Archaic perceptions of impotence, dependence, and control are so primitive that they need to be somehow elaborated and transformed into more acceptable images.[11] There is always the possibility that overwhelming emotions stream in, demanding to be made meaningful within some interactive language. In certain early conditions experienced as a painful state but not yet truly suffered, there is a worrisome concentration of 'concrete thoughts'; they derive from our inability to distinguish between feeling and thinking, words and objects – and thus induce a paralysis of metaphoric attempts. The concretized experience of either images or symbolic expressions (which are not tangible entities) may be caused by an insufficient capacity to tolerate the ambiguity of images or the multiple meanings of language. Kitayama suggests that metaphors indicating situations which are uncertain, obscure or ambiguous are the most important among the non-consensual expressions of a phatic community.[12] In the absence of these metaphors some of our intuitions would remain sadly concrete – insufficiently mentalized. Some ambiguities are systematically concealed in standard epistemologies and there is a silent collusion in rendering them obscure inasmuch as they somehow oppose an epistemology of clear demarcations. And yet, in our life-world, occasions are inevitably created in which we must confront emerging situations of ambiguity and confusion. But then our unconscious domain of ambiguous and contradictory experiences also provides the potential for our intellectuality: 'We must not forget', says Wittgenstein, 'that even our more refined, more philosophical doubts, have a foundation in instinct.'[13] We are eminently human to the extent that we manage a roundabout access to instinctual depths, for otherwise we could only elucidate or expand areas of current literalness. The germinative area for metaphorical processes may then extend between human instincts, on the one side, and a propositionally structured space, on the other. Indeed whenever there are difficulties in expressing a nascent thought or intuition, we must strive to create some metaphoric expression or else endure the oblivion and waste of our more personal creative thoughts. Human metaphoricity thus develops in conjunction with the creation of an intermediate epistemic space of ambiguities, extending between the individual self and the communal epistemology. Kitayama reminds us that the Japanese word *hashi* is equivalent to 'bridge' in English; the word *hashi* means not only 'bridge' but also, with a slight difference in pronounciation, 'edges' and 'chopstick'. In the effort to present a picture of these meanings 'ambiguously and metaphorically' so as to make his language enjoyable to English-speaking people, Kitayama tells us that the Japanese 'bridge' means a bridging chopstick between two edges.[14]

The problem with any intraepistemic consensual logic is that it can lead the psychic system to stagnate into 'local minima', and waste innovative thoughts in less than perfect solutions. Because the revision of individual parts must increase dreaded 'disorder' at each step, there is no provision or encouragement for breaking up a pattern approximating to the standard solution if this implies a short-term worsening of the overall goodness of the organization. Eiser remarks that this sort of difficulty is similar to that experienced when trying to solve puzzles such as Rubik's cube: the puzzle is made up of rotatable smaller cubes with different colours on each side, and its aim is to make each face of the cube show squares of a single colour. To achieve this, it is often necessary to break up imperfect patterns, that is, to rotate the smaller cubes so as, in the short term, to increase the mix of colours on each face of the large cube, temporarily damage the organization, and cause some state of instability.[15] Thus, even though metaphoric processes are conditions for attaining personhood, they may exhibit destructuring features; indeed chaos and ambiguity may even need to be introduced so as to provide an escape route from the dominance of a set of hidden constraints.

Humans indeed exhibit the linguistic ability not only to recognize and make use of what is culturally canonical, but also to identify deviations which potentially constitute the source of stories, accounts, narrations. Humans, of course, develop a sense of what is appropriate by giving it shape in relatively stable epistemologies functioning as a cognitive frame within which propositional assertions are commensurable. Such epistemic structures, however, *also* function as a background against which to interpret and give meaning to the innumerable forms of deviation from 'normal' ways of shaping our view of the world. And such deviations become conspicuous by means of metaphoric narratives through which we can attempt further interpretations of our individual insights with respect to a basic frame of reference. A capacity to renegotiate meanings by means of metaphoric constructs which often take shape in a variety of narratives is one of the salient achievements of our cultural evolution. Participation in a cultural heritage in fact involves an ability both to appreciate the principles of normality and to understand deviations. The latter can be incorporated into narrative accounts in such a way as to generate a variety of further shareable meanings. Humans thus also develop an ability to share metaphors of their own challenging and fascinating diversities.

In this perspective we can see how it becomes possible to proceed indefinitely beyond a given situation and into contexts which are not immediately factual. A dynamic process is constituted by its own past and by the way it generates linguistic attractors which direct its own future behaviour; it is thus a process shaped by and shaping its own history. When two different approaches are metaphorically connected in such a way that they support one another, the link between them is strengthened. And if we ask what might happen with a strengthened connection, we can hypothesize that subsequent relational activity will be likely to utilize, or travel along, that same connection; it may thus even expand its field of attraction to interact with yet more thoughts that are simultaneously active. In a socio-psychological language it could be said that

> there is a drive towards the strengthening, the overlearning, of associations that are already formed. Initially rather weak, or shallow, attractors become stronger and deeper through being repeatedly approached, and the connecting routes . . . through which they are approached become deeper and wider too, that is, more likely to be activated across a range of input configurations.[16]

MEANING, CONVERSATION AND PLAY

We could regard a metaphoric sort of language as prior to literal talk in terms of individual development and, in general, prior to the development of 'higher' logical functions; this 'priority', however, does not suggest that metaphoric competence is more important, or dominant, with respect to literal language. It rather entails that non-literal preconditions may influence the development of our propositional achievements. And such preconditions can only be marginalized at the price of unduly circumscribing our understanding of language, or – practically – of impairing the qualitative development of our linguistic life. There could be developmental risks in trying to confine the appreciation of language to such circumscribed areas as demonstration, deduction, argumentation, for in fact neglected but *constitutive* dimensions of language might irreversibly atrophy. Such neglected but constitutive dimensions of language are sometimes described in psychoanalytic dialogues. And yet such subtle and complex affectual expressions may not fall into the realm of rare or exceptional interactions, since they can actually be more directly related to our daily life: the basis and root of creative intellectual achievements.[17] And the sort of intellectual outlooks inclining to dispense with the linguistic development of our inner lives, might appear as our highest evolutionary achievements, unwittingly damaging our cultural habitat and thus, ultimately, allowing its extinction.

The propensity to allow for, and utilize, a convergence of different levels of linguisticity pertaining to different functions of our mental life, could be conceptualized as a synergy – as an inclination to let qualitatively different acts work collaboratively. The idea of a cognitive synergy could thus be employed to designate the occurrence of incompatible properties being experienced simultaneously in relation to the development of one's identity. This is the case, for instance, when the simplest narratives can be both disturbing and reassuring in an enlivening way. And indeed, if the language which is spoken is 'dead', even dialogue impedes the development of inner life.

One of the important factors in determining which state of mind prevails at a given time is whether the individual feels fairly secure, or threatened in some way. If one feels secure then, other things being equal, one can maintain the playful mental state in which the fullness of personal experience can be enjoyed – and the more intense the experience the better it is. If one feels somehow threatened, then removal of the source of threat naturally becomes a priority. If a playful dimension cannot be created or maintained, the serious-minded state will prevail and the synergies involved in the work of metaphor might be felt as irritating, even to the point of eliciting anger. Apter suggests that in certain states of mind, characterized by the search for intense experiences, synergies are typically sought out and appreciated.[18] The 'tension' which they help to induce is experienced as a form of enlivening excitement, and the more vivid the experience the more it is valued. This is the state of mind in which people, for instance, do such things as enjoying drama, watching sports, or reading novels. There are, however, different states of mind characterized by the pursuit of goals which are felt to be highly important and unavoidable: if the former state of mind can be described as playful, then the other state is to be regarded as 'serious'. Since in the latter state the pursuit of a goal takes precedence, this means that the immediate pleasures which can be experienced are relegated to the background. In this state the intensity of personal experience serves no useful purpose, and arousal is felt as unpleasant anxiety rather than life-enhancing excitement;[19] anything that increases the sharpness of experience, including exposure to synergies, will be generally avoided. If a synergy does happen to be experienced it will probably be felt as annoying or worrisome. With respect to these inner conditions, terms such as anomaly, ambiguity, incongruity and dissonance, all of which have unpleasant connotations, tend to be invoked; they in fact tend to describe intractable human conditions.

The principal divergence between representational and relational concerns could be seen as the outcome of at least two basic human propensities unfolding through metaphors that depict cognition as a (serious) process of reproducing the world, *and* metaphors depicting it as a (playful) creative enterprise, inventing structures for whatever it encounters, and ultimately generating a variety of 'worlds'. Bruner and Fleisher Feldman call these approaches 'reproductive' and 'productive' theories of cognition.[20] Each outlook is committed to a different view of the cognitive function: one emphasizing how the contents of consciousness mirror the world – or distort it – and the other focusing on those acts of meaning that not only influence structure but also enhance experience itself.[21] The reproductive outlook on cognition functions by means of the pervasive mirroring metaphor in which the outside world sends messages that are reflected by the mind inside us. In contrast to such an outside-to-inside metaphor of reproductive cognition, Bruner and Fleisher Feldman point out metaphors of the interactive generation of knowledge. They mention for instance the metaphors of illumination (expressed in the language of search lights, spotlights, and footlights), creative synthesis (expressed in the language of masonry, mental chemistry, and construction), assignment of meaning (expressed in the language of semantic networks, encoding and decoding), and topography (expressed in the language of cognitive maps, schemata, and topological representations), to name only a few of the major categories.[22]

And the playful mind, enjoying variety, even considers the possibility of having been initiated into the wrong intellectual tribe, and of refusing its identifying language games: the intention grows to interpret the fundamentals of one's epistemology as simply instruments used to inculcate a local standard vocabulary. As Nietzsche reiterates, 'serious' work tends ever more to coincide with legitimate concerns, while the inclination to play tends to be called a 'need for recreation' and, somehow, begins to be a source of shame.[23] The playful mind appears more inspired by metaphors of making rather than by the paradigms of representing, by an ideal of playful creativity *rather than* diligent work performed according to intraepistemic criteria. 'Pleasure precedes business', remarks Quine; and he also adds: 'The child at play is practicing for life's responsibilities . . . Art for art's sake was the main avenue . . . to ancient technological breakthroughs. Such also is the way of metaphor: it flourishes in playful prose and high poetic art, but it is vital also at the growing edges of science and philosophy.'[24] And the type of imagination we select in science, or any other enterprise, reveals our personal history and describes the sort of liveable mental space that each of us manages to create. 'The course of the world is a playing child'[25] – says one of Heraclitus' fragments. And it resonates with Heidegger's counsel to think of being as starting from play, rather than thinking of play starting out from ratiocination.[26]

In the perspective so far illustrated we could better appreciate the later Wittgensteinian inclination towards an interactive – rather than a semantic – outlook on meaning; attention to its living, interpersonal, and playful nature can be illustrated with a sequence of three consecutive remarks drawn from his *Investigations*: 'We want to say: "When we mean something it's like going up to someone, it's not having a dead picture (of any kind)." We go up to the thing we mean.' Secondly:

'When one means something, it is oneself meaning'; so one is oneself in motion'
... And finally: 'Yes: meaning something is like going up to someone.'[27] With
this same outlook we can easily concede that conversation is play, and not primarily
work, or research, or education.

That conversation is profoundly interwoven with our biological life becomes
apparent from innumerable examples deriving from the circumstances of language
acquisition. Lieven is among those who point out that the interactions between
certain very young children and their (playful) parents give the impression of being
proper conversations.[28] This may be in part due to the adults' effectiveness in
keeping the conversation going despite the 'inadequacies' of the children (such as
interrupting, failing to answer, not knowing the words), and in part to the child's
capacity in taking turns. Life-enhancing adults treat children as partners from a
very early age and, initially, they accept almost anything (e.g. a burp) as constituting
the baby's turn. As the children grow older, adults may become more stringent in
their criterion of what is an acceptable utterance, although they are still willing to
accept almost any conversational opening on the part of the child and to fill in for
the child whenever necessary. The most striking feature in the protocols of infant
speech with which investigators are confronted is that virtually all such speech is
a conversation between a child and a parent.[29] And such parent–child pairs differ
markedly in how they talk to each other because children have effects on adults as
well as the other way around. Thus a very marked degree of individual difference
in children–adults interactions becomes obvious. One child–mother pair may
approach a 'full' dialogic interaction while another pair may interact very differently and at least on the surface may not be having a conversation[30] – while still
other pairs might virtually avoid all interaction. But then, when having no conversation or interaction, what could they be having? To attempt a minimum answer
to this unavoidable question, we could acknowledge that an excessive avoidance
of conversational interaction may ultimately herd the subject through a sequence
of 'maturing' stages describable perhaps as animal husbandry directed to the breed
homo sapiens. Those inchoate interactions offering biological satisfaction while
unmindful of dialogic needs represent crucial passages where affectual and cognitive damage may occur.[31] In fact, even though there is no 'need' to converse and
no cogent explanation could be given for advocating the necessity of playful
conversation, these early 'language games' may profoundly influence the quality,
rigour, and creativity of human ratiocination: subsequent events may in fact
originate in experiences which these 'unnecessary' and playful interactions have
initiated.

SYMBOLIC PLAY AND AFFECTUAL SYNERGIES

There is a significant difference between metaphor itself and the improper use of
terms, such as resorting to the overextension of a word to make up for an insufficient
vocabulary, because, of course, once the appropriate word is learned the improper
one can be abandoned.[32] Genuine metaphoricity does not coincide with a compen-
sation for linguistic shortages; indeed, a young child may improperly rename an

object even though he knows the correct word for it – and thus may succeed in highlighting a feature that is especially meaningful for him. He can stage a pretence because he knows that the thing 'out there' does not coincide with the thing he is naming and using. Even while reluctant to recognize special interactive qualities in young children, an 'Apollonian' thinker such as Piaget has had to recognize that the non-conventional use of words *can*, at times, be founded on some form of pretence, or 'fiction'. Piaget insists that such uses are 'simple' images or temporary confusions which do not express proper concepts; and yet the very fact that instances of 'pretence' must be recognized, somehow implies the admission that the non- conventional conjunction of terms on the part of children cannot be simply reduced to a lexical or semantic error.[33] Winner remarks that whenever a child renames an object without previously transforming it through a fictional action, the metaphor remains based on some degree of physical resemblance, such as calling the letter 'J' 'walking stick', calling balloons 'apples', or a pencil 'large needle'.[34] Winner reports case-studies of children's language in which the *deliberate* renaming of objects is clearly at work for a variety of purposes.[35] In this early stage of development the sort of metaphors in which we are more interested are those involving a symbolic play, that is, involving attempts to make transformations and stage pretences.[36] These can be differentiated from the more descriptive or representational sort of metaphors primarily deriving from the perception of a physical similarity, and without the support of much creative fiction. If a young child renames an object by creating a fictional interaction with it and dealing with it as if it were something else, this is the more interesting sort of phenomenon illuminating the life-and-language synergies of our individual development.

Symbolic play is thus the condition for the embryonic metaphors rooted in a *functional* similarity created by means of *fiction*. In a case-study described by Winner, a young child puts a ribbon around the support of a microphone and says that 'the microphone needs a bib'; he also puts his leg inside a waste basket saying that 'he needs a boot'. In these cases the relation with the objects is largely created and not entirely discovered, or recognized; the child, in fact, does not (simply) perceive a measure of resemblance between the function of certain objects, but creatively perceives their potential for being drawn into a fictional dynamics, such as for instance needing a bib or a boot.[37] Thus the recognition of a similarity significantly differs from imaginatively creating functions and roles by means of a much deeper *personal* involvement.

Winner also points out that this form of metaphoricity originating from fiction does not possess the direction which more commonly characterizes metaphors constructed by adults.[38] In these metaphors the vehicle is used to redirect our attention toward the topic, which in fact constitutes the focus of a metaphor. When we (adults) say that 'the world (topic) is a jungle (vehicle)', it is our interpretation of the world (topic) and not that of the jungle (vehicle) which we wish to transform. If we say that 'Richard is a lion' and 'Sophia is a star', Richard and Sophia function as topics with respect to 'lion' and 'star' functioning as vehicles, in a situation normally focused on the topic and not quite transformable by shifting the focus on to the vehicle. In children's metaphors originating from fictional play there is no such fixed direction: the topic is more like a means to create an imagined object, and consequently the vehicle itself might turn out to be the focus of the metaphor. When the child calls the ribbon 'bib', he is not suggesting that ribbons can be seen in a new way because the ribbon – *per se, qua* ribbon – is not so important and other items could perform the same bib role; the child is here using the ribbon as if it were a bib. Children's metaphors may thus appear as lacking the typical asymmetry which characterizes adult metaphors.

The identities which are forged through metaphoric processes can be experienced in different ways: as both safe and risky, secure and adventurous. Part of the emotional intensity associated with such arousals of interest may derive from the creation of some sort of synergy. Apter remarks that it is quite possible that, at any moment, one of the characteristics of an identity which is being experienced synergically will constitute the focus of attention while the other will be relatively marginal.[39] Over time, too, it is likely that there may be reversals between which aspect of the synergy is in the foreground and which in the background. There may be moments when the two different components are present as the focus of attention at the same time, and at these moments the metaphoric synergy will be especially strong. This is particularly likely immediately after a reversal of attention between topic and vehicle, since it seems that the aspect receding into the bacground may take a little longer to do so than the aspect coming into the foreground, with the result that a condition may be created when they overlap at the focus of attention: they could be said to take the centre of the stage together.[40] Apter also points out that until the new 'information' has been properly assimilated, thus relegating the old property to the background, there is likely to be a brief period of excitement and pleasurable bewilderment. Following this, the synergy will be of a weaker form in that it more comfortably connects the new meaning in the foreground with the old meaning now occupying the background. This whole process can be referred to as a 'reversal synergy'.[41] All sudden changes in the nature of an identity should produce a reversal synergy to same degree, but it would seem that the strength of the synergy is appreciable only if the displaced property was previously a silent and well-established part of the identity in question, and the change to the new property was relatively unexpected or sudden. These remarks thus tend to converge with the suggestion that in children's symbolic metaphors there is the possibility of changing the direction of the expression because either the topic or the vehicle may be the focus of attention. It is probably a question of a greater mobility in the balance between symmetries and asymmetries and thus, possibly, of a greater measure of participation in unconscious modes of being.[42]

A 'characterizing' asymmetry can only be locally or temporally circumscribed because in an evolutionary perspective the topic can well soar to a lexical status such that it can function as a vehicle. If we think of a classical example such as 'Richard is a lion', and conceive the possibility that 'Richard' may reach a linguistic status comparable to Tarzan, Rambo, Batman (or whatever the current equivalent), we could easily envisage a metaphor such as 'This lion is a Richard'. We are thus inextricably interwoven in a pattern implying life and culture, logic and history. Thus in an open evolutionary outlook we would hardly experience surprise in seeing that the literal meaning of an utterance may be metaphoric or that the metaphoric meaning can be literal.

A synergy may occur when some new property, not previously part of either the centre or the fringe of experience, is suddenly perceived to be a property of the identity and made the focus of attention; it then ousts some contrasting property, relegating it to the periphery of awareness as a previous property of identity.[43] If a parent, for instance, tells a child something explicitly hurtful, this emerging hostility pushes the loving properties of the parent to the margin of awareness, where they remain as previous characteristics of the parental identity. A strong, if transient, synergy occurs in such cases, since the appearance of the new meaning is more or less instantaneous, while the old meaning may take a short time to recede so that the two opposite meanings temporarily absorb attention together. Apter also directs his attention to the more complex form of cognitive synergy in which one identity is superimposed on another identity which contrasts with it in a number of ways. An example can be afforded by any object that a small child, who is not offered proper toys, uses as a model for something else, such as a house, a person, a boat, or a weapon. In such cases, whatever is available for playing suggests another object different from itself, and usually larger, mightier, or more complex.[44] So the unofficial 'toy' – which is usually something that adults discard – becomes the bearer of at least two meanings, both of which are essential to the playful activity: it is a discarded piece of wood *and* a horse as well. A piece of wood which is not used to represent anything other than itself would no more be a toy than a real toy-horse. The interest of 'toys' derives from the fact that two identities are conceptually made to overlap. The toy object both is and is not something, even in the case of official toys. Its significance as a toy is therefore a synergic quality which emerges from this 'contradiction', together with the excitement that playing with it engenders. Any object allowed to float on water may share a number of properties with a real boat although in other respects it will be quite different. Apter suggests that 'There is therefore a set of relationships between the two identities, some of which are non-contradictory when the two identities are equated, and some of which are contradictory.'[45] The discrepancies are, as it were, kept together by the similarities so that an area is created which is suitable for mental 'leaps', generating links.

Matte Blanco claims that Freud's fundamental discovery is not so much the characteristics of our unconscious mind, but its symmetrical form of logic; and although Freud did not directly state the principles of symmetrical logic, his arguments were based on some implicit notion of this kind.[46] 'Symmetrical logic' is a general description used to refer to logical operations governed in part by what Matte Blanco calls the principle of symmetry; this principle states that whenever A has a given relation with B, then B must also have, or must be treated as having, the same relation to A.[47] If, for instance, we consider a proposition implying an asymmetrical relation such as 'A parent feeds a baby', this describes a situation whose converse – 'A baby feeds a parent' – is not the same as the original relation. But whenever the initial discrimination is either disregarded, or not yet attained, we could lapse or remain within symmetry and 'think' that if a parent is feeding the baby, then the baby is feeding the parent. In well-regulated literal contexts this is obviously regarded as faulty logic; and yet, immature psychic experiences of this sort can be profoundly interwoven in our life and language. A suckling infant may have no clear idea whether food comes from an outside donor or from the omnipotence of his desire. But, an early forced recognition that fantasy and desires cannot generate food may prematurely convince the nascent mind that nothing good may come from within and that only the outside reality has any goodness. These fragmentary remarks may only indicate that the function of symmetrical non-propositional schemata is more subtly pervasive than we are inclined to think. And, obviously, there is no way of deciding whether the experiences of entering life, or of leaving it, are biological or cultural events because presumably they are both.

In the case of young children symmetrical paradigms may be at work implying that 'since' they love their parents, then they must be equally loved by them. Such underdeveloped logic reverberates in our culture to the point that it is commonly believed that a loved child becomes a loving person. These symmetrizations often resonate in a variety of beliefs, such as in the self-fulfilling 'prophetic' paradigms of the type 'Since they hate me, then I hate them'. Indeed a statement of the type 'My enemy is good', is logically quite acceptable although affectually difficult to utter on account of profound links with primal symmetries influencing our linguistic behaviour. Thus the condition of not being exclusively ruled by the prevalent asymmetry of adult logic offers a unique opportunity to explore interactions that metabolically bring together immature experiences and mature language.

THE GENERATION AND USE OF LINKS

A synoptic historical glance may reveal that one of the major forces behind cultural evolution is the 'fateful' invention of a written language by the Sumerians; archaeological evidence seems to demonstrate that writing was in fact born in Mesopotamia.[48] Even though pictograms existed in that area, the most they could do was to enumerate objects or depict situations: they could not be used to communicate complex utterances, evaluations or thoughts as one could do in spoken language. Representation by pictograms virtually came to an end, and the written tradition was initiated, when the human mind became capable of achieving an unhoped for connection between signs and sounds, between two entities which do not resemble each other in the least. A proper written language, capable of communicating the visible and the invisible, can only be recognized when the signs 'acquire' a phonetic value, that is when specific sounds are linked with them. The hiatus that separates the pictogram and hierogliph from phonetic signs is in fact so great that we can legitimately consider the conjunction of graphic signs and sound vibrations as one of the major leaps forward in the itinerary of hominization. Possibly, the peaceful and agricultural Sumerians heeded the surrounding concert of nature and conversations so devotedly as to recognize the beauty and fascination of different, distinct sounds. The capacity to appreciate a sound so well that it can be sufficiently differentiated from others may be the precondition for linking it to a sign and thus inaugurate the immense perspective of our written tradition – from which we 'quickly' arrived at a telematic civilization.

Indeed, a superb metaphoric talent must be at work for affirming that a certain sound vibration *is* a specific sign, or that a certain sign *is* an identifiable sound vibration. Since the essential mark of metaphor is to express a link between something relatively well known (the semantic vehicle), and something which – although of greater importance – is more obscurely known (the semantic topic), and since it must make its point by means of some linking element, it appears that a metaphor presupposes some vehicular image or connecting motion. Thus it is not so important to determine whether or not saying that the sound 'Ssss' is an 's' (or that the design 'S' is the voice vibration 'Ssss') would count as a proper metaphor. In the Sumerians' case, more relevant than the focus of the metaphor is the connecting motion, the metaphoric process itself, the act of metabolically linking something to something else. By devotedly listening they identified specific sounds and were thus able to use them; if they had not creatively listened they might not have elements to metaphorize with. This linkage of sign and sound released the specifically human joy that comes from supplementing biological reproduction with cultural fertility, from transplanting our symbolic achievements in the most varied places and distant times. In Galileo's *Dialogue on the Great World Systems* the connectionist mentality is epitomized by Sagredus who intervenes in the discussion between Simplicius (a follower of Ptolemy) and Salviatus (a Copernican). Sagredus represents an irrepressible imaginative aspect of the empirical-minded Galileo, and he says:

> But, above all other stupendous inventions, what sublimity of mind must have been his who conceived how to communicate his most secret thoughts to any other person, though very far distant either in time or place, speaking with those who are in the Indies, speaking to those who are not yet born, nor shall be this thousand, or ten thousand years? And with no greater difficulty than the various collocation of twenty-four little characters upon paper? Let this be the seal of all the admirable inventions of man and the close of our discourse for this day.[49]

Metaphoric efforts can be seen as transferences of meaning whereby we 'gracefully' introduce further dimensions into our analysis and thus enrich our potential comprehension. The force of these efforts resides in their capacity to hold in interactive tension the use of similarities and differences between the considered elements. The assessment through metaphor of both what 'is' and what 'is not' constitutes one of the instruments which expand our understanding. Thus metaphoric constructs function as mediating instruments which draw on imagery as part of their power for sharpening thought. We could almost see in the robotic use of isolated words and concepts a tacit obligation to abide by their stricter sense, even though a consistent use of the stricter sense can be an overlooked source of misunderstanding. Enlivening synergies are established through the conjunction of different identities and the creation of intermediate concepts. If there were only fixed bits of reality to cope with and no metaphoric devices to play with them, our cognitive and affectual life might be significantly restricted. Wittgenstein points out that 'A main source of our failure to understand is that we do not *command a clear view* of the use of our words. Our grammar is lacking in this sort of perspicuity. A perspicuous representation produces just that understanding which consists in "seeing connexions". Hence the importance of finding and inventing *intermediate* cases.'[50] He thus explicitly underwrites the importance of either 'finding' or 'inventing' instruments whereby we can appreciate connections; and even the intermediate cases constitute connectives between different situations which could not be utilized in the form of discrete, unrelated items.

We might roughly describe the use of language by explaining how the words connect together to provide sentences. But if we think of the origin of linguisticity in humans or of the evolution of language in culture, perhaps we should proceed somewhat differently. We can only 'confer' meaning to novel uses of words if we can grasp the sense of the overall message in which they are used and have enough familiarity with other aspects of a sentence to make reasonable hypotheses about their new roles. Metaphoric language is thus an interpersonal linguistic occurrence and its use must be sustained by internalized schemata in ways that cannot be accounted for in compositional semantics. 'Rejection of compositional semantics', say Arbib and Hesse, 'has a more than technical significance. It implies, indeed, nothing less than a new theory of knowledge.'[51] Quite simply we could say that humans master their connective skills through the extensive and inescapable practice beginning almost as early as the onset of speech itself. Such experience with metaphoric construction and construal enhances the growth of conceptual hierarchies and contributes to the development of abstract thought. And because metaphor renames not only sensed objects and events, but superordinate abstractions as well, it also provides the individual's earliest linguistic exercise with the conceptual apparatus from which logical powers will emanate. Language development, in fact, interacts with and influences concept formation in a manner so fundamental that psycholinguists can rarely avoid talking about both at once.

The boundary between metaphor and nonsense frequently appears to be flexible and permeable for indeed, if read literally, metaphor would not make much sense as its most salient characteristic is its semantic absurdity, its transgression of lexical constraints. More precisely, metaphor violates the conditions governing normal application of its terms by joining words whose semantic markers are incompatible. In the celebrated Aristotelian definition, in fact, 'metaphor consists in giving the thing a name that belongs to something else.'[52] In Richards's more relational outlook we have 'two thoughts of *different* things active together and supported by a single word, or phrase, whose meaning is a resultant of their interaction'.[53] And yet, however 'implausible' they are, we could not properly function without metaphoric passages. In the human condition as new beliefs and desires appear which challenge our customary mental habits, we generally refer to them as 'contradictions', at the more formal end of the spectrum, and as 'tensions', towards the more affectual end. One of the properties of an identity may be more central than the other at a given time, so that one property may come to the front while the other, opposite, property recedes. It is thus legitimate to wonder how much of what we affirm in the way of a justifiable belief connects and in fact overlaps with the expression of a desire. Rorty suggests that it is common to treat desires as if they were beliefs. This is done by regarding 'the imperative (optative) attitude toward the sentence S "Would that it were the case that S!" as the indicative attitude: "It would be better that S should be the case than that not-S should be."[54] Through this approach any web of beliefs can be considered not just as an attitudinal conglomeration but as a coalition of desires which induce behavioural consequences. In certain cases the formation of a new belief-desire will provoke a notable, conscious and deliberate rearrangement of our sentential attitudes which Rorty calls 'inquiry' or 'scientific breakthrough':

> As one moves along the spectrum from habit to inquiry – from instinctive revision of intentions through routine calculation toward revolutionary science or politics – the number of beliefs added to or subtracted from the web increases. At a certain point in this process it becomes useful to speak of 'recontextualization'. The more widespread the changes, the more use we have for the notion of a 'new context'.[55]

In the wake of this language we could say that a new texture has to be woven to accommodate life to major changes. Good metaphors appear as the indispensable instruments for reweaving new webs of belief-desires. And in this same language it becomes possible to ask which are the metaphoric shifts which induce weaving of new webs and which instead might only produce knots and tangles, that is, contexts or textures which are not propitious to the development of mental life.[56]

RECIPROCITY AND SILENCING

Protection of the right to free speech could be conceived – in an 'abstract' liberal view – as the promotion of some disembodied idea of freedom, where 'freedom' is something we automatically have unless someone interferes with it; and of course free speech would be all too easily achieved in such a lifeless, solipsist perspective. On the basis of normal cognitive and vocal resources a person would thus be free to speak unless obstacles are created which impede speech acts. Hornsby considers this approach in order to demonstrate that it is rooted in a misconception about the way language operates.[57] She puts her argument in the terms of Austin's 'speech act theory' and shows that the 'liberal' view ultimately assumes that speech is simply a matter of *locution* and ignores its function of *illocution*. In Austin's model[58] a locution is a linguistic act which simply consists in producing sounds belonging to a given language, organized according to a given grammar and possessing a specific meaning; the locutionary act thus consists in the merely factual aspects of speech – as logically detachable from those features which it would exhibit if it were also considered as an illocution. An illocution is in fact a speech act which is more than a locution because it *produces* something in the saying. By treating utterances as simple locutions we deny their illocutionary force and thus also ignore the unity of the speech act of the speaker: what he wants to say he cannot say at all whenever the transformational aspects of the illocution are not appreciated. Whenever the illocution is treated as if it were a locution, the metaphoric force for really saying what he would like to say is tacitly annulled. Metaphor, in fact, is an indivisible process of both construction and construal.

Hornsby and Searle[59] seem to converge in suggesting that shared understanding is the crucial element of illocution. If person *A* is trying to tell person *B* something, as soon as *B* recognizes that *A* is trying to tell it to *B*, *A* has succeeded. Unless *B* recognizes that *A* is trying to tell *B* it, *A* does not fully succeed in telling it to *B*. What person *A* relies on, then, in order to tell *B* something is *B*'s being open to the idea that *A* might be telling *B* what in fact *A* means to tell *B*; unless *B* can readily entertain the idea that *A* might be doing this, *B* could hardly take *A* to be doing it. Hornsby, then, goes on to argue that silencing is the process of depriving a person of his illocutionary potential: 'It may work by affecting people's mind-sets and expectations in such a way that reciprocity fails. Where reciprocity does fail, what someone might attempt to do, she will not be recognized as attempting to do, thus cannot be understood as having done, and therefore, given the nature of illocution, simply cannot (successfully) do.'[60] And if reciprocity is the condition of linguistic communication, it is *a fortiori* a condition for metaphoric constructions. Reciprocity in fact obtains when people are able to recognize one another's speech as it is meant to be taken, and thus to ensure the success of attempts to perform the less conventional and more expressive speech acts, the listener being an essential complementary partner in an integral view of language. 'The speaker's doing what she does with her words is the product of her attempt *and* the hearer's recognition of it', says Hornsby.[61]

It is interesting that it should be emphasized that communication is a relation between people, and that, as such, it requires understanding on the listener's part not only of the meaning of the utterance but also of the intended performance. If the intended performance is neglected, the metaphoric potential is silenced. Whatever the particular language, Hornsby remarks that 'it is a condition of its normal successful use – of speaker's intended communicative acts actually being performed – that people be sufficiently in harmony, as it were, to provide for recognition of speaker's meaning.'[62] And of course it is only under these circumstances that we can make use not only of 'language' but of the condition of reciprocity. No matter how extensively argued this position is, it is perhaps an approach requiring transformations for which we may not be sufficiently mature.

Hornsby's invoked notions of 'harmony' and 'reciprocity' resonate with Davidson's 'principle of charity' and at least in part coincide with it. 'Since charity is not an option, but a condition . . . it is meaningless to suggest that we might fall into massive error by endorsing it . . . Charity is forced on us: whether we like it or not, if we want to understand others, we must count them right in most matters.'[63] And also: 'Widespread agreement is the only possible background against which disputes . . . can be interpreted. Making sense of the utterances and behaviour of others, even their most aberrant behaviour, requires us to find a great deal of reason and truth in them.'[64] Davidson also suggests that if the agreement on plain matters that is assumed in communication escapes notice, it is because the shared truths are too many and too dull to bear mentioning: 'What we want to talk about is what's new, surprising or disputed.'[65] And this is what we usually struggle to express through metaphoric efforts, provided there is a sufficient background of 'charity', 'reciprocity' and 'harmony'.

If there is reason to analyse language so that the complex formal dynamics of communication are progressively elucidated, there is also reason to monitor those barely noticed ways of silencing which pre-emptively forbid a person to success-fully say what he is actually saying. So it is not quite right to say of the unconstrued metaphoric efforts that they are wasted as could be said of the utterances that are drowned out, refused, or misunderstood. From the point of view of the unlistened person who is not taken as he would mean to be taken, there is something pointless about saying the things he says because he cannot do what he intends to do by saying what he says. This condition does not render people inaudible, but rather unable to communicate.[66] Just as it is more or less automatic that an attempt to say something is successful when certain socially defined conditions obtain, so one simply cannot communicate when certain conditions do not obtain. Just as reci-procity may secure communication, so the absence of conditions that ensure reciprocity may prevent communication: to the extent that reciprocity fails a person, he has been deprived of his illocutionary potential and cannot do with language what he may want to do.[67]

Hornsby reports the case of a magistrate in the process of recommending the acquittal of a man accused of rape and quotes Judge David Wild saying: 'Women who say "no" do not always mean "no". It is not just a question of saying "no".'[68] In the instance lucidly analysed by Hornsby it is the case of a person rendered unable to perform a specific illocutionary act by saying 'No'. But then, we could use the discussion as an illuminating paradigm to take better notice of those innumerable occasions in which individuals cannot properly succeed in saying 'Yes'. If it is legitimate to transform into the affirmative the statement of Judge Wild – 'Women who say "Yes" do not always mean "Yes". It is not just a question of saying "Yes"' – would imply a massive devaluational attitude and would tend to cast doubt on statements such as 'Yes, I will pay', 'Yes, I can do that', and 'Yes, I understand' – let alone metaphoric expressions aiming to create greater precision or transform outlooks. Even though it is quite easy to speak it seems often impossible to speak successfully. If it is so difficult to say 'No' successfully under adverse circumstances, it is perhaps even more difficult effectively to say 'Yes', if 'Yes' is tacitly implied, or silently exclaimed, as a preamble to affirmations such as constructive projects, innovative descriptions of reality, or illuminating met phors. That a refusal is not understood is a deplorable occurrence, although comparatively less consequential than the pervasive failure to communicate af-firmative utterances. The tragedy implicit in this and similar examples is that cumulative failure to grant reciprocity and construal of metaphoric expressions does not so much impede or prohibit language as it actually prevents its success-ful use.

BODILY PROJECTIONS

Resisting the surrounding pressures of pure thinking, Johnson innovatively explores the ways in which rationality arises from, and is conditioned by, the patterns of our bodily experiences. He proposes a theory of how basic concepts such as balance, limit, force, and transitivity develop from our corporeal experiences and are metaphorically extended to create abstract meanings and rational connections.[69] His enlightening contributions, however, tend to ignore the more interpersonal and dialogic aspects of these developments. The processes he describes cannot be regarded as automatic ones since the detachment from a relational matrix can in fact significantly inhibit their course.

Books on the philosophy of language generally assume that meaning is first and foremost something *sentences* have and also reasonably maintain that the meaning of words or phrases depends upon their role within sentences. This exclusive focus on sentence structure has contributed to the widely held view that an account of meaning as propositional is all that is required. Johnson's contribution can be seen as a non-traditional inquiry into the nature of meaning, attempting to probe beneath the level of propositional content, as it is usually defined, and to ask how propositional structure is possible.[70] The enterprise leads him down into the image schematic structures of somatic events, through which we are able to have coherent experiences that we can comprehend. He thus intends to treat 'linguistic meaning' as a sub-case of meaning in a much broader sense. He claims in fact that it is possible to question the assumption that only words and sentences have meanings: 'Although linguistic meanings are subject to elaborate analyses of human intentionality that would not be possible without the complex structure of propositions and speech acts, it does not follow that all meaning is merely propositional in nature.'[71]

In this view the notion of metaphorical projections could provisionally be conceived as a pervasive mode of producing knowledge, implemented by projecting patterns from one domain of experience on to an as yet unstructured area. So conceived, our metaphoric function is only partially related to metaphor-as-a-figure-of-language; it rather comes across as constitutive of both our cognitive development and self-creation. It is through our metaphoric capacity that we utilize patterns that obtain in any of our life experiences in order to structure novel and more abstract areas of concern. In Johnson's view bodily experience not only determines a dynamic pattern of our perceptual interactions by constraining the 'input' to metaphorical projections, but it also determines the nature of the projections themselves, that is, the kind of links that can occur across domains.[72] Metaphorical projections are experiential patterns of meaning that are essential to most aspects of our rational endeavours; thus, they are not arbitrary but rather they are highly constrained by basic aspects of our bodily experience.[73] This research strategy is almost the mirror image of the Cartesian approach, where corporeal experiences are regarded as an unfortunate hindrance to mental development. 'Indeed', says Descartes, 'in our early years, our mind was so immersed in the body, that it knew nothing distinctly, although it perceived much sufficiently clearly; and because it even then formed many judgements, numerous prejudices were contracted from which the majority of us can hardly ever hope to become free.'[74]

Exploring one of the instances of image-schematic structures derived from very early experiences of containment, Johnson remarks:

> Our encounter with containment and boundedness is one of the most pervasive features of our bodily experience. We are intimately aware of our bodies as three-dimensional containers into which we put certain things (food, water, air) and out of which other things emerge (wastes, air, blood, etc.) . . . If we look for a common structure in our many experiences of being *in* something, or for locating something *within* another thing, we find a recurring organization of structures: the experiential basis for *in–out* orientation is that of spatial boundedness. The most experientially salient sense of boundedness seems to be that of three-dimensional containment (i.e., being limited or held within some three-dimensional enclosure such as a womb, a crib, a room).[75]

The problem is that the experience of spatial containment, *per se*, would only afford a very weak structure if it were not, in turn, supported by a sense of containment in time, that is by a sense of temporal continuity, by a structure which is essential to hold together our experience as long as it endures, lasts and resists in time. For, indeed, the organizing force of the in–out image schema is ultimately dependent upon the continuing 'mental' performance of the schema itself. And the degree of stability which is attained is profoundly dependent upon the symbolic and affectual vicissitudes of the developing person.

It is often suggested that metaphor is ubiquitous in language and that the existence of non-metaphorical language is questionable. In fact, even when we talk about abstract concepts, we employ linguistic derivatives emerging from a concrete domain. Whenever we talk of the mind we use spatial models to describe phenomena which are clearly non-spatial in character: we have ideas 'in' or 'on' our minds, and thoughts may 'pass through' it. Our basic method for understanding typically non-sensory concepts still derives from concrete experiential situations. Johnson invites us to

> consider, for example, only a few of the many *in–out* orientations that might occur in the first few minutes of our ordinary day. You wake *out* of a deep sleep and peer *out* from beneath the covers *into* your room. You gradually emerge *out of* your stupor, pull yourself *out* from under the covers . . . stretch *out* your limbs, and walk *in* a daze *out* of the bedroom.[76]

These examples, of course, typically refer to a mature person and not to an immature one, whose sense of in and out might be developed or distorted by innumerable interactive experiences. The *in–out* orientation scheme involves a sense of separation, differentiation, and enclosure which, in turn, entails a sense of restriction and limitation. And yet, when the embodied schema is too weak to function because its potential development has not been sufficiently nurtured by an appropriate dialogic approach, we may have a mind which cannot contain thoughts, make abtractions and distinctions, establish links, and 'inhabit' a body with sufficient confidence.

Johnson remarks that it is a matter of great significance that patterns such as containment, limit, stability, accessibility and transitivity, which exist preconceptually in our experience, can give rise to rational entailments (which we can describe propositionally);[77] he says,

> What is important is that these recurrent patterns are relatively few in number, that they are not propositional in the objectivist sense, and that they have sufficient internal structure to generate entailments and to constrain inferences (and thus to be propositionally elaborated).[78]

But then again how do these structures *generate* rational entailments? The answer could be that a wealth of interactive support is necessary for these structures properly to develop and thus transform biological behaviour into logical creativity. Although we gratefully recognize that a schema is a recurrent pattern in our ordering activity and that such regularity emerges for us at the level of our corporeal movements through space, our manipulation of objects and our perceptual interactions, it should be remarked that such experiences are *necessarily* interpersonal because an isolated infant only exists as a hypothetical abstraction. Whatever goes on at the bodily level is in fact highly charged with affectual, cultural and interpersonal dynamics which influence the development of those very same image schemata – thus to be regarded as potential and non-automatic sources of structure.

Johnson says: 'Image schemata exist at a level of generality and abstraction that allows them to serve repeatedly as identifying patterns in an indefinitely large number of experiences, perceptions, and image formations for objects or events that are similarly structured in the relevant ways.'[79] Perhaps such 'objects or events' are not just 'similarly structured in the relevant ways' but can be similarly structured on condition that the metaphoric projection is successful in linking up with the endless sequence of impacts with the world. And, as usual, metaphoric projections are constantly a matter of construction and construal – an essentially dialogic phenomenon. 'There are those few days when the synapse connections are being established and then, fairly suddenly, the baby becomes a little *homo erectus*.'[80] But then, why is it that under conditions of extreme interactive deprivation this would probably not happen? The major point in Johnson's view is that 'the *meaning* of balance begins to emerge through our *acts* of balancing and through our *experience* of systematic processes and states within our bodies . . . The key word here is "structure", for there can be no meaning without some form of structure or pattern that establishes relationships.'[81] He also says, 'If you observe a one-year-old learning to walk, you see its initial clumsy attempts to distribute mass and forces properly . . . and you will often see the toddler's arms held out to form a balancing horizontal axis relative to the vertical axis.'[82] Although we also 'observe' infants, we primarily share affectual interactions with them. A hypothetical isolated infant only observed from a distance might not succeed in achieving upright balance. These remarks are intended to suggest that not only bodily schemata influence the domain of our linguisticity but also that communicative language is an essential factor in shaping our human experiences. Johnson reiterates that it is necessary to appreciate that balancing is an attitude that we learn in our physical life and not by grasping rules or concepts. 'First and foremost, balancing is something we *do*. The baby stands, wobbles, and drops to the floor. It tries again, and again, until a new world opens up – the world of the balanced erect posture.'[83] But then, if it is the case that the bodily schema of balance is metaphorized into different abstract domains, it is also to be recognized that the acquisition of the balanced erect posture depends on affectual and cultural factors in the absence of which it is just not acquired. As a response to Johnson's insight in describing the emergence of meaning through embodied schemata, it could be suggested that even the development of image schemata derived from bodily experience is to some extent dependent on conditions of dialogic metaphoricity. Indeed, physical schemata are metaphorically projected on to abstract symbolic relations, while at the same time metaphorical language is essential in the development, distortion, or even elimination of such precious schematic functions. At the utmost extreme, a severely traumatized person might not even know whether or not he 'inhabits' his own body.

Thus the development of cognitive schemata which can be extended on to different domains might 'appear' as a quasi-automatic process, immune from conflicts, hindrances and distortions. And yet the essential decisive question regards the intervening factors which either enhance or impede such development. Out of the Middle Ages comes a chronicle of Salimbene de Adam from Parma (1221–88) in support of the idea that the processes of human development are far from automatic. He narrates how Frederick II of Sicily wished to discover which had been the first language spoken on earth, wondering whether it had been Hebrew, Greek or Latin. The logically inclined King arranged for a number of new-born babies to be kept in isolation, with the injunction that they be seen only for feeding and that no one should ever talk to them. The enlightened monarch had worked out that the language which the secluded infants would spontaneously begin to speak would be the first language that had ever existed on earth. The result of the experiment is unknown, as not one of the children survived. And the chronicler asks: 'How could they have survived without the cuddles, gestures, smiles and endearments of their nurses?'[84]

10 Vicissitudes of self-formation

LIFE AND LANGUAGE SYNERGIES

To the extent that the more 'normal' theories of language, mind and knowledge have a definite cultural effect they may also succeed in somehow benumbing our intellectual life – for a while at least – by obliquely discouraging the expression of further pressing questions. Even though in the form of an enlightened 'liberation' from confusion, some philosophical outlooks may quietly encourage intellectual repression. A perplexing aspect of our more rigorous philosophies, in fact, is not so much that they fail to yield 'solutions' of the problems they focus on but that they do not see the problems closely surrounding their foci of attention; or they even obscure them completely. The theoretical representation of cognition does not necessarily show what minds do when they cognize, although it may none the less be a description that is adequate for particular purposes. Indeed, only philosophical questions that have achieved great popularity come to appear as worthy of intellectual scrutiny. Being insufficiently articulated may thus cause even the most 'urgent' of practical and theoretical questions to be excluded from cultural life. We could condense the issue in the words of Putnam by saying that 'the question that won't go away is how much what we call "intelligence" presupposes *the rest* of human nature'.[1]

Since the results of past philosophies are usually judged to be inadequate, we should expect even the most prestigious elucidations of our contemporary culture to appear somehow defective in due time. And this realistic lack of confidence might become an essential part of our approach, not something that facts alone could repeatedly teach us. In our ineradicable dependence on linguisticity, it is then a question of creating provisional balances of conceptual beliefs, to be constantly re-optimized in the process. Most philosophical endeavours at coping with the constraints of the mind–body problem, for instance, have traditionally sought a reduction to one mode or the other. As a response to such excessively schematic outcomes, we might then attempt to develop a vocabulary more capable of articulating the experience of ourselves as living subjects, as creatures inexorably involved in a life cycle – the biological pre-condition for forming desires, beliefs and knowledge. And a philosophy really hospitable to the appreciation of metaphoric processes is in a comparatively more propitious condition to encompass the complexity of our bio-cultural life. Conversely, a faithful appreciation of our life-complexity is a prerequisite for the construction and construal of a metaphoric linguisticity. In such a life-dependent perspective, then, there is no neutral time out, from which to claim or seek the next best step. Arbib and Hesse, for instance, are among those thinkers who constantly argue that human thought is not purely abstract: 'There is no pure cognition', they insist, 'because we are essentially embodied. Our thought enters into, and helps constitute, our actions, emotions and desires. To come to terms with the thinking subject is to come to terms with the actions and practices its thoughts are implicated in.'[2]

The moment the philosophical community inclines toward a Davidsonian vocabulary whereby beliefs, desires and intentions are a condition of language while language is also a condition for them,[3] the 'unbreakable' distinction is virtually bypassed between language as the contemporary substitute for mind (spirit, intellect. . .), and the life of creatures throbbing with fantasies, conflicts and aspirations – as the contemporary substitute of body and nature.

As the very beginning of development is profoundly influenced by cultural circumstances, in the human domain biological events and linguistic interactions should only be distinguished for the purposes of exposition and discussion. One cannot envisage such a thing as a natural mind developing language in a vacuum: 'Culture rather than nature', remarks Bruner, 'has become the world to which we must adapt and from which we draw our resources for doing so.'[4] Thus a fuller concept of human understanding increasingly requires a pattern of interactions with nature and persons, rather than a reduction to the aseptic semantic network that often permeates western philosophy – a network which, of course, can be aptly isolated for purposes of circumscribed elucidation.

Out of the range of possible outlooks through which we select a focus of attention we may thus choose to approach language primarily as a means of interaction and secondarily as an instrument of synchronic representation; the life and language synergies may then begin to appear in the full diachronic dimension affecting human development. In fact, even though constrained by external conditions and biological inheritance, self creation is also influenced by the demands of the story that the individual is intent upon 'inventing'. And the story itself relies upon metaphoric assumptions which function almost like genes in the effort of self-development. Basic metaphors can be identified which guide one's life journey by the constant process of shaping a diachronic, enduring structure of the self.[5]

Weak but repeated attempts to tell one's life story not only constitute accounts, given in the here and now, of events which took place in the there and then; in the endeavours of recounting one's story the narrator and protagonist tend actually to coincide in the 'end', an end which then functions as an inaugural opportunity for re-examining the underlying assumptions of self creation. At the 'end' of the story metaphoric links can be found telling us whether words are instruments or weapons, precious or worthless, whether the individual or the group *really* exists, whether danger comes from the inside or from the outside. As such connecting structures become less obscure, the person in the making may also try to reveal the so far hidden guidelines of events in his development.

In this perspective metaphoric guidelines which tend to function as self-fulfilling prophecies may come closer to being rationally scrutinized. We could perhaps think of a self-fulfilling prophecy as a metaphor which predetermines the occurrence of what it implies, suggests or intimates on account of its having been sufficiently well proclaimed and absorbed. Behaviour deriving from a believed prophecy thus tends to create preconditions for the occurrence of the prophesied event in the sense of generating the sort of contexts which could not have been produced in the absence of the 'oracular' metaphor. At the start such 'predictive' metaphors cannot be assessed as either 'true' or 'false', while in a diachronic perspective they seem subtly to create conditions which support their soaring truth value. There may be cases in which a believed assumption that is regarded as a bit of reality produces the sort of event which it implies: what seems to make a difference is the course of action chosen as a reaction to the believed development of the situation. And the sort of action which we consider a reaction to the behaviour of others may produce in them just that specific conduct which then 'justifies' our own doings.

'Invented' reality could be thought of as transforming itself into factual reality through a full belief in the invention. And whenever the components of belief and conviction are absent, the 'prophecy' may remain without effect. Through a more accurate monitoring of the 'prophecies' which fulfil themselves, our capacity for eschewing them might be optimized. In fact, a metaphoric prophecy which we diagnose as just a metaphor cannot properly fulfil itself. But then, such diagnoses can only be the derivatives of our elaborate narrative endeavours: as soon as a 'trick' becomes clear, we are no longer bound to a naïve way of playing the game and even no longer constrained by it.

In the history of hominization, knowledge of the 'healing' effects of prophecies is as common and ancient as the 'unavoidable' consequences of spells. And a basic feature of such outlooks is the power deriving from a belief in the fixity of things. But then, the nature of these convictions may range all the way from simple superstitions to theories resting upon empirical observation. Perhaps in past centuries it was easier to identify self-fulfilling prophecies by attributing them to hopelessly romantic and oracular thinkers; but the problem is that today most prophetic metaphors are expressed in the lucid public language of scientific publications and of benevolent 'educators': we may still be far from appreciating the scope of the self-fulfilling forecasts utilized in our enlightened culture. In a linguistic approach linked to the exploration of beliefs and desires we inexorably move in the direction of discovering that we actually contribute to the creation of relevant features of our reality; we thus incline more to the study of interaction than to the scrutiny of representation. We consequently face an expulsion from the earthly paradise of 'objective' reality. And although it may be a tough reality, which causes us various degrees of difficulty, it none the less is a 'reality' for which we are only minimally responsible, for we only have a small effect on something that we find 'out there'.

Arbib and Hesse often argue that metaphoricity is crucial for language and that the nature of our embodiment helps us create the metaphors through which we organize our multiple experiences – which are not primarily representations.[6] The very notion of an *essentially embodied subject* suggests, moreover, that such a reconciliation has been made necessary as a remedy against the detrimental effects of the persistent disembodiment perpetrated by a philosophical tradition more focused on accurate representation than on the synergies of interaction. And an 'excess' of attention to objective representations, which tend to marginalize inter-active issues, is not without consequences. In Nagel's view the limit of objectivity with which we are most concerned is one that derives from the process of detachment by which objectivity is attained. Of course an objective standpoint is identified by dismissing the more subjective, or even just human, perspective but there are things (he remarks) that cannot be adequately understood from a maxi-mally objective standpoint, however much it may extend our understanding beyond the point from which we started. Qualifying features are essentially connected to particular points of view and the project of obtaining a thorough account of the world in detached, objective terms inevitably leads to false reductions or to the 'outright denial that certain patently real phenomena exist at all'.[7]

Different styles of metaphoricity cannot be intended as indirect statements about the world but rather, in the language of Cooper, as 'little dramas' through which the world in its essential features is introduced.[8] The important affinity charac-terizing non-literal accounts of human life lies in the dynamic conception of the world they share. The 'little dramas' referred to by Cooper may indeed indicate complex and difficult relations which are not comparable with the emblematic cases of a mirroring language. The richness of nature and culture may constantly be defying conventional classifications. Should such richness be tacitly denied by indirectly endorsing the ultimate value of our literal vocabulary, the individuals constrained by it would tend to be excluded from life itself inasmuch as a caricature of reality would come to be enforced upon them.

'Truth' plays the role of the pivotal notion in the discussion of how language relates to the world, and those with a basic leaning to semantics want to hear of it more than anything else. The later process of hominization is of course being implemented by means of conscious reflection on truth problems. But our capacity for critical reflection on knowledge now unfolds with the support of unlimited symbolic ways of formalization, and thus increasingly loses *contact* with its biological roots. Contemporary ratiocination is capable of unprecedented achieve-ments even though it does not clearly perceive and include its own evolutionary background;[9] whenever this biological background becomes evident, people react almost as if they were ashamed of it, and so tend to ignore it. And yet the successful evolution of our independent intellectual functions thus seems to depend today upon a capacity seriously to re-establish contacts with our evolutionary heritage: the detached dominance of our conscious propositional reason may be as unviable as insufficient development of rationality itself.

Metaphors do not only connect different semantic fields but also different evolutionary levels within our inner world. Although the same person may express utterances of an incompatible quality, it is through personal metaphoric language that their potential for being linked is expressible. Through the development of a truly maturational language we may thus start to opt for integrative conditions which we could not formerly envisage, and to develop a distrust for former accepted desires underlying our divisive convictions. And although most theorists end up using metaphors to break the hold of a limiting metaphor, the problem remains of somehow reconnecting divergent views within the individual or the intellectual community. The condition of feeling split between parts of oneself, in fact, is more likely to be remedied through an epistemic shift towards wholeness rather than through an intellectual exacerbation of the split. In Bateson's view the only exit from a condition of feeling split comes through a move to a complementary mode, or *surrender* to a larger context, in which a system may shift from an increasing polarity to a concern for a larger range of needs.[10]

FROM BIOLOGICAL LIFE TO DIALOGIC EXISTENCE

If we speak of the biological function of our metaphoricity the expression may come across as incongruous as in fact metaphor is generally regarded as a typically symbolic activity, and thus quite distinct from our existence as living organisms. A possible way, then, to think of a 'biology of metaphor' is by reference to experiences of our development which are influenced by metaphorical language and which may enhance or impede the fruitfulness of life. And in the life cycle of humans biological and cultural events are more profoundly interwoven than we are prepared to allow. It appears to be increasingly acknowledged that the acquisition of language requires more care from parental figures than was previously suspected and that relevant communicative interactions are well in force before the immature person is able to master the 'normal' language for expressing them verbally. In a 'biological' outlook it almost seems that the developing self is motivated to achieve consensual language in order to extend its own pre-existing communicative patterns.[11] A capacity for making relationships characterizes those early ways of knowing things from which our rational knowledge is laboriously derived.[12] In fact, although we may never be fully cognizant of being bonded, we are none the less conscious of our acute *dis*ease when we are not suitably related or when we are hopelessly bound to inadequate compensatory contexts. And of course, although interaction seems necessary, there is no logical necessity that it be regarded as a sufficient condition. The complexity of our syntactic rules and languaging is such that we might even regard it as being learned 'instrumentally', that is, as a means for fulfilling certain previously operative goals. In a similar approach Bruner remarks that nowhere in the higher animal kingdom are highly skilled and recombinable acts ever learned 'automatically' even when they are nurtured by strongly developed biological predispositions.[13]

As metaphors lead to the creation of ever new worlds of experience, to which one could not otherwise gain access, a developing ability to use metaphor cannot be reduced to a mere linguistic inclination for a 'transfer' of meanings. Were there no such original drive towards the expansion of significance it would be hard to see why a subject in the making should strive to learn or 'invent' a language: without such preliminary attributions of significance reality would look so threadbare and restricted as not to elicit any responsive commitment. If our nascent thought is unable to endow with inspiring connotations a (possible) surrounding world, that same external world will be unable to 'emit' signals which arouse interest or cognitive wonder, and which ultimately demand both serious and playful involvement.

The outcome of fictitious relations based on the non-construal of metaphoric messages and on the indifferent staging of literalist responses is inevitably associated with a lifeless language which may only function as a deadening filler. This sort of non-construing language can be highly manipulative and even suitable for determining a cognitive space which is only apparently free of conflicts, but which ultimately leads to nullifying vital relations. Speakers become tied into a sort of benumbed state which is perhaps the most widespread and most concealed of all forms of degradation. Paradoxically, the more our life can be described as 'intimate', 'profound', 'subjective', the more its development is dependent upon the quality of the interpersonal relationships which affect the crucial distinction between mirroring and relating.[14]

There could be something secretly reactionary and idealistic in contemporary outlooks whereby what there is and how we know it cannot go beyond what we can properly think about. Situations in which a subject does not succeed in expressing something which he already 'knows' are indeed precious and crucial, since they constitute passages in which he is searching for a bearer of meaning which he could share with others for the purpose of developing 'real' consensual communications. Meaning may derive from interpersonal negotiations regarding something on which there is a measure of agreement because it is sufficiently shared. And meanings which have been reciprocally agreed upon are of course such that they develop, change and are an issue of dispute within the relation.

Whenever the interlocutor who putatively has greater responsibility within a bi-personal field is not sufficiently aware of how challenging it is to make contact with the depths of his own self in order to attempt authentic construals, the relationship will be steered toward literalness in such a way as to avoid the risk of attempting unexpected, disquieting connections. The more 'responsible' one in the dyad might only take the pathways which are already well known and which present no threat to the epistemology he inhabits: this would be an irresponsible, yet an unnoticed and respectable way of dealing with the intelligence of interlocutors.

Bollas suggests that we may originally perceive parental figures not so much as persons but as 'forces' capable of transforming our inner world and external surroundings; initially we may not quite realize that this transformation is induced by identifiable persons.[15] So we could then say that the *experience* of persons precedes our *knowledge* of them – which is perhaps a view that most of us would readily accept. We could even hypothesize that the developing person may live through the most intense affectual experiences by journeying through 'atmospheres' whose origin he cannot correctly identify. But then, if our very early, intense experiences actually precede, and possibly shape, our ensuing ways of knowing, they can only be expressed in terms which exceed the boundaries of any literality.

If we could think of some 'primitive' form of logic which interacts with the mature logic of parental figures in ways which are more 'pragmatic' than 'cognitive', we could then say that the nascent mind 'knows' the basic rules of interactive life; what it knows, however, is not organized in terms of discrete propositions and we could not say that it properly thinks what it well knows. What it knows is not cognitively or mentally representable even though its fantasies and metaphoric expressions tend accurately to reflect some of the crucial circumstances he faces in negotiating a relationship with adult figures. There are early experiences, then, that we know of although we cannot quite think of them. One of the axes of psychoanalytic culture is in fact the persuasion that analysis not only offers an opportunity to re-live interactions, but also that it creates an opportunity for an entirely new experience: attention and nurture are provided for those selfsame experiences in such a way that they are no longer just somehow 'known' but profoundly thought through by the individual. And of course whatever is known but not sufficiently thought cannot be 'appropriately' or 'properly' articulated, but only metaphorically communicated, provided that a vital alliance is at work allowing for an enlivening exchange of constructs and construals.

In life-enhancing language games the early expressions of the nascent personality are met with construals inducing the belief that language is an enriching instrument and a path to self-formation. But in those pseudo-construals whereby actual life tends to become sadly detached from linguistic life there is no interpretive reaction to the metaphoric inventions of the evolving individual, but instead a steady directing towards the literalness of 'adult' language. A centrifugal sort of language, leading away from the core of the nascent self, is firmly established; and through it we come to believe that life and language are ultimately to be dissociated inasmuch as one's own language is to be regarded as inessential to projects of self creation. This inner centrifugal force seems contrary to any kind of formation, education, growth, *Bildung*: it is the unseen (and thus unquestioned) equivalent of intimating that there is no logic whatsoever in the individual and that real logic is only to be found in the dominant epistemology; to this one must seek access and adhere if one aspires to be something more than a mere natural being. Adhering to a constant deviation from what is personal to what is conventional one is ultimately deprived of any instruments for self-reflection and thus for appreciating the inner life of others – as if we could look *at* others without even trying to see into them.

An atrophy in the potential for generating metaphors may result in an inability to generate any models and consequently in a submission to whatever paradigms are offered by the surrounding culture.[16] With this insight attention could be profitably directed away from the classic instruments of social control and on to the everyday workings of our linguistic and educational tradition. A new emphasis could be placed upon the unnoticed indoctrinating influence of the ongoing discourses, which necessarily reverberate in life-shaping experiences more secretly and surely than any form of overt authority. Lakoff and Johnson point out, for instance, that a metaphor 'by virtue of what it hides can lead to human degradation.'[17] To explain their thesis they cite the 'Labour is a resource' metaphor whereby most contemporary economic theories treat work *as* a natural resource and speak of it in terms of cost and supply thus dismissing the distinction between meaningful and dehumanizing labour. Languaging, too, could ultimately be treated as a 'resource'.

Since metaphors function by highlighting particular features of the conditions described, other features are made to remain concealed, including ones that are of the highest survival relevance. If we consider the early phases of human development we could appreciate that certain dominant metaphors afflicting infancy not only obscure specific capacities, but actually cause them to atrophy by consistently ignoring their function. The ultimate danger is a 'genetic' damage which actually prevents the development of a human potential: a loss which cannot even be protested by the individual because there is no way of arguing that a certain 'unknown' quality of life has been excluded from development. Unless inner connections are somehow appreciated we can concur with a detrimental cognitive mechanism which some authors have termed 'foreclosure'; in Laplanche and Pontalis's gloss of Lacan, 'Foreclosure consists in not symbolizing what should have been symbolized.'[18] Whenever a metaphor is not construed, and thus basically denied, it is like suggesting to the interlocutor that he should relinquish, or let go, that part of his mental life which is concerned with whatever his metaphoric expressions try to point out. This attitude may drive a person to retreat from full self-development by allowing the extinction of more and more vital parts of the mind.

The metaphors dealt with in most philosophical works commonly refer to abstract contexts, usually well detached from the appreciation of affectual contingencies. There seems to be a tacit agreement to keep language segregated from lived lives in such a way that scrutiny of linguistic behaviour be relatively aseptic and confortably amenable to analytic processing.[19] In academically oriented works we encounter such classical metaphoric examples as 'Juliet is the sun', 'Richard is a lion', or 'John is a mouse', which are obviously not meant as having anything to do with the actual lives of any Juliet, Richard or John. In a different perspective, however, when a metaphoric genre is directed toward a particular developing person such expressions may function as 'metabolic' constraints actually influencing the course of development.[20]

A salient feature of dead metaphors is that they are unquestionably the most successful inasmuch as they have gained access and citizenship into the domain of literal language – the reservoir of our descriptive vocabulary for assessing what is and what is not in the world. And whatever 'is not' in the world might be out there enduring neglect and silently yearning to become symbolized. Whatever metaphor successfully sinks into the lexical literality of *any* phatic community becomes a powerful instrument for appreciating something and ignoring something else. If, for instance, 'Richard is a lion' and 'John is a mouse' become literal in the comparatively short life cycle of a family linguistic community, such 'tangible facts' as Richard's courage and John's fearfulness become totally natural, like the obvious realities incorporated into the literal linguisticity of any epistemology. Such dead metaphors spring to life in daily language so powerfully that Richard, against his own nature, may be compelled to act 'brave' to the point of jeopardizing his life, while John may similarly restrain his natural responses and equally endanger his own life. Migrating in search of novel vocabularies can be one of the solutions sought for psychic survival. Language itself thus comes to produce intricate and enduring synergies with the human life cycle.

That attention to these factors is rather rare could also be indicated by the total absence of children in philosophy, an exclusion which might even be the sign of a 'statutory' detachment from life itself. Indeed, the image of the lovely infant has a relatively recent origin. There was nothing poetical about the infant in our less recent history, not even in literary works. Possibly symbols of impotence, 'incapable of speech', and totally dependent upon others, children had no cultural relevance, and philosophy dispensed with the topic.

PRIMAL INTERACTIONS

Although it is widely acknowledged that metaphor intervenes in cognitive growth, the question whether its intervention is generally formative or potentially impairing remains scarcely explored or hardly even thematized. And yet the fact that these questions rarely obtrude does not exempt us from suspecting the presence of obscured, anti-cognitive features of metaphoricity. As metaphors concur in the shaping of meaning, understanding and rationality, they ought to be viewed as capable of also introducing constraints and blind spots which might ultimately be detrimental to cognitive and affectual maturation. In the wave of an increasing interest in metaphor, its 'negative' functions are rarely scrutinized.

The early phases of linguisticity, especially, occupy a strategic position with respect to the unfurling of our cognitive progress. The uniquely human factor of personal significance enters into our basic approach to language inasmuch as it proceeds from early experiences where the resources and potentials of life become ciphered in order to influence the course of behaviour. By unobtrusively introducing a metaphor one may instil a particular way of seeing the world, a way of disclosing a dimension which really matters or else establishing a pre-emptive closure for the potential existence of contexts which might really have significance. Deriving from a joint process of constructions and construals our metaphors establish, or annul, prospects for further dimensions of the world – both 'inner' and 'outer'. In fact, we actually understand a metaphor – that is, perform our construal – by participating in its vision. And even when the 'vision' is actually a damaging cause of blindness, we may perhaps accept the damage for the sake of preserving our cultural participation in construals. For indeed, to check the empirical validity or logical consistency of a metaphor in advance of this participation would come close to missing the metaphorical nature of the expressions we try to construe. And all this connects with an interactive outlook on language: an approach in which we do not think of metaphors as of 'abstract' utterances which hardly matter to anyone. The unique metaphoricity of humans entails in fact a potential to enlighten and blind, to nourish and poison.

With this outlook, then, a metaphor can function as an explicit psychological act intended to shape or shatter mental reality, while personal experiences could even be conceptualized as a sequence of living metaphors; in the language of Wheelwright we could say that what really matters in a metaphor is the psychic depth at which the things of the world, whether actual or fancied, 'are transmuted by the cool heat of the imagination'.[21]

As we know, when we look at the cards of a Rorschach test – or at a worn and irregular surface – we may begin to see different objects or scenes. It would be incorrect of course to say that the surface 'contains' whatever representation is seen or might be seen in it. And yet, if what is seen becomes sufficiently 're-designed' and verbally described, it is that particular intuition-perception which is usually said to correspond to whatever appears on the discoloured or abraded surface. These same aspect-perception experiences could apply to a wide variety of interactive scenarios, not only to spotted surfaces. The distinction between veridical perception and psychic projection is then much less secure in all those quite numerous cases where a measure of aspect-perception dynamics is involved. In an interpersonal perspective the question of course is whose aspect-perception should count as a perception. Probably we shall want to say that this is a matter of degree, that is, the degree to which a majority of observers will be disposed to see 'a mental surface' or an interactive 'scene' as such and such a picture or event. Indeed, without the 'genius' of our inner life we could not see as much in either physical surfaces or human activities. It is probably a question of a complex and controversial balance of fluctuating interactions constantly involving one's mind, other minds and the world.

The intersubjective appreciation of a metaphor may similarly be enforced, under certain circumstances, so as to endorse the specific cognitive operations of the person generating the metaphor or propagating a particular interpretation of events.[22] For instance, if a developing person gets the fixed idea that he is worthless, indeed redundant, there is not much cognitive input from reality that will change this fundamental personal outlook. With differing levels of complexity, humans seem to develop at their earliest opportunity a global view of reality; with this they supplement what they know nothing about with derivatives from that same general view of themselves in the world. When confronted with surprising situations we are 'tempted' to produce an explanation which may account for the 'new' data in terms of our innermost picture of things. Our basic metaphors thus provide the symbolic channels whereby we incorporate new experiences on our own terms. Metaphors can thus be arresting inasmuch as they compel as well as invite us to enter their figurative ground in order to grasp them. In fact the copular 'is' which could be described as creating connection may as easily involve an 'abuse' which entraps the interlocutor. Metaphor both opens and forecloses. Its radically perspec-tival nature – its capacity to create perspective through incongruity – can also turn into a restrictive perspectivism. For instance, in any macro- or micro-community in which repressive metaphors seem to thrive – and thus tend to become literal – certain restrictive and distorting mental attitudes are reinforced that may eventually degrade the quality of life in the phatic community.

In human interactions reciprocity often depends on the hypothesis that most aspects of one's inner life could ultimately be shared. And yet whenever we injudiciously presume that a particular interlocutor has no resources for expressing his inner world, we tend to make use of our own metaphoric capacities to give voice to the other's inner experiences. As soon as such a momentous assumption is made within a two-person interaction, one of them is gradually deprived of the opportunity to exercise his own metaphoric resources.[23] Such an appropriation, moreover, is uniquely unnoticeable and difficult to oppose inasmuch as it comes across as an offer, as an interpretive gift, which is made to the other. It is the sort of linguistic gift which fills the other while atrophying the symbolic capacity of the recipient, who is overcome by the colonizing attitude of the linguistically more developed agent. Such an interaction not only implies that one person regards himself capable of vicariously metaphorizing for the less gifted partner but also that no expressive potential is being perceived in the individual whose metaphoric opportunities are being usurped. Whenever our efforts to shape and decipher are 'educationally' voiced by someone else, these 'formative' offers ultimately denude and sterilize our own inner linguisticity. The theft, moreover, is disguised by the personalized quality of the 'gift'.

Whenever the exploration of one's behaviour is consistently taken over, that is, articulated, by others, the sort of intimate language for coping with the vicissitudes of hope and despair, attachments and separations, may not properly develop; this language may be entrusted, or surrendered, to the managers of standard metaphors that are gradually converging into a collective literal vocabulary.[24] And one particular person may have no idea why an inner life is not found in him. Anything such as an inner world is then only to be found in 'special' others, recognizable as geniuses, stars or heroes. Such a surrender of profound experiences to the vicarious symbolizing of expert managers of language could be seen as colluding in the theft of one's inner life. Indeed the territorial and predatory heritage of our hominization is thus transferred from the biological to the dialogic level and enacted in the symbolic domain, in the sense that we now have to cope more with culture than with nature.

It is possible that anyone suffering from an addiction to literal language may have collaborated in being systematically deprived of his own expressive resources. Having relinquished contacts with the roots of one's self – what we often call the unconscious – one no longer faces the challenge and burden of constantly attempting to translate messages from the inner world into shareable language; the subject consequently restricts linguisticity to elements borrowed from, or imposed by, the authorial authority of the more competent, non-listening speakers. If this hypothesis is pursued one step further we may legitimately think that whoever has been deprived of the burden of articulating inner life will tacitly identify with 'educators' and ultimately internalize an intrusive and predatory style only suited to deprive still others of the challenge of expressing an inner world.[25] And yet, while loss and detriment may be quite real, the 'gain' of predators is totally non-existent and unusable: nothing is being truly gained by unwittingly silencing others and by only exercising our own narcissistic languaging. Having introjected such a relational style we may go on imposing our articulations to others and illusorily conquering their inner space: damage is perpetrated while no benefit is reaped. And of course such deceptive predatory styles may be adopted both by individuals and by coalitions of persons unconsciously sharing the same attitude. Once personal language has a tendency to become fiction by imitative recourse to a standardized vocabulary, hardly any progress or growth can be made.

The surrender of one's inner language may be tacitly realized in our memory although it may not be thought out with sufficient clarity; Bollas suggests that it may be something which sadly defines the boundaries of our life even though it lies beyond any clear comprehension and only leaves the 'conviction' that some persecutory external element has stolen something lively inside us.[26]

Whenever authorial discourses impose their rule, the subject cannot use his inner space as his own, and personal experiences which could be indirectly expressed ultimately enhance the vocabulary which dominant figures use for the maintenance of their own myth. If any personal need is ever expressed which appears to be stout refusal of the imposed myth, it may provoke anger, since the speaker is perceived as interfering with the established order. And yet, a human being may respond to metaphoric constraints in the way he would react to the threat of annihilation. If we think for instance of metaphoric expressions such as 'You are my life', 'You are my guardian angel', or 'You are my hope', the developing person to whom they are addressed may feel forced into a certain role, one that would put him at the disposal of those who engage him with these metaphorical devices.[27]

The maturing individual may resort to defensive manoeuvres in order not to sink into a depersonalized state in which he may only function as a false self whose authentic qualities have been surrendered to the originators of the metaphoric language. In any such predicament language and life are profoundly interwoven and indeed essential to one another. Under these circumstances the nascent personality might resort to any hostile behaviour as a defence from such destructive language games. The individual may intuitively try to survive by being 'bad', since being 'good' may be felt as a serious danger to the core of his identity.

Indeed, some of the frequently quoted metaphors in the profusion of literature are expressions such as 'Richard is a lion' and 'Juliet is the sun'. Here again we are confronted with the scholarly style of books resonating with the creative language of literary works while the formative or damaging effects of metaphoric expressions remain perplexingly ignored. And yet, if an infant were only attended to by satisfying his biological needs and if he were not encouraged by the innumerable metaphors of caring adults, there would be virtually no mental growth. By converse, the denial of the infant's symbolic potential and the manipulative use of metaphoric language by the authorial authority of those who do the talking can be equally detrimental to cognitive development. Denying the inner life of a little boy who is terrified with a cliché such as 'But you are always such a tiger', or else stifling an angry girl with an equivalent utterance such as 'But you are my little angel' are common ways of using metaphors to impede psychic life.

As one of the frequently quoted metaphors, 'Richard is a lion' exudes historical resonances; and yet the idea that 'Richard is a lion' might be conveyed to an ill little boy in the sort of intimate spirit that transforms the torments of physical illness into an experience of mental growth, appears quite remote from the style of contemporary investigations. In fact these considerations may entail questions regarding the *absence* of any such metaphors and the devastating results of human nurturing unaided by the use of creative language, or impaired by the sort of language that official culture seems to value. Similar questions may be posed about the far more enigmatic experience of death, as we can only speculate on what it would be like to suffer the loneliness or the sort of language offered by our prestigious literature.

It seems, almost, that the dynamics of cognitive expansion and narcissistic contraction constitute the polar opposites between which linguisticity swings. 'The drive towards the formation of metaphors is the fundamental human drive, which one cannot for a single instance dispense with in thought', says Nietzsche, 'for one would thereby dispense with man himself.'[28] And dispensing with someone else's humanity is in effect inflicting irreversible damage. In fact, if we regard the efforts to assimilate an earlier object of interest to another one as the precursor of human metaphoricity, we could expect that when such attempts repeatedly end in failure, the experience may lead to a sense of paralysis that inhibits the life of the mind. To enhance a transition towards further metaphoric connections there should be widespread encouraging interpretations rather than the customary negative responses. Whatever their 'ultimate' structure metaphoricity and thinking do not develop automatically and irrespectively of the interactive context within which they originate.

It may be appropriate to invoke in this connection Bion's reflections on the psychoanalyst's effort to understand the dynamics of the relation with the analysand. In his view formulations can be judged by considering how necessary is the existence of the analyst to the thoughts he expresses: 'The more his interpretations can be judged as showing how necessary *his* knowledge, *his* experience, *his* character are to the thoughts formulated, the more reason there is to suppose that the interpretation is psychoanalytically worthless.'[29] Simply worthless, or actually detrimental? Such interpretations, in fact, may be focusing on his own way of seeing things and not on the unity of perceptual experiences his client is trying to convey on the basis of a negotiated agreement.

The often unnoticed refusal to respond to metaphoric endeavours cannot be regarded as a direct attack on a developing mind. And yet, a nascent person whose linguistic creativity is not sufficiently appreciated may perceive parental attitudes as destructive of all mental activity, almost as if they were attempting to induce a schism between life and mental life – an obscure way of opposing the course of evolution. An example appearing in a book primarily dealing with formal and structural aspects of metaphor refers to a young child who has suffered from earaches but has not yet learned the term 'earache': he wakes one might and comes into his mother's room holding his ear and saying, 'Mummy, an elephant stepped on my ear'.[30] While the text, of course, pursues concerns of reference and truth, in a maturational perspective one could think that if the metaphor were not construed, he might revert into muteness and feel as forlorn as a prisoner whose supervisors are forever against him. The situation would be even worse if the child did not even think of the metaphor or dare express it, as if he could not venture to voice a difficulty for fear of retaliation or increased misery. In this case we could even say that nothing happened and that all was quiet on the front of the child's inner life. And while earaches may come and go, inner devastations can have lasting effects.

When construction and construal fail to create a synergy, a developing person cannot be said to possess a criterion whereby he may at least perceive himself as an individual. When parental presence is excessively detatched and conventional, the subject in the making is 'genetically' damaged in his potential for becoming a thinking individual. In fact if we regard reproductive organs as a biological symbol of the capacity to generate, we may be able to see in the drama of Oedipus a mythical quandary spun from 'mental' experiences of a drastic and dramatic nature. The metaphoric capacity is stifled not by inflicting damage to something existent, but rather by obtusely refusing to construe non-literal messages and thus impeding the growth of thought. The point at issue is not the damage to something functioning but the failure to allow something to exist and function. Thus Oedipal vicissitudes linked to the desire to attain something and the concomitant anxieties of retaliation can be viewed as an account in fable form – a story that we can visualize – of the more crucial (and more difficult to grasp) experiences affecting the development and inhibition of mental life.

The task of mediating relations between antithetical parts of the self involves an effort progressively to bring forth meaningful inner life, an effort which entails both opposing, and coping with, the mechanisms of dividing, separation and fragmentation which lead, inevitably, towards a state of inanimation. In this sense, also, language does interact with life. Those processes of endless fragmentation result in the negation of any interactive potential and in mental degradation: they steadily conspire in the extinction of mental life. And the regressive separation of thoughts and affects is one of the most damaging threats to the life of the mind – however hidden from view this process may be.

Examples of the resolution of conflicts by regression include the tendency to give up one's individuality by becoming, for instance, an undifferentiated member of a group. Such a condition is attained throught the adhesion to primitive para-digms which are all the more powerful for promising release from tensions and conflicts. Once we are absorbed into a regressive gestalt there is no more need for the metaphoric efforts by which we try to mediate between diverse inclinations, prospects and functions. It might be generally conceded that all addictions have that same quality of familiarity and 'comfort' in spite of their obviously devastating nature.

As we know, in the vicissitudes of our adult life a transformational event may be given significance and then dissolve again, may promise a longed-for-enlightenment and then fall back into a sense of disillusionment. Our search for a salvational stance could be described in terms of endless discussions which point to future results of our endeavours even though the whole project may belong to our remote history.[31] Perhaps the vast genre of metaphoric expressions indicates that we are looking for some transformational context and aspire to establish intimacy with any epistemic outlook which seems to promise to bring about a transformation of our own selves – cognitively and even affectually.

Perhaps the quality of the atmosphere in which we behave is created by the prevalent metaphors with which we describe culture and nature. These, in turn, partially depend on the beliefs of individuals. Living within any social structure each person is still to some extent an individual and the conflict-prone gap between individual and social schemata is where we may attempt to shape possible worlds. Our contemporary culture is characterized by an externalization of our resources of memory and knowledge which are increasingly entrusted to computing devices, thus taken out of ourselves and placed into external mechanisms in order to optimize results. Similarly, even our deepest metaphoric endeavours have to be somehow externalized to enable the sort of construal which will enhance interaction and cognition. Here too externalization is instrumental in optimizing the development of our innermost structures. This essential and unbreakable reciprocity between subjective structures and external dynamics thus poses for us the most challenging of questions.

RECEPTION AND TRANSMISSION OF METAPHORS

In a developmental perspective, the communicative function of language not only precedes but also influences our cognitive efforts for accurate representation. Intractable difficulties seem to arise from a philosophical tendency to privilege the representational function of language, disconnected from its listening and communicative role. With an outlook of self creation we may better scrutinize how much we depend on external agents for our own intellectual life: our metaphoric efforts are in fact meaningful to the extent that our constructions are met with adequate interpersonal interpretation. The life of our metaphors depends, then, on interlocutors while at the same time it constitutes the core of our individual inner life. In the early developmental phases, moreover, construal can rarely be offered by peers and is usually to be obtained from various parental figures.

It is only through the creative listening of others that our expressions of the experiences we live through, but cannot yet think of, can be linked with maturer levels of articulation. The process may start out with the deliberate patience of a listener who is willing to receive the sort of projections in which someone entrusts to another what he believes he knows but cannot yet think.[32] By way of reciprocity, an authentic listener might also get to know something about the speaker even though he may not be ready to think it out in any logical way. But then we should ask in which way what is known, but not yet thought, may gradually reach the stage of being both known and thought; and also ask which are the aspects of the dialogic interaction that either facilitate or hinder this linguistic evolution. A capacity for construal of the metaphoric expressions of the immature person speaking out from his unthought 'knowledge' and trying to reach out for those who inhabit the thinking literalness of any standard epistemology, constitutes the essential element of the enterprise. An appropriate response to non-literal dialogic attempts convinces the evolving individual that the inner world that he somehow knows, can be thought about and articulated. If his metaphoric efforts were not listened to and were met by an absence of construal, no consensual thinking could properly develop.

The nascent mind may even get to learn that parental figures cannot act in co-operation, that the original bi-personal field is not a safe place for real growth, and that this must be sought or 'bought' elsewhere from whatever figures seem to sell adulthood. By not being offered construals to metaphoric constructs, the developing individual may ultimately learn that he is as resourceless as the emissaries of the adult world. The stage is then set for the potential surrender of responsibility to whoever makes a 'professional' claim for privileged access to truth, emancipation, progress.[33]

When striving to belong to any exclusive or elitist subgroup we try to tune in with the metaphoric subtleties that we perceive or imagine to be at work in it. But then, as we also strive towards individuation, our utmost concern is to verify whether or not we have an inner mental core which can think its own thoughts. This more basic and vital enterprise can only be attempted through very special metaphoric efforts which are effective to the extent that they are shared. Indeed, for qualitative developmental leaps some special intimacy is indispensable. Thus, the needs to belong and to develop can often be in contrast in our symbolic itinerary. For instance, understanding the metaphors of a 'mentally ill' person indicates that we can share the profound reasons for such language and also implies that we actually recognize their personal reasoning as such instead of as incoherent thinking, or in other words, as 'insanity'.

Our native curiosity can be seriously affected by cumulative lacks of response, to the point that we may opt for an adhesive dependence on the official producers of collective metaphors. The original capacity to absorb may tend to atrophy as absorption only exacerbates the sense of being blocked. Indeed we may even opt for a defensive acquiescence and for a retreat from lucidity. Persistent experiences of non-construal may also induce an epistemic climate of distrust in the value of communication and an increased compensational valuing of tangible objects. The long-term symptoms of the symbolically unbonded individual include a degradation of interpersonal linguistic relations and the increasing demand for concrete goods which can be manipulated, clung on to, and which are not *per se* sources of anxiety. Primary experiences in which we learn that disappointment derives from dialogic interactions, and consolation (or escape from such frustration) comes from the use of tangible things, may reverberate in the culture at large. Indeed, by 'getting ahead in the world' we often indicate the acquisition of conditions and goods suitable to compensate for any potential scarcity of meaningful bonds.

We might envisage a minimum of ordinary interpretive competence as characteristic of any 'representative' member of a phatic community: such representative members will adequately cope with metaphors bringing along a variety of evocations which may be aptly developed in an extended paraphrase. But then, we also have extraordinary metaphors, which cannot possibly be construed on the basis of a minimal interpretive competence provided by the standards of the speech community. Whenever it is the case that such a metaphor is successfully and knowingly uttered in place of something literal, the expression entails a further dimension of profound interpersonal significance – hardly amenable to a paraphrase. This is due to a valuational attitude presupposed by the originator of the utterance and justifiably attributed to his listener. Such an element is not of the type to be included in an attempted literalization of the message inasmuch as it could not describe the creative way in which we expect the metaphor to be received.[34] The shared use of particular utterances may in fact differentiate a subset, or sub-group, from those who only share in the ordinary interpretive competence of the community at large. And those who can interpret an extraordinary utterance will probably also be able to appreciate a range of related expressions such as veiled or indirect messages circulating for the creation and maintenance of a more intimately woven subset. Cooper points out that sometimes what unites interpreters of a metaphor will be just the kind of bond connecting users of slang or technical jargon.[35] The utterance of a metaphor may be regarded as a signal that the speaker takes his hearers to belong to a subset distinguished by a special bond of intimacy; in fact, in what might be called a full metaphorical exchange (comprising the utterance itself, its appropriate interpretation by the listener, and a capable assessment of that interpretation by the speaker), the intimacy between interlocutors, presupposed by the original utterance, will eventually be reinforced. The generation of this sort of closeness is similarly suggested by Cohen in the remark that intimacy is achieved through 'the awareness that not everyone could make that offer or take it up'.[36]

It is common knowledge that certain family groups are scarcely communicative and inclined to be 'cold', in the sense that parental figures may have difficulties in expressing whatever affection they experience or whatever lovability they may appreciate in the younger members. The evolving individual may systematically have to recognize that his construction of affectionate metaphors is not met with any construal or is even interpreted as an offensive intrusion. Whatever the reasons for these circumstances, the case may be that the adult world consistently refuses to appreciate metaphorical efforts to transform an 'atmosphere' and establish bonds of mutual recognition. The unformed personality may thus develop a hidden mistrust in affectionate relations of any authenticity. And love can even be replaced by hatred as a basic affect which may enliven interactions. Since the non-construal of loving metaphors is experienced as hostility, one may ultimately find out that his most authentic affectual attitude to parental figures has become animosity. Persons in the making may even develop arguments justifying why they should be angered by adult figures and why such a relationship should be the only possible paradigm. To strengthen the structure, moreover, interlocutors may strive to be hateful, and to secure some attention they will endeavour to reinforce the dynamics by developing into reliable targets of hostility – a condition still preferable to being an unbonded person. Paradoxically, self-creation projects whose course is threatened by a chronic lack of responsiveness, may be rescued by means of hostile metaphoric exchanges as the only possible style of achieving some relatedness. These evolving individuals detest parental figures not so much in order to destroy them but rather in order to keep them alive as partners in an inseparable relation.

By irritating others and eliciting hostility they seem to gain some guarantee of a provisional interactive life.

But what is the language of these interactions? Certainly not a literal language employing the linguistic terms in which we can only try to describe metaphorically such a mode of human interaction. What is at work is a constant weaving and reweaving of metaphorical contexts in which life and language join together in a metabolic process which extends from the extremes of impeding inner life to the enhancement of self-creation.[37]

Notes

1 CONNECTIONS BETWEEN LANGUAGE AND LIFE

1 Plato, *Phaedo*, 66a, in *Collected Dialogues*, edited by E. Hamilton and H. Cairns, Princeton, N.J.: Princeton University Press, 1961, p. 48.
2 R. Rorty, 'Introduction', in *Philosophy and the Mirror of Nature*, Oxford: Blackwell, 1980, pp. 3–13.
3 Aristotle, *Poetics*, paragraph 22, 1459a 5–8. *The Complete Works of Aristotle*, Revised Oxford Translation, edited by J. Barnes, vol. II, Bollingen Series LXXI.2; Princeton, N.J.: Princeton University Press, 1985, pp. 2234–5.
4 Aristotle, *Rhetoric*, 10–15, p. 2239.
5 W. V. O. Quine, 'Two Dogmas of Empiricism', in *From a Logical Point of View*, New York: Harper Torchbooks, 1961, p. 41.
6 'Beliefs, desires and intentions are a condition of language, but language is also a condition for them. On the one hand, being able to attribute beliefs and desires to a creature is certainly a condition of sharing a convention with that creature' (D. Davidson, *Inquiries into Truth and Interpretation*, Oxford: Clarendon Press, 1985, p. 280).
7 The story appears in *Genesis* 11: 1–9.
8 A comparable issue is discussed in J. Amati Mehler *et al.*, 'The Babel of the unconscious', *International Journal of Psycho-Analysis*, 71, 1990, pp. 569–83.
9 See P. A. Parker, 'The metaphorical plot', in D. S. Miall (ed.), *Metaphor: Problems and Perspectives*, Brighton: Harvester Press, 1982, pp. 133–57.
10 These problems are discussed in various parts of G. Corradi Fiumara *The Other Side of Language: A Philosophy of Listening*, London and New York: Routledge, 1990, and *The Symbolic Function: Psychoanalysis and the Philosophy of Language*, Oxford and Cambridge, Mass.: Blackwell, 1992.
11 R. Rorty, *Philosophy and the Mirror of Nature*, pp. 316–18, 333.
12 T. Hobbes, *Leviathan*, edited by C. B. Macpherson, Harmondsworth: Penguin Books, 1968, pp. 116–17.
13 T. Hobbes, *Leviathan*, Oxford: Basil Blackwell, 1960, p. 28.
14 T. Hobbes, *Leviathan*, Penguin Books, p. 81.
15 H. Feigl, 'Positivism in the twentieth century (Logical Empiricism)', in P. P. Wiener (editor in chief), *Dictionary of the History of Ideas. Studies of Selected Pivotal Ideas*, New York: Charles Scribner's Sons, 1974, p. 547.
16 L. D. Smith, 'Metaphors of knowledge and behaviour in the behaviorist tradition', in D. E. Leary (ed.), *Metaphors in the History of Psychology*, Cambridge: Cambridge University Press, 1990, p. 240.
17 Ibid., p. 240.
18 H. Feigl, 'Positivism in the twentieth century (Logical Empiricism)', p. 547.
19 The term 'revolutionary' is used in a general Kuhnian sense. See T. S. Kuhn, *The*

Structure of Scientific Revolutions, 2nd edn, Chicago and London: University of Chicago Press, 1970.

20 R. Rorty, *Objectivity, Relativism, and Truth: Philosophical Papers*, vol. I, Cambridge: Cambridge University Press, 1991, p. 2.

21 W. V. O. Quine, 'Indeterminacy of translation again', in D. Davidson and J. Hintikka (eds), *Words and Objections: Essays on the Work of W. V. O. Quine*, Dordrecht: Reidel, 1969, pp. 7–8

22 R. Rorty, *Philosophy and the Mirror of Nature*, p. 3.

23 Ibid., p. 12.

24 J. Stewart, 'Beyond the symbol model: notes toward a post-semiotic account of the nature of language', unpublished paper presented in May 1993 at the International Communication Association on the theme 'Beyond Representation: Communication Issues in Discourse, Theory and Philosophy of Language', p. 16. The book that will include a version of the paper is the forthcoming *Language as Articulate Contact: Toward a Post-semiotic Philosophy of Communication.*

25 J. Stewart, 'Beyond the symbol model', p. 16.

26 Aristotle, *De Interpretatione*, 16a, in *The Basic Works of Aristotle*, translated by E. M. Edghill, edited by R. Mickeon, New York: Random House, 1941, p. 40 (quoted in J. Stewart, 'Beyond the symbol model', p. 3).

27 J. Stewart, 'Beyond the symbol model', p. 3.

28 E. M. Barth, 'Waiting for Godot: on attitudes towards artefacts vs. entities, as related to different phases of operation in cognition', *Epistemologia*, XIV, 1991, pp. 77–104 (emphasis added).

29 J. Stewart, 'Beyond the symbol model, p. 4.

30 A. Danto, 'Philosophy as/and/of literature', in A. J. Cascardi (ed.), *Literature and the Question of Philosophy*, Baltimore, Md. and London: Johns Hopkins University Press, 1989, p. 23.

31 Ibid., p. 6.

32 J. Stewart, 'Beyond the symbol model', p. 4.

33 Ibid., p. 12.

34 The notion of possible worlds is extensively discussed in J. Bruner, *Actual Minds, Possible Worlds*, Cambridge, Mass.: Harvard University Press, 1986.

35 D. Davidson, *Inquiries into Truth and Interpretation*, p. 153.

36 J. Martin Soskice, *Metaphor and Religious Language*, Oxford: Clarendon Press, 1985, p. 15. Richards remarks that 'Our skill with metaphor . . . is one thing – prodigious and inexplicable; our reflective awareness of that skill, quite another thing – very incomplete distorted, fallacious, over-simplifying' (I. A. Richards, *The Philosophy of Rhetoric*, Oxford: Oxford University Press, 1936, p. 116).

37 J. Martin Soskice, *Metaphor and Religious Language*, p. 15.

38 D. Cooper, *Metaphor*, Oxford: Blackwell, 1986, p. 196.

39 See J. Bruner, *Acts of Meaning*, Cambridge, Mass. and London: Harvard University Press: 1990, p. 118.

40 'Human values, viewed in objective, scientific perspective, stand out as the most strategically powerful causal control force now shaping world events. More than any other causal system with which science now concerns itself, it is variables in human value systems that will determine the future. Any given brain will respond differently to the same input and will tend to process the same information into quite diverse behavioral channels depending on its particular system of value priorities. In short, what an individual or society values, determines very largely what it does' (R. W. Sperry, *Science and Moral Priority: Merging Mind, Brain, and Human Values*, New York: Columbia University Press, 1983; Oxford: Blackwell, 1983, p. 109).

41 Aristotle, *Poetics*, 1459a 5–8.

42 G. Galilei, *Il saggiatore*, edited by L. Sosio, Milan: Feltrinelli, 1965, p. 45.

43 M. Arbib and M. B. Hesse, *The Construction of Reality*, Cambridge: Cambridge University Press, 1986, p. 158.

44 E. F. Kittay, *Metaphor: Its Cognitive Force and Linguistic Structure*, Oxford: Clarendon Press, 1987, p. 326.

45 T. S. Kuhn, *The Structure of Scientific Revolutions*, 2nd edn, Chicago and London: University of Chicago Press, 1970. See also T. S. Kuhn, 'Second thoughts on paradigms', in F. Suppes (ed.), *The Structure of Scientific Theories*, Urbana, Ill. : University of Illinois Press, 1974.

46 N. Goodman, *Languages of Art*, Indianapolis, Ind.: Bobbs–Merrill, 1968, p. 80. The increasing number of scholars includes Hesse, Barbour, MacCormack, Boyd, Kuhn, Gould, Neisser, Eccles.

47 S. C. Pepper, 'Metaphor in Philosophy' in P. P. Wiener (Editor in Chief), *Dictionary of the History of Ideas. Studies of Selected Pivotal Ideas*, New York: Charles Scribner's Sons, 1974, p. 197. Danto goes as far as to suggest that philosophical texts may be kept alive as metaphors when they have long since stopped seeming plausible as structural hypotheses, as 'a tribute to their vivacity and force, their status as literature being a consolation prize for failing to be true' (A. Danto, 'Philosophy as/and/of Literature', p. 21).

48 M. Johnson, *The Body in the Mind: The Bodily Basis of Meaning, Imagination, and Reasoning*, Chicago and London: University of Chicago Press, 1987, pp. xxiv–xxv.

49 Cooper suggests that Black's primary aim is to analyse metaphor, rather than to account for why we engage in it, but at various points he ventures just such an account. A metaphor, he says, is an utterance with two subjects: a primary one spoken about metaphorically in terms of a secondary one. The point of such an utterance is not to give figurative expression to what could be put literally, nor is it to state a single comparison or set of comparisons. Rather, it is to provide, by means of a secondary subject, a 'model' or 'filter' with whose help we can achieve new understanding of the primary subject (D. Cooper, *Metaphor*, pp. 144–5).

50 Aristotle, *Rhetoric* (W. R. Roberts, translation), in W. D. Ross (ed.), *The Works of Aristotle*, vol. 11, II. 1354–1420, Oxford: Clarendon Press, 1924.

51 'People carry in their heads what appears to them to be a total model of the universe because what they have no information about they fill in from their world modeling. Starting from their current picture of the world, when confronted with something new they "tell a story" to fit the new data . . . What we already know provides the "equipment" through which we incorporate new data' (M. Arbib and M. B. Hesse, *The Construction of Reality*, p. 35).

52 D. Hume, *Treatise on Human Nature*, edited by L. Selby-Bigge, Oxford and London: Oxford University Press, 1973, I, iii, 8; quoted in H. Blumenberg, *Paradigmi per una metaforologia*, Bologna: Il Mulino, 1969, p. 19.

53 B. Leondar, 'Metaphor and infant cognition', *Poetics*, 4, 1975, p. 281.

54 See M. Arbib and M. B. Hesse, *The Construction of Reality*, p. 161.

2   THE LIFE OF LANGUAGE

1 We could speculate, with Fraser, that our ancestors discovered some novel uses for already existing faculties, something which 'catapulted' them into new modes of survival. Then again in the evolution of language they may have linked some new uses with already existing capacities, which then projected early creatures into our more recent modes of behaviour such as articulate languages, social and individual planning, sophisticated control of the environment. In each case a few judicious (or chance) selections from the domain of imagery may have done the linkage, provided it received communal reinforcement – echoes, as it were – from the minds of other humans ready to make similar metaphoric links. A desire may have prevailed to use the discovery for the

offspring or pass to them such consequential novelties (J. T. Fraser, *Of Time, Passion and Knowledge: Reflections on the Strategy of Existence*, Princeton, N. J. : Princeton University Press, 1990, p. 272).

2 See G. Corradi, *Philosophy and Coexistence*, Leyden: Sijthoff, 1966.

3 G. Bateson, *Mind and Nature: A Necessary Unity*, New York: Bantam Books, 1979, p. 8.

4 'A language may be viewed as a complex abstract object, defined by giving a finite list of expressions (words), rules for constructing meaningful concatenations of expressions (sentences), and a semantic interpretation of the meaningful expressions based on the semantic features of individual words . . . . Thought in this way, a language is abstract in the obvious sense that it is unobservable, changeless, and its components are for the most part also unobservable and changeless. Expressions may, if we wish, be viewed as acoustical or two dimensional spatial shapes that could, on occasion, inform actual utterances or inscriptions, but the expressions themselves remain abstract and their existence independent of exemplification' (D. Davidson, 'The second person', a paper presented at the University of Rome in 1993, p.1; an earlier version of this unpublished paper appeared in J. Sebestik and A. Soulez (eds), *Wittgenstein et la philosophie aujourd'hui*, Paris: Méridiens Klincksieck, 1992, under the title 'Jusq'où va le caractère public d'une langue?'.

5 L. Wittgenstein, *Philosophical Investigations*, translated by G. E. M. Anscombe, Oxford: Blackwell, 1988, paragraph 23, p. 11 e (emphasis added).

6 P. Wheelwright, *Metaphor and Reality*, Bloomington, Ind.: Indiana University Press, 1962, p. 71.

7 H. Putnam, *Reason, Truth and History*, Cambridge: Cambridge University Press, 1981, p. 22n.

8 See R. Fiumara, 'Il cervello come macchina darwiniana', *Bollettino di Psichiatria Biologica*, 1988, IV, (3), pp.63–6.

9 The historicity of languages is indirectly indicated by Goodman: 'A schema may be transposed almost anywhere. The choice of territory for invasion is arbitrary; but the operation within the territory is almost never completely so. We may at will apply temperature predicates to sounds or hues or personalities or to degrees of nearness to a correct answer; but which elements in the chosen realm are warm, or are warmer than others, is then very largely determinate. Even where a schema is imposed upon a most unlikely and uncongenial realm, antecedent practice channels the application of the labels' (N. Goodman, *Languages of Art*, Indianapolis, Ind.: Indiana University Press, 1968, p. 74.

10 Nietzsche's often quoted remark on the primacy of metaphor reads as follows: 'What then is truth? A mobile army of metaphor . . . which after long usage seem to a people fixed, canonical and binding. Truths are illusions of which one has forgotten that this is what they are – metaphors that have become worn out and without sensous force' (F. W. Nietzsche, 'Über Wahrheit und Lüge im aussermoralischen Sinn', *Werke*, III, Ulstein, 1979, p. 314).

11 D. E. Cooper, *Metaphor*, Aristotelian Society Series, vol. 5; Oxford: Blackwell, 1986, p. 119.

12 Ibid., p. 119. The authors quoted by Cooper are H. W. Fowler and P. Newmark.

13 J. Hobbs, 'Metaphor, metaphor schemata, and selective inferencing', Technical Note No. 204, *SRI International*, Cambridge Computer Science Research, Menlo Park, Calif., 1979; reported in C. Cacciari and P. Tabossi (eds), *Idioms: Processing, Structure and Interpretation*, Hillsdale, N. J., Hove and London: Lawrence Erlbaum Associates, 1993, p. 32.

14 G. Lakoff and M. Johnson, *Metaphors We Live By*, Chicago and London: University of Chicago Press, 1980, p. 4.

15 C. S. Peirce, *Writings of Charles S. Peirce: A Chronological Edition*, general editor, M.

H. Fisch, volume 1, 1857–1866; Bloomington Ind.: Indiana University Press, 1982; Lowell Lecture XI, ms 132, November 1866, p. 497.

16 Ibid., p. 497.

17 Ibid., pp. 497–8.

18 A. Einstein, *Ideas and Opinions*, London: Souvenir Press, 1954, p. 8.

19 R. Nozick, *Philosophical Explanations*, Oxford: Clarendon Press, 1981, p. 418.

20 'Value is not merely something that exists out there (or in us); it is also something to which we are to have, when possible, a certain relationship. Values are to be thought about, maintained, saved from destruction, prized . . . We are to care about, accept, support, affirm, encourage, protect, guard, praise, seek, embrace, serve, be drawn toward, be atttracted by, aspire toward, strive to realize, foster, express, nurture, delight in, respect, be inspired by, take joy in, resonate with, be loyal to, be dedicated to, and celebrate values' (ibid., p. 429).

21 Ibid., p. 417. He also remarks, 'Despite our recent talk of atemporal structures, we should emphasize that the organic unifications occur not only at one time, for temporal slices only, but also in the functioning of entities or systems over time. Thus, the goal-seeking and purposeful behaviour of people in accordance with long-term plans further unites what otherwise would be more disparate parts of their existence. For this reason, psychological explanations that have no place for purposeful behaviour undermine an important component of the organic unity of people's lives, and so these nonteleological psychologies are seen as reducing our value' (ibid., p. 427).

22 Ibid., p. 613.

23 'Thus, the view that organic unity gives rise to new value allows value creation *ex nihilo*: the creation of intrinsic value out of nothing of intrinsic value. There need not be atoms of value, since there can be valuable molecules composed of valueless atoms. (However, the parts without intrinsic value might have another kind of value, representing their capacity to participate in wholes that have intrinsic value.)' (Ibid., p. 424).

24 F. Coulmas, 'Idiomaticity as a problem of pragmatics,' in H. Parret and M. Sbisà (eds), *Possibilities and Limitations of Pragmatics*, Amsterdam: John Benjamins, 1981, pp. 139–51.

25 R. Nozick, *Philosophical Explanations*, p. 416.

26 Ibid., p. 416.

27 Commenting on the lucid, sedate, and impersonal style of academic papers, Danto remarks that 'the professional philosophical paper is an evolutionary product, emerging by natural selection from a wild profusion of forms Darwinized into oblivion through maladaptation, stages in the advance of philosophy toward consciousness of its true identity' (A. Danto, 'Philosophy as/and/or literature', in A. J. Cascardi, (ed.), *Literature and the Question of Philosophy*, Baltimore and London: Johns Hopkins University Press, 1989, p. 8).

28 It would be difficult to single out utterances and their purported meanings if we could, for instance, *listen* to the sound of a congress hall during an interval, or of a classroom during a break; there is possibly a hum of human sounds creating an hermeneutic dimension which supplements the discrete utterances which are the object of "pure' knowledge. And that resounding noise is as human and as real as the cognitive messages which could be extracted from it.

29 It is significant that Davidson must specify: 'I shall be talking about real second people, not the words we use to address them.' D. Davidson, 'The second person', p. 1.

30 D. Davidson, 'The social aspect of language', unpublished paper presented at the University of Rome in 1993, p. 7.

31 Live language and academic language may resemble one another primarily with regard to their lexical or structural appearance but of course it would be a mistake to suppose that things which resemble one another in one respect may be similar in others. Peirce points out that 'There is no greater nor more frequent mistake in practical logic than to suppose that things which resemble one another strongly in some respects are any more

likely for that to be alike in others' (C. S. Peirce, *Collected Papers*, vol. 2, Cambridge, Mass.: Harvard University Press, 1934–1948, p. 634). Indeed the sort of thing which we call 'language' is primarily the textual jargon of texts or the academic language of philosophers of a linguistic persuasion.

32 All thinkers have made the 'linguistic turn' and that is no longer an issue, for the question is where that turn leads. For mainstream philosophical analyses it leads to the semantic ideal of natural languages. For still others it leads to the pragmatics of natural languages, that is to a study of the language in use and of linguistic practices.

   If we begin to strive and compete for 'good' metaphors, the problem of truth will cease to be a problem. The problem of truth will vanish not so much because of a final, perennial assessment of methodology and truth conditions but because new and, it is hoped, more vital concerns may prevail in our cultural scenario.

33 Indeed there is no need to surrender one's view of reality in order to accommodate that of the interlocutor, for it is precisely this discrepancy between the two that we may draw upon for indications of something ulterior or unforeseen; however illiterally conveyed it may bear a truth still to be learned.

34 In a metaphoric-metabolic perspective, the ideal of logical consistency is no longer at the heart of language and, conversely, logical discrepancies may be heuristically valued as sources of potential new meanings. In a synoptic view, Arbib and Hesse suggest that normal science seeks to reduce instability of meaning and inconsistency by developing logically connected theories within an internally commensurable epistemic frame; revolutionary science attempts metaphoric leaps which generate new meanings and which may be conducive to innovative formulations (M. Arbib and M. B. Hesse, *The Construction of Reality*, Cambridge: Cambridge University Press, 1986, p. 157).

   Bertrand Russell suggested that 'There is a tendency to use "truth" with big a T in the grand sense, as something noble and splendid and worthy of adoration. This gets people into a frame of mind in which they become unable to think' (*An Outline of Philosophy*, London: George Allen and Unwin, 1970, p. 265).

35 'While the body is highlighted in deceptive modes, it tends to be taken for granted at times of accurate perception. The revelatory power of the body rests precisely upon its self effacement. Moreover . . . this self effacement is most marked in the case of abstract thought. Insofar as such thinking is regarded as the royal road to truth, this road seems to lead away from the body. When the body reclaims attention it is in the guise of an obstacle on the path . . . Thus a "disembodied" state is highly to be valued' (D. Leder, *The Absent Body*, Chicago and London: University of Chicago Press, 1990, p. 133).

36 Ibid., p. 5.

37 A. Danto, 'Philosophy as/and/of literature', p. 6.

38 Ibid., p. 6

39 D. Leder, *The Absent Body*, p. 154. Perhaps the greatest immediate gift of a renewed physics is that of restoring wonder and awe to the heart of science. As Merchant points out, the shift in the root metaphors from world–as–organism to world-as-mechanism rendered nature inert, passive, devoid of the sense of living energy which characterized earlier relationships to nature. The drawbacks of a mechanistic model have taken a long time to surface. The metaphor of world-as-organism has a long history in western philosophy but the shift to a mechanistic model of the universe has made the recovery of organismic models a significant achievement (C. Merchant, *The Death of Nature: Women, Ecology and Scientific Revolution*, San Francisco: Harper and Row, 1980, p. 193).

40 Ibid., p.79.

41 D. Cooper, *Metaphor*, p. 141.

42 D. Leder, *The Absent Body*, pp. 126–48.

43 L. Wittgenstein, *Philosophical Investigations*, paragraph 115, p. 48e.

44 By seminal metaphors we could indicate an irrepresentable, unconscious pre-existent form. By 'irrepresentable' one could not mean completely unmanifest, but only not

representable by means of a spatial model or in the words of a conventional language. If schemata are to be made a part of our generally accepted notion of our cognitive claims, they must have a place in the evolutionary progress of life and in the ontogeny of the self. Thus for their origins we ought to look to experiences that have been common to humans, such as the transitional stages of growth, reproduction, survival.

45 G. Lakoff and M. Johnson, *Metaphors We Live By*, p. 4.
46 To try to understand a person's experience of his 'position' we may resort to colloquial speech which, again, supplies us with a variety of expressions. The territorial metaphor is clear in one of the writings of R. D. Laing. He remarks that in ordinary language we use expressions such as: 'To put someone on the spot; to give someone room to move; to have no elbow-room; to be put in an awkward position; to make someone feel small; to know where one is with someone; to pull someone or to be pulled in opposite directions; to turn the screw on; to know where one stands; to have the ground taken from under one's feet; to be based in, tied in a knot, caught, set upon, cornered, entangled, trapped, smothered' (*Self and Others*, London: Tavistock Publications, 1969, p. 146).
47 When symmetrization prevails differences between elements of any category tend to disappear as in the domain of affects all that is known has the characteristic of a set. A consequence is that distinctions of hierarchy and proportion, which are typical of logic, tend to vanish. This implies that a member of a set can be known only as identical to the whole class. In a prevalently symmetrical perspective, then, an absent father is identical to all fathers, or a depressed mother to all mothers, a careless doctor to all doctors. In this way Matte Blanco introduces the idea of infinite experiences in our approach to human interactions. And once we are alerted to this possibility we can notice allusions to infinite experiences in everyday language. This in turn entails that our awareness of beliefs and desires can be linked to a rich variety of differences in the area of our beliefs and desires: they are indeed pointers to the breadth and depth of our linguistic life. We have finally come to confront in philosophy the *life* of our language. See I. Matte Blanco, *The Unconscious as Infinite Sets: An Essay in Bi-Logic*, London: Duckworth, 1975; *Thinking, Feeling and Being: Clinical Reflections on the Fundamental Antinomy of Human Beings in the World*, London: Routledge, 1989.
48 A. Danto, 'Philosophy as/and/of literature', p. 22.
49 Ibid., p. 22. See also U. Eco, *Lector in fabula: La cooperazione interpretativa nei testi narrativi*, Milan: Bompiani, 1979.
50 A. Danto, 'Philosophy as/and/of literature', p. 23.
51 A hypothetical isolated person, only concerned with representational knowledge, is a candidate for a tragic destiny. In fact, we are constantly linked with a variety of relations: to the extent that these relations are insufficient, or damaged, such inadequate links constitute a 'destiny' which is a threat to personal life.
52 M. Arbib, *The Metaphorical Brain*, New York: Wiley – Interscience, 1972, p. vi.
53 Ibid., p. vi.
54 M. Arbib and M. B. Hesse, *The Construction of Reality*, p. 156.
55 Ibid., p. 157.
56 J. R. Eiser, *Attitudes, Chaos and the Connectionist Mind*, Oxford and Cambridge, Mass.: Blackwell, 1994, p. 43.

3   THE INTERDIGITATION OF FIELDS

1 D. Davidson, 'What metaphors mean', in *Inquiries into Truth and Interpretation*, Oxford: Clarendon Press, 1985, p. 262.
2 M. Cavell, 'Metaphor, dreamwork and irrationality', in E. LePore (ed.), *Truth and Interpretation: Perspectives on the Philosophy of Donald Davidson*, Oxford: Blackwell, 1986, p. 495. Italics added. It is worth remembering, in this connection, that the Sumerians' capacity for imagining linkages between such reciprocally alien elements as

signs and sounds created the general pattern for the writing styles which has significantly transformed the story of hominization.

3 I. Kant, *Critique of Pure Reason*, translated by N. Kemp Smith, New York: St Martin's Press, 1965, A138, B177.

4 P. F. Strawson, 'Imagination and perception', in *Freedom and Resentment and Other Essays*, New York and London: Methuen, 1974, p. 45.

5 Ibid., p. 46.

6 M. Cavell, 'Metaphor, dreamwork and irrationality', p. 495.

7 McGuinness suggests that the implications of Wittgenstein's technical philosophy for his philosophy of life were not always apparent to him, though no doubt they were unconsciously part of his motivation. 'But now, in this the worst summer of danger and defeat, somewhere between the shells and the bullets, he began to feel that the two were connected; that grasping the essence of propositions or of an operation had something to do with adopting the right attitude towards life. No longer does his attitude towards his philosophy merely exhibit the same structure as his attitude towards life: the two are now identified. The critic of Russell is fused in the reader of Dostoevsky.' And also: 'Tomorrow perhaps I shall be sent out, at my own request, to the observation post. Then and only then will the war begin for me. And – possibly – life too. Perhaps nearness to death will bring light into my life' (Diary 4.05.16). (B. McGuinness, *Wittgenstein, a Life: Young Ludwig (1989–1921)*, London: Duckworth, 1988, p. 243 and p. 240.

8 M. Johnson, *The Body in the Mind: The Bodily Basis of Meaning, Imagination and Reasoning*, Chicago and London: University of Chicago Press, 1987, pp. xxiv–xxv.

9 Ibid., pp. xxiv–xxv.

10 P. F. Strawson, *Freedom and Resentment and Other Essays*, p. 57.

11 L. Wittgenstein, *Philosophical Investigations*, translated by G. E. M. Anscombe, Oxford: Blackwell, 1988, p. 197e.

12 Ibid., p. 197e.

13 Ibid., p. 212e.

14 P. F. Strawson, *Freedom and Resentment and Other Essays*, p. 57.

15 L. Wittgenstein, *Philosophical Investigations*, p. 212e.

16 'The behavioural disposition includes, or entails, a readiness for, or expectancy of, other perceptions, of a certain character, of the same object' (P. F. Strawson, *Freedom and Resentment and Other Essays*, p. 59).

17 M. Cavell, 'Metaphor, dreamwork and irrationality', p. 495.

18 In fact, while most theorists of metaphor ascribe two meanings to a metaphorical sentence, Davidson argues that a metaphorical sentence means nothing beyond what it really says. Metaphor is a particular use of language, and not a particular kind of meaning and while it is propositional in character, the 'seeing as' response it prompts is not (E. LePore, 'Truth and meaning' in E. Le Pore (ed.), *Truth and Interpretation*, pp. 25–6).

19 See, for instance, E. F. Kittay, *Metaphor: Its Cognitive Force and Linguistic Structure*, Oxford: Clarendon Press, 1987, ch. 3, para. 2, 'A relational approach to meaning', pp. 121–39.

20 He refers to the Harvard Center for Cognitive Studies. See also J. Bruner, *Acts of Meaning*, Cambridge, Mass. and London: Harvard University Press, 1990, p. xvi.

21 F. M. Berenson, *Understanding Persons: Personal and Interpersonal Relationships*, Brighton: Harvester Press, 1981, p. 121.

22 L. Wittgenstein, *Philosophical Investigations*, paragraph 241, p. 88e.

23 J. Bruner, *Acts of Meaning*, p. 72.

24 Aristotle, *Poetics*, paragraph 22, 1459a 5–8, pp. 2234–5. *The Complete Works of Aristotle*, Revised Oxford Translation, edited by J. Barnes, vol. III, Bollingen Series LXXI.2, Princeton, N. J.: Princeton University Press, 1985.

25 D. Davidson, 'A nice derangement of epitaphs', in *Inquiries into Truth and Interpretation*, pp. 173–4.

26 In connection with the problem of 'dissolving' boundaries, Arbib and Hesse maintain

that 'Both schema theory and the network view of science have led to a theory of language in which metaphor is normative, with literal meaning as the limiting case. The resulting epistemology combines coherence and correspondence criteria of truth and *dissolves the barriers* between "objective" science and nonscience' (M. Arbib and M. B. Hesse, *The Construction of Reality*, Cambridge: Cambridge University Press, p.171).

27 Ibid., p. 155.

28 Aristotle, *Poetics*, paragraph 22, 1459a 5–8.

29 M. Midgley, *Wisdom, Information and Wonder: What is Knowledge For?*, London and New York: Routledge, 1989, p. 70.

30 In the perspective of valuational hierarchizations, Foucault remarks: 'Humanity installs each of its violences in a system of rules and thus proceeds from domination to domination' (M. Foucault, *Language, Counter-Memory, Practice: Selected Essays and Interviews*, edited by D. Bouchard, Ithaca, N. Y.: Cornell University Press, 1977, p. 151.

31 'I have learnt in other fields of study how transitory the "assured results of modern scholarship" may be . . . And the interesting thing is that while I lived under that dynasty I felt various difficulties and objections which I never dared to express. They were so frightfully obvious that I felt sure they must be mere misunderstandings; the great men could not have made such very elementary mistakes as these which my objections implied' (C. S. Lewis, 'Fern-seed and elephants', in *Christian Reflections*, Glasgow: Collins Fount Paperbacks, 1981, p. 203).

32 In this connection see, for instance, S. Toulmin, *Human Understanding*, vol. I, Princeton, N. J. : Princeton University Press, 1972, p. 505.

33 A propensity towards a 'maturation' of thinking ultimately suggests that it is a question of developing a problem-solving style more suited to approaching 'frustrating' questions than to the well-structured problems presented within the literalness of the epistemology through which we are sojourning. A further concern is the extent to which, on certain crucial occasions, the imagination of a scientist may be guided by his, perhaps implicit, fidelity to one or more themes. 'Adherence to such preconceptions may help or impede the scientist', as Einstein once wrote to de Sitter. The thematic structure of scientific work, one that can be thought of as largely independent of the empirical and analytical content, emerges from the study of the options that were in principle open to a scientist (G. Holton, *The Scientific Imagination: Case Studies*, Cambridge: Cambridge University Press, 1978, p. viii).

34 See R. J. Sternberg, *Metaphors of Mind: Conceptions of the Nature of Intelligence*, Cambridge: Cambridge University Press, 1990, p. 5.

35 S. Toulmin, *Human Understanding*, p. 478. He further remarks that 'This is where our "ecological" approach comes into the picture . . . Instead of leaving us wandering . . . in an abstract world of "methodological research programmes" whose very names are inherited from the arguments of the formal logicians, it requires us to focus . . . on the historically-developed problems . . . with which our rational enterprises are concerned' (ibid., p. 480). And also: 'Propositional systems and formal inferences are legitimate instruments, among others, for the purposes of rational investigation and scientific explanation, but they are no more than this' (ibid., p. 480).

36 'Abandoning the theoretical pattern of formal "systems" characterized by static interactions, in favour of the alternative schema of "populations" subject to historical evolution, forces methodological changes on many of the human sciences' (S. Toulmin, *Human Understanding*, p. 505). We may, in fact, set about relating the 'life of ideas' to the life cycle of the institutions which conceive and transmit them, thus reintegrating the theoretical to the practical aspects of research.

37 M. Midgley, *Wisdom, Information and Wonder: What is Knowledge For?*, p. 58.

4 THE OPPOSITIONAL METAPHOR

1 L. Wittgenstein, *Culture and Value*, translated by P. Winch, edited by G. H. von Wright, in collaboration with H. Nyman, Oxford: Blackwell, 1980, p. 56e (1946).

2 See G. Corradi Fiumara, 'Midwifery and philosophy', in *The Other Side of Language: A Philosophy of Listening*, London and New York: Routledge, 1990, pp. 143–68. In *Euthydemus* 227d, 288d, and 295, Socratic maieutics is significantly contrasted with Euthydemus' belligerent approach. Plato, *The Dialogues of Plato*, Oxford: Clarendon Press, 1925.

3 R. Nozick, *Philosophical Explanations*, Oxford: Clarendon Press, 1981, p. 6. Nozick says that we often search for statements that our partners will accept and which will lead to the conclusions we want them to reach. Recognizing the deductive connections, a person must accept the conclusion, or else struggle to reject one of the statements he previously accepted – once he sees where it leads. So the clever discussant will identify premises that the interlocutor will not abandon. And he further remarks that 'The terminology of philosophical art is coercive: arguments are *powerful* and best when they are *knockdown*. Arguments *force* you to a conclusion; if you believe the premises you *have to* or *must* believe the conclusions . . . and so forth. A philosophical argument is an attempt to get someone to believe something, whether he wants to believe it or not. A successful philosophical argument, a strong argument, *forces* someone to a belief' (p. 4).

4 Wittgenstein suggests that even more profound convictions scarcely show in our world-view. 'I know whether I am talking in accordance with my conviction or contrary to it. So the conviction is what is important. In the background of my utterances. What a *strong* picture. One might paint conviction and speech ("from the depths of his heart"). *And yet how little that picture shews*!' (L. Wittgenstein, *Remarks on the Philosophy of Psychology*, translated by G. E. M. Anscombe, vol. I, Oxford: Blackwell, 1980, paragraph 808, p. 143e).

5 This thesis is advocated and extensively elaborated by J. Moulton in 'A paradigm of philosophy: the adversary method', in S. Harding and M. B. Hintikka (eds), *Discovering Reality: Feminist Perspectives on Epistemology, Metaphysics, Methodology and Philosophy of Science*, Dordrecht, Boston, Mass. and London: Reidel Publishing Company 1983. She further specifies: 'Of course, it will be admitted that the Adversary Method does not *guarantee* that all and only sound philosophical claims will survive, but that is only because even an adversary does not always think of all the things which ought to be criticized about a position, and even a proponent does not always think of all the possible responses to criticism' (p. 153).

6 G. Lakoff and M. Johnson, *Metaphors We Live By*, Chicago and London: University of Chicago Press, 1980, p. 4.

7 Ibid., p. 4.

8 Ibid., p. 4. They further argue: 'The most important claim we have so far is that metaphor is not just a matter of language, that is, of mere words. We shall argue that, on the contrary, human *thought processes* are largely metaphorical. This is what we mean when we say that the human conceptual system is metaphorically structured and defined' (ibid., p. 6).

9 J. Moulton, 'A paradigm of philosophy: the adversary method', p. 153.

10 'It is in this sense that the "argument is war" metaphor is one that we live by in this culture; it structures the actions we perform in arguing' (G. Lakoff and M. Johnson, *Metaphors We Live By*, p. 4).

11 Ibid., p. 5. And they add: 'We talk about arguments that way because we conceive of them that way – and we act according to the way we conceive of things.'

12 'What distinguishes metaphor is not meaning but use – in this it is like assertion, hinting, lying, promising, or criticizing. And the special use to which we put language in metaphor is not – cannot be – to "say something" special, no matter how indirectly. For a metaphor *says* only what shows on its face – usually a patent falsehood or an absurd truth. And this plain truth or falsehood needs no paraphrase – its meaning is given in the literal

meaning of the words' (D. Davidson, *Inquiries into Truth and Interpretation*, Oxford: Clarendon Press, 1985, p. 259). Davidson thus clarifies his position: 'I depend on the distinction between what words mean and what they are used to do. I think metaphor belongs exclusively to the domain of use. It is something brought off by the imaginative employment of words and sentences and depends entirely on the ordinary meaning of those words and hence on the ordinary meanings of the sentences they comprise' (ibid., p. 247).

13 R. Nozick, *Philosophical Explanations*, p. 4.

14 L. Wittgenstein, *Remarks on the Philosophy of Psychology*, vol. I, paragraph 710, p. 130e, italics added.

15 J. Moulton, 'A paradigm of philosophy: the adversary method', p. 154.

16 J. Bruner, *Acts of Meaning*, Cambridge, Mass. and London: Harvard University Press, 1990, pp. xi–xii.

17 This is the approach which Moulton named the 'adversary paradigm'. She further specifies that, 'The reasoning used to discover the claims, and the way the claims relate to other beliefs and systems of ideas are not considered relevant to philosophic reasoning if they are not deductive'. ('A paradigm of philosophy: the adversary method', p. 153).

18 In fact, 'Metaphors as linguistic expressions are possible precisely because there are metaphors in a person's conceptual system. Therefore, whenever . . . we speak of metaphors, such as "Argument is war", it should be understood that *metaphor* means *metaphorical concept*' (G. Lakoff and M. Johnson, *Metaphors We Live By*, p. 6).

19 'If we want to understand the fervour of the reformers, we need always to bear in mind how heavily the Hegelian influence loomed over them. Just as the earlier empiricists were always tacitly shooting at something they called "the schoolmen" – that is, at the degenerate relics of medieval Aristotelianism, still lingering in the universities, so what the nineteenth-century rebels had in their sights, apart from Christianity, was nearly always German idealism' (M. Midgley, *Wisdom, Information and Wonder: What is Knowledge for?*, London and New York: Routledge, 1989, p. 185).

20 Ibid., p. 240.

21 See chapter 23, 'Philosophizing out in the world', ibid., pp. 239–54.

22 D. Davidson, *Inquiries into Truth and Interpretation*, p. xvii. 'Disagreement and agreement alike are intelligible only against a background of massive agreement' (p. 137). And also: 'The basic methodological precept is, therefore, that a good theory of interpretation maximizes agreement. Or, given that sentences are infinite in number, and given further considerations to come, a better word might be *optimize*' (p. 169).

   The nascent 'principle of charity' advocated by Davidson might resonate with Taylor's analysis and criticism of 'The two–person prisoner's dilemma supergame'. He says: 'The Prisoner's Dilemma is by definition a non-cooperative game. The Prisoner's Dilemma supergame is thus also a non-cooperative game. Either agreements may not be made (perhaps because communication is impossible or because the making of agreements is prohibited) or, if agreements may be made, players are not constrained to keep them. It is the possibility of cooperation in the *absence* of such constraints that I am interested in here' (M. Taylor, *The Possibility of Cooperation: Studies in Rationality and Social Change*, Cambridge: Cambridge University Press, 1987, p. 61).

23 C. K. Ogden, *Opposition: A Linguistic and Psychological Analysis*, Bloomington, Ind. and London: Indiana University Press; New York: Midland Books, 1967, p. 21, italics added.

24 Aristotle, *Metaphysics*, Books I–IX, translated by H. Tredennick, Cambridge, Mass.: Harvard University Press, 1980, Book IX, paragraph II, 4, p. 435.

25 D. Davidson, *Inquiries into Truth and Interpretation*, p. 197.

26 Ibid., p. 27.

27 Ibid., p. 153.

28 G. Lakoff and M. Johnson, *Metaphors We Live By*, p. 4.

29 G. Moulton, 'A paradigm of philosophy: the adversary method', p. 157.

30 Ibid., p. 149.
31 Ibid., p. 150.
32 Ibid. pp. 147–53. Introducing his paper 'Imagination and perception', Strawson points out that the paper 'belongs to the species *loosely ruminative* and *comparative-historical* rather then to the species *strictly argumentative* or *systematic-analytical*' (P. F. Strawson, *Freedom and Resentment and Other Essays*, London and New York: Methuen, 1974, p. 45). The 'nobler' species, however, rarely compares in innovative force with the former one, which is possibly less inspired by adversarial concerns.
33 L. Wittgenstein, *Remarks on the Philosophy of Psychology*, paragraph 1132, p. 197e.
34 The quotations from Ulpian, Bocer and Azo are to be found in E. Peters, *Torture*, Oxford: Blackwell, 1985, p. 1; they are reported by Barry Allen in *Truth in Philosophy*, Cambridge, Mass. and London: Harvard University Press, 1993, p. 21. It should be noted, however, that Ulpian also writes that 'Torture is a fragile and dangerous thing and that the truth frequently is not obtained by it. For many defendants, because of their patience and strength are able to spurn the torments, while others would rather lie than bear them, unfairly incriminating themselves and also others'. Cited in John Teduschi, 'Inquisitorial law and the witch', in B. Ankarloo and G. Henningsen (eds), *Early Modern European Witchcraft*, Oxford: Oxford University Press, 1989, p. 100.
35 R. Descartes, *Discourse on Method*, translated by John Veitch, London: Dent and Dutton-Everyman, 1937, part IV, p. 26.
36 This synoptic view is put forward by M. Midgley in *Wisdom, Information and Wonder*, p. 71.
37 Ibid., p. 240.
38 'A perspicuous representation produces just that understanding which consists in "seeing connexions". Hence the importance of finding and inventing *intermediate cases*' (L. Wittgenstein, *Philosophical Investigations*, translated by G. E. M. Anscombe, Oxford: Blackwell, 1988, paragraph 122, p. 49e).
39 See G. Corradi Fiumara, *The Other Side of Language: A Philosophy of Listening*, London and New York: Routledge, 1990, pp. 184–6.

5   THE MATURATION OF KNOWLEDGE

1 The term 'normal' is, of course, used in a Kuhnian sense as highlighted in *The Structure of Scientific Revolutions*. Cooper appropriately points out that in order to mark the crucial difference, from the semantic point of view, between fresh metaphorical utterances and the ones belonging to established practice, we should reserve the noun 'metaphor' for the former alone (D. Cooper, *Metaphor*, Aristotelian Society Series, vol. 5, Oxford: Blackwell, 1986, p. 179). Cacciari points out that several relationships can exist between a sentence and its referent apart from its being literal or figurative: a sentence in fact can be literal, metaphorical, vague, indeterminate, anomalous, polysemous, indirect, ambiguous, etc. Thus the literal-metaphorical distinction is only one of many and also a rather controversial one (C. Cacciari and P. Tabossi (eds), *Idioms: Processing, Structure and Interpretation*, Hillsdale, N. J., Hove and London: Lawrence Erlbaum Associates, 1993, p. 30).
2 D. Davidson, 'Thought and talk', in *Inquiries into Truth and Interpretation*, Oxford: Clarendon Press, 1985, p. 169. Putnam argues that philosophical work trying to reduce rationality to what language we are using or what culture we belong to retains a measure of irrationality, inasmuch as this sort of work does not allow for a comparative critique of cultural traditions. But then, we have no reason to believe that our epistemic communities only provide algorithms to be automatically employed by all. In equating the contingent with the desirable there is a risk of fostering an excessive degree of cultural solipsism and closure, segregating cultures into narcissistic islands. According to Putnam it would be a mistake to relinquish the normative notion of justifiable truth, since we

need to accept that reason is both natural and transcendent and that 'philosophy, as culture-bound reflection and argument about eternal questions, is both in time and in eternity' (H. Putnam, 'Why reason can't be naturalized', in K. Baynes, J. Bohman and T. McCarthy (eds), *After Philosophy: End or Transformation?*, Cambridge, Mass. : MIT Press, 1987). The most profound concern of a thinker is the serious fear that the part of philosophy which is assigned to 'eternity' may actually indicate no more than a tacit decision to be self- perpetuating and overruling – a juvenile attempt permanently to upgrade an epistemic position.

3 R. Rorty, *Objectivity, Relativism, and Truth. Philosophical Papers*, vol. I, Cambridge: Cambridge University Press, 1991, p. 166. In a perspective in which we no longer regard 'meaning' as the complementary term of a two-elements relation between language and some extraneous domain, whether this be the world or a metalanguage, we can take meaning to be a cluster of significant relations in the dynamics of our linguisticity. We could thus relinquish the question 'What does a metaphor mean?', and substitute the question 'How does a metaphor work?'.

4 Toulmin suggests that once a discipline has well-established strategies, any factors enhancing conceptual variations or distorting the procedures of critical judgement will come to be regarded as obstacles to the 'evolution' of the discipline. And when we deal with a prestigious epistemology, geographical and gender barriers exist only to be ignored (S. Toulmin, *Human Understanding*, vol. 1, Princeton, N.J.: Princeton University Press, 1972, p. 392).

5 What we may also gain from an awareness of this danger is a measure of greater freedom in playing with figures and backgrounds in the exploration of our philosophical language.

6 G. Labouvie-Vief, 'Wisdom as integrated thought: historical and developmental perspectives', in R. J. Sternberg (ed.), *Wisdom: its Nature, Origins and Development*, Cambridge: Cambridge University Press, 1990, p. 70.

7 M. Arbib and M. B. Hesse, *The Construction of Reality*, Cambridge: Cambridge University Press, 1986, p. 150. Of course there is no suggestion that language is always and everywhere metaphorical. Scientific models, in fact, are usually expressed in some locally stable and commensurable language, and possibly also in the form of deductive arguments. As Arbib and Hesse suggest, these are the instances in which language is clearly literal rather than metaphoric. Such cases, however, cannot be used to entail that 'science', in general, is characterized by its own special, literal language in which meanings are exclusively derived from 'empirical states of affairs ("truth conditions")', and for which truth is explicated by a simple correspondence theory.' From the increasing successes of scientific models one cannot altogether deduce that they are ideally suited to be true descriptions of the basic structure of the world (p. 158).

8 D. Cooper, *Metaphor*, p. 223.

9 R. Descartes, *Philosophical Letters*, translated and edited by A. Kenny, Minneapolis, Minn.: University of Minnesota Press, 1970, p. 112.

10 R. Descartes, 'The principles of philosophy', in E. Haldane and G. R. T. Ross (eds), *The Philosophical Works of Descartes*, Cambridge: Cambridge University Press, 1911, p. 252.

11 Albert Memmi argues that the colonialist approach removes situations from possible evolution by placing them out of time and history. 'What is actually a sociological point becomes labeled as being biological, or preferably, metaphysical. It is attached to the colonized's basic nature. Immediately the colonial relationship between colonized and colonizer, founded on the essential outlook of the two protagonists, becomes a definitive category. It is what it is because they are what they are, and neither one nor the other will ever change' (*The Colonizer and the Colonized*, Boston, Mass.: Beacon Press, 1967, p. 85).

12 And yet we should also be aware of an emerging culture which dissolves 'thing' and 'noun', perhaps every bit as much as the world of experience inaugurated by modern physics. Bateson repeatedly cautions against the dangers of noun language: 'There are

no "things" in the mind'. Bateson seeks to replace a substance-oriented materialistic outlook with a vocabulary of pattern and communication by constantly favouring concepts like form, order and balance which ultimately link with relationships and organization (M. C. Bateson, *Our Own Metaphor*, New York: Knopf, 1972, p. 275).

A common notion of literal language often used in linguistics as well as in psychological literature is the one proposed by Katz and Fodor in 1963, based on the 'anonymous letter criterion': a person receives an anonymous letter containing only a single sentence, and no specification whatsoever about motives, circumstances, or any contextual information. It is presumed that what the addressee will understand is the *sentence meaning*, that is, its semantic interpretation or literal meaning, rather than the *utterance meaning*. The latter in fact requires contextual information that is totally absent in the anonymous letter case. Yet evidence coming from different linguistic phenomena such as indirect speech acts, conversational implications and irony has been used to question the plausibility of the notion of literal language as well as of the assumption of a hypothetical 'zero context'. It is argued that the proposal does not take into account linguistic presuppositions, background knowledge, and comprehension processes. (J. J. Katz and J. Fodor, 'The structure of semantic theory', *Language*, 39, 1963, pp. 170–210).

13 P. Ricoeur, *The Rule of Metaphor*, translated by R. Czerny with K. McLaughlin and J. Costello, Toronto: University of Toronto Press, 1977. See also P. Ricoeur, 'The metaphorical process as cognition, imagination, feeling', *Critical Inquiry*, 5(1), 1978, pp. 143–60.

14 Paracelsus knew that some 'diseases that deprive man of his reason' come quite unnoticed by the patient; and inveterate physician, chemist and astrologer that he was, he began to seek the aetiology of the 'suffocation of the intellect' (Paracelsus, 'The diseases that deprive man of his reason' (1512), translated by G. Zilborg, in H. E. Sigerist (ed.), *Four Treatises*, Baltimore, Md.: Johns Hopkins Press, 1941, pp. 135–212).

15 For a discussion of this issue see G. Corradi Fiumara, *The Symbolic Function: Psychoanalysis and the Philosophy of Language*, Oxford, and Cambridge, Mass.: Blackwell, 1992, p. 107.

16 See chapter entitled 'Pseudosymbolic language' in *The Symbolic Function*, pp. 80–108.

17 The risks of personal closeness and listening are explored in G. Corradi Fiumara, *The Other Side of Language: A Philosophy of Listening*, London and New York: Routledge, 1990, especially in chapters entitled 'Dialogic interaction and listening', pp. 113–26; 'Midwifery and philosophy', pp. 143–68; and 'Paths of listening', pp. 169–83.

18 J. Bruner, *On Knowing: Essays for the Left Hand*, New York: Atheneum, 1966, pp. 4–5.

19 G. Corradi Fiumara, *The Symbolic Function*, p. 103.

20 The constitution of objects can now be interpreted as the (universal) projection on to the world of the classificatory presuppositions of scientific theories, carrying not only these classifications but also theoretical ontologies of fundamental entities and their properties.

21 M. Black, 'More about metaphor', in A. Ortony (ed.), *Metaphor and Thought*, Cambridge: Cambridge University Press, 1980, p. 34, and in *Dialectica*, 31 (3–4), 1977, pp. 431–57.

22 D. Cooper, *Metaphor*, p. 145.

23 The issue is extensively discussed in 'Folk psychology as an instrument of culture', the third chapter of J. Bruner, *Acts of Meaning*, Cambridge, Mass. and London: Harvard University Press, 1990, pp. 33–66.

24 G. Labouvie-Vief, 'Wisdom as integrated thought: historical and developmental perspectives', p. 73.

25 S. Freud: 'Where id was, there ego shall be.'

26 C. Bollas, *L'ombra dell'oggetto: Psicoanalisi del conosciuto non pensato*, Rome: Borla, 1989, p. 24, the translation of *The Shadow of the Object: Psychoanalysis of the Unthought Known*, London: Free Association Books, 1987, p. 16.

27 G. Ryle, *The Concept of Mind*, London: Hutchinson, 1949, p. 26.

28 The 'compulsion' to change the world by means of our rational powers could be thus

exemplified: 'Archimedes, that he might transport the entire globe from the place that it occupied to another demanded only a point that was firm and immovable; so also, I shall be entitled to entertain the highest expectations, if I am fortunate enough to discover only one thing that is certain, certain and indubitable' (R. Descartes, *Discourse on Method*, part II, trans. by J. Veitch, London: Dent and Dutton/Everyman, 1937, p. 85).

29 R. Rorty, *Philosophy and the Mirror of Nature,* Oxford: Blackwell 1980, p. 231.
30 M. Midgley, *Wisdom, Information, and Wonder. What is Knowledge for?*, London and New York: Routledge, 1989, p. 102.
31 Ibid., p. 102.
32 R. J. Sternberg, *Metaphors of Mind: Conceptions of the Nature of Intelligence*, Cambridge: Cambridge University Press, 1990, p. x.

6 THE RELATIONSHIP BETWEEN DIGITAL AND ANALOGIC STYLES

1 J. Bruner, *Acts of Meaning*, Cambridge, Mass. and London: Harvard University Press, 1990, p. 4.
2 Refusing to recognize latent dynamics and opting for a starting-point exclusively based on logical grounds it is possible that we inadvertently allow the most archaic of mental mechanisms to infiltrate into the domain of rationality. For a discussion of this issue, see chapter 12, 'The philosophy of listening: an evolutionary approach' (paragraphs entitled 'Phylogenetic perspectives', 'Listening and hominization', 'Prospects of communication') in G. Corradi Fiumara, *The Other Side of Language: A Philosophy of Listening*, London and New York: Routledge, 1990, pp. 184–98.
3 J. Bruner, *Actual Minds, Possible Worlds*, Cambridge, Mass.: Harvard University Press, 1986.
4 I. Matte Blanco, *Thinking, Feeling and Being: Clinical Reflections on the Fundamental Antinomy of Human Beings and World*, New Library of Psychoanalysis, no.5, London and New York: Routledge, 1989, p. 92.
5 Ibid., p. 92.
6 Ibid., p. 27.
7 And also, when there is symmetrization within a particular category or equivalence class, the individual elements are collected together by some thought (or propositional function), which regards them as sharing something in common, and becoming the same in every respect. With symmetrization the differences of degree within the class are abolished. Elements disappear and the only thing that remains is 'parentness', 'richness', 'threateningness'. For a fuller discussion of this issue see I. Matte Blanco, *The Unconscious as Infinite Sets: an Essay in Bi-Logic*, London: Duckworth, 1975.
8 It is true that open language cannot be as exact as responsibly closed language can be about the things and relations with which the latter properly deals. Nor can it be as exact in the *same way* as closed language is. On the affirmative side, however, let it be observed that a somewhat vague description or an allusion may, with reference to a problematic situation, be more relevantly precise that the use of a more logical technique would be. Where more humanly important situations are invoked the employment of alien forms of exactitude is *a posteriori* meaningless and absurd (P. Wheelwright, *Metaphor and Reality*, Bloomington, Ind.: Indiana University Press, 1962, p. 42).
9 J. Bruner, *Acts of Meaning*, p. 6. Also see H. A. Simon, *The Science of the Artificial*, Cambridge, Mass.: MIT Press, 1981.
10 R. Rorty, 'Inquiry as recontextualization: an anti- dualist account of interpretation', in *Objectivity, Relativism and Truth: Philosophical Papers*, vol. 1, Cambridge: Cambridge University Press, 1991, p. 95.
11 Ibid., p. 95.

12 E. von Hartmann, *Philosophy of the Unconscious*, translated by W. C. Coupland, London: Kegan Paul and Trench, 1931, p. 1.
13 J. Bruner, *On Knowing: Essays for the Left Hand*, Cambridge, Mass.: Harvard University Press, 1962, p. 2.
14 Just as we may come to perceive a continuum between literal and metaphorical meanings, so we can relinquish inherited, defensive dichotomies between the natural sciences on the one hand and the hermeneutic disciplines on the other.
15 In Rorty's view the line between the respective domains of epistemology and hermeneutics is not a matter of the difference between the 'sciences of nature' and the 'sciences of man', nor between the theoretical and the practical; the difference is purely one of familiarity (*Philosophy and the Mirror of Nature*, Oxford: Blackwell, 1980, p. 321).
16 This general contention regarding the metaphorical nature of thought is worth stating and pondering, since forgetting the metaphorical nature of our concepts invites 'hardening of the categories' and various sorts of myths and cults (S. Toulmin and D. E. Leary, 'The cult of empiricism in psychology and beyond', in S. Koch and D. E. Leary (eds), *A Century of Psychology as Science*, New York: McGraw-Hill, 1985, pp. 594–617).
17 S. Freud, 'Fragment of an analysis of a case of hysteria', 1905, Standard Edition, vol. 7, p. 65, note.
18 M. Johnson, *The Body in the Mind: The Bodily Basis of Meaning, Imagination and Reasoning*, Chicago and London: University of Chicago Press, 1987, p. 23.
19 Central to the set of assumptions that connote a systems theory is the notion of synergy, a term selected to indicate that the operation of a total system is not reductible to, or predictable from, the behaviour of separate parts within the system (B. B. Fuller, *Operating Manual for Spaceship Earth*, Carbondale and Edwardsville, Ill.: Southern Illinois University Press, 1969, p. 71).
20 M. Johnson, *The Body in the Mind*, p. 10.
21 Dreams are said to constitute an archaic and predominantly visual language. The images of this language are its words. And even though they mostly are objects, actions and fantasies of the waking state, both the syntax and the semantics of the language are unique. The rules of its syntax are connections such as one would tend to ascribe to infancy or archaic humanity. And since it is a question of being connected it would be more appropriate to look for links rather than schemata.
22 T. Nagel, *The View from Nowhere*, New York and Oxford: Oxford University Press, 1986, p. 6.
23 Ibid., p. 6.
24 'It is another property of the human mind that whenever men can form no idea of distant and unknown things, they judge them by what is familiar and at hand. This axiom points to the inexhaustible source of all the errors about the principles of humanity that have been adopted by entire nations and by all scholars. For when the former began to take notice of them and the latter to investigate them, *it was on the basis of their own enlightened, cultivated and magnificent times that they judged the origins of humanity, which must . . . by the nature of things have been small, crude and quite obscure. Under this head come two types of conceit, one of nations and the other of scholars*' (G. Vico, *The New Science of Giambattista Vico*, revised translation of the third edition of 1744; translated by J. G. Bergin and M. H. Fisch, Ithaca, N Y: Cornell University Press, 1968, Section II, p. 60 (emphasis added)).
25 M. Arbib and M. B. Hesse, *The Construction of Reality*, Cambridge: Cambridge University Press, 1986, p. 34.
26 Hierarchies are systems of objects or ideas structured according to ascending levels of complexity, abstraction or control. The deepest mystery, perhaps, may lie not so much in the information input, but rather in the nature of its processing which may take place primarily in the right hemisphere of the brain and hence cannot be expressed in language (R. W. Sperry, *Science and Moral Priority: Merging Mind, Brain and Human Values*, New York: Columbia University Press, 1983; Oxford: Blackwell, 1983, p. 58).

27 J. Bruner, *Acts of Meaning*, pp. 3–6.

28 R. W. Sperry, *Science and Moral Priority*, p. 58.

29 P. Wheelwright, *Metaphor and Reality*, p. 16.

30 R. R. Hoffman, E. L. Cochran and J. M. Nead, 'Cognitive metaphors in experimental psychology', in D. E. Leary (ed.), *Metaphors in the History of Psychology*, Cambridge: Cambridge University Press, 1990, p. 211.

31 R. Rorty, *Objectivity, Relativism and Truth*, p. 208.

32 M. Arbib, and M. B. Hesse, *The Construction of Reality*, p. 38.

33 A. M. Muratori, 'Il continuo e il discreto in psicoanalisi; contributo alla teoria della conoscenza', in A. M. Muratori (ed.), *Il 'continuo' e il 'discreto' in psicoanalisi*, Rome: Borla, 1987.

34 P. A. Parker 'The metaphorical plot', in D. S. Miall (ed.), *Metaphor: Problems and Perspectives*, Brighton: Harvester Press, 1982, pp. 151–2.

35 Ibid., p. 152.

36 J. Derrida, *De la grammatologie*, Paris: Éditions de Minuit, 1967; Italian translation: *Della grammatologia*, pp. 54–5.

37 W. V. O. Quine, 'A postscript on metaphor', *Critical Inquiry*, 5(1), 1978, pp. 161–2.

38 Ibid., p. 162.

39 Ibid., p. 162.

40 The notion of commensurability is explored by Rorty in *Philosophy and the Mirror of Nature*, especially pp. 315–21 and 323–32. Searle points out that the best we can do in paraphrases is reproduce the truth conditions of a metaphorical expression, even though a metaphorical utterance does more than just convey its truth conditions. For instance, it reveals a capacity to create language or to identify aspects of reality which standard language cannot grasp. At the very least metaphor conveys its truth conditions by way of another semantic vehicle whose truth conditions are not part of the truth conditions of the utterance. It gives testimony to a capacity successfully to use an instrument for a further purpose with respect to its 'primary' purpose. At the same time metaphoric expressions challenge the hearer on the same grounds inasmuch as he is invited to construe what the speaker means and to contribute much more than just passive uptake; part of the achievement is dependent upon the capacity to use a semantic vehicle different from the one which is communicated (R. Searle, 'Metaphor', in A. Ortony (ed.), *Metaphor and Thought*, Cambridge: Cambridge University Press, 1980, p. 123).

41 The prevalence of formalized aspects in linguistic philosophy is such that thought and action converge in a timeless paradigm and in an increasingly more restricted choice of vocabulary; the realm of research thus becomes restricted to one epistemology only and no epistemological migrations are possible.

42 L. E. Olds, *Metaphors of Interrelatedness: Toward a Systems Theory of Psychology*, Albany, N. Y.: State University of New York Press, 1992, pp. 115–36. Things have contexts, but only persons have perspectives. The essential excuse for writing, then, is to unveil as best one can some perspective that has not already become ordered into a public map. All writing to be sure is perspectival in the most general sense; for even the most banal cliché or the most plainly factual report is formulated from a certain trend of associations and expectations. The difference is not between the perspectival and the universal; for every universal, at least every humanly intelligible universal, is perspectivally conceived. No, the difference is between perspectives that have become standardized and perspectives that are freshly born and individual (P. Wheelwright, *Metaphor and Reality*, p. 16).

43 A thought-provoking contribution in this direction is offered in E. C. W. Krabbe, R. J. Dalitz, and P. A. Smit (eds), *Empirical Logic and Public Debate: Essays in Honor of E. M. Barth*, Amsterdam and Atlanta, Ga.: Editions Rodopi, 1993.

44 H. Putnam, *Realism with a Human Face*, edited and introduced by J. Conant, Cambridge, Mass.: Harvard University Press, 1990, p. 308.

45 P. A. Parker, 'The Metaphorical Plot', in D. S. Miall (ed.), *Metaphor: Problems and Perspectives*, p. 136.

46 Ibid., p. 136.

47 R. Vernon, 'Politics as metaphor: Cardinal Newman and Professor Kuhn', in G. Gutting (ed.), *Paradigms and Revolutions: Applications and Appraisals of Thomas Kuhn's Philosophy of Science*, Notre Dame, Ind. and London: Notre Dame University Press, 1980, p. 246.

48 D. E. Leary, 'Psyche's muse: the role of metaphor in the history of psychology', in D. E. Leary, *Metaphors in the History of Psychology*, p. 5.

49 J. Bruner, *Acts of Meaning*, p. 8.

50 L. E. Olds, *Metaphors of Interrelatedness*, p. 46.

51 R. R. Hoffman, 'Cognitive metaphors in experimental psychology', in D. E. Leary, *Metaphors in the History of Psychology*, p. 207.

52 D. E. Leary, 'Psyche's muse: the role of metaphor in the history of psychology', pp. 10–11.

53 Ibid., pp. 1–78.

54 Ibid., p. 18.

55 R. R. Hoffman, 'Cognitive metaphors in experimental psychology', p. 214.

56 Although the term 'wave' was first applied to sound in a metaphorical sense, Kittay asks whether it is still appropriate to say that it is meant as a metaphor. We do in fact take sound to have the same essential properties as a wave and to have these properties in a way not true of light, to which the application of the term 'wave' is more likely to be metaphorical (E. F. Kittay, *Metaphor: Its Cognitive Force and Linguistic Structure*, Oxford: Clarendon Press, 1987, p. 19).

57 L. E. Olds, *Metaphors of Interrelatedness*, p. 20.

58 Wheelwright remarks that ordinarily one is more successful at communicating fullness and intensity to a few persons of similar sensitiveness than to a heterogeneous many. 'Fit readers find, though few', said John Milton, expressing a very serious writer's advice. But there is always risk, for fit readers may not actually be found and at best their fitness will be less than perfect. The risk is the price that is paid for trying to speak with honest and fresh imagination instead of dully falling into set linguistic routines (*Metaphor and Reality*, p. 44).

59 Language that is closed in this manner, by default, may be indefinitely susceptible to ambiguities; and such ambiguities, unlike the creative ambiguities, serve no good purpose (ibid., p. 38).

60 Ibid., p. 164.

61 This illuminating approach is drawn from O. Kitayama, 'Metaphorization – making terms', *International Journal of Psycho-Analysis*, 68(4), 1987, pp. 499–509.

62 The unambiguous information-bearing carrier may be called a signal. This definition embodies the classical concept of Newtonian, or 'billiard ball' causality as the limiting case where the information approaches zero and only energy is transmitted. Causal events have reliably traceable lines for some finite distance. This pathway may be repeated and predicted according to known laws of energy and information transmission. This gives us a certain psychological feeling of security which we accept as an 'explanation'. And yet, in 'real life' no path is isolated, but is constantly intersecting with other paths.

63 R. Rorty, *Objectivity, Relativism and Truth*, p. 167. To sketch a tentative distinction between two different sorts of knowledge contexts in which rearrangements can be attempted, we could think of new attitudes toward some of the items previously in our conceptual frame of reference, or else of the creation of new attitudes toward unforseen 'truth-value bearers' which were previously regarded as irrelevant. There is thus a distinction between two senses of inquiry which is at least in some respects similar to the distinction between inferential processes and creative work, playing a game successfully and creating new successful games.

64 D. Cooper, *Metaphor*, Aristotelian Society Series, vol.5, Oxford: Blackwell, 1986, p.

151. If the semantic collisions are obvious, it is the illuminating collusion which is properly metaphorical. As members of a phatic community we are projected in standardized and taken-for-granted language games whereby we tend to speak and think and see in a communal way. As the adequacy of words is taken for granted, reality and language are so intimately interwoven that the rift that separates the two remains concealed. Semantic collisions often help dissolve this too intimate union. As language gains a certain autonomy from reality we are induced to appreciate the usually forgotten distance that separates words and things. There is a language of childhood, a highly creative one, that does little more than recall us to an awareness of this distance. The revelatory power of such language does not lie in the fact that it gives us more complete descriptions or transforms our semantic space. Its force springs rather from its capacity to reveal the usually passed- over inadequacy of language. Revealing this inadequacy it rekindles the conflict between language and all that transcends it as its ground and measure (K. Harries, 'Afterthoughts on metaphor', *Critical Inquiry*, 5(1), 1978, pp. 167–74.

65 L. Wittgenstein, *Culture and Value*, translated by P. Winch, edited by G. H. von Wright, in collaboration with H. Nyman, Oxford: Blackwell, 1980, p. 62e.

66 M. Douglas, *Purity and Danger*, London: Routledge and Kegan Paul, 1966.

67 L. Wittgenstein, *Culture and Value*, p. 62 e.

68 Ibid., p. 76 e.

69 Ibid., p. 80 e.

70 See G. Corradi Fiumara, 'The question of anomalies: a connection between Wittgenstein and Freud', in *The Symbolic Function: Psychoanalysis and the Philosophy of Language*, Oxford and Cambridge, Mass.: Blackwell, 1992, pp. 21–4.

7 DETACHMENT AND PARTICIPATION

1 In Johnson's view 'Understanding is not only a matter of reflection, using finitary propositions, on some preexistent, already determinate experience. Rather, *understanding is the way we "have a world", the way we experience our world as a comprehensible reality.* Such understanding, therefore, involves *our whole being* – our bodily capacities and skills, our values, our moods and attitudes, our entire cultural tradition' (M. Johnson, *The Body in the Mind: The Bodily Basis of Meaning, Imagination and Reasoning*, Chicago and London: University of Chicago Press, 1987, p. 102).

2 N. Malcom, *Ludwig Wittgenstein: A Memoir*, London: Oxford University Press, 1958, p. 39.

3 M. Johnson, *The Body in the Mind*, p. 103. As is well known, one of the pivotal texts is Max Black's *Models and Metaphors*, an extremely influential work which continues to hold a central position in contemporary discussion. In his work, however, there seems to be a tacit acceptance of the idea that metaphors are relatively inconsequential unless they are cognitive, that is, unless they meet this classical test of respectability. He starts out by saying that the questions he should like to see answered concern the 'logical grammar' of metaphors. And he concludes: 'No doubt metaphors are dangerous – and perhaps especially so in philosophy. But a prohibition against their use would be a willful and harmful restriction upon our powers of inquiry' (M. Black, *Models and Metaphors: Studies in Language and Philosophy*, Ithaca, N. Y.: Cornell University Press, 1962, pp. 25, p. 47).

4 Rorty, with Peirce, has a propensity to paraphrase talk about the object as talk about the practical effects which the object will have on our conduct. Once we relinquish the distinction between context and thing contextualized there follows a decreasing interest in the search for entities which are what they are independent of culture and those which are culture-dependent.

5 'There is no way to divide the world up into internal relations, nor into intrinsic versus

extrinsic properties – nor, indeed, into things that are intrinsically relations and things which are intrinsically terms of relations.' And also: 'For once one sees inquiry as reweaving beliefs rather than discovering the natures of objects, there are no candidates for self-subsistent, independent, entities save individual beliefs – individual sentential attitudes' (R. Rorty, 'Inquiry as recontextualization: an anti-dualist account of interpretation', in *Objectivity, Relativism and Truth: Philosophical Papers*, vol. 1. Cambridge: Cambridge University Press, 1991, pp. 93–110.

6 M. Arbib and M. B. Hesse, *The Construction of Reality*, Cambridge: Cambridge University Press, 1986, p. 155.

7 G. Lakoff and M. Johnson, *Metaphors We Live By*, Chicago and London: University of Chicago Press, 1980, p. 4.

8 M. Arbib and M. B. Hesse, *The Construction of Reality*, p. 156.

9 Arbib and Hesse comment in this connection that 'There is no "fact" to which "argument" corresponds that has the natural character of "war", "logic" or "negotiation". The extended metaphors are not in that sense true or false but are appropriate or inappropriate, more or less revealing, more or less useful, depending on the context of application and upon their coherence with evaluative judgements made about particular situations' (*The Construction of Reality*, p. 156).

10 N. Malcom, *Ludwig Wittgenstein: A Memoir*, p. 39.

11 M. Arbib and M. Hesse, *The Construction of Reality*, p. 160.

12 Ibid., p. 159.

13 T. Nagel, *Mortal Questions*, Cambridge: Cambridge University Press, 1979, p. 206.

14 H. Putnam, *Representation and Reality*, Cambridge, Mass.: MIT Press, 1988, p. 89.

15 S. Langer, *Philosophy in a New Key: A Study of the Symbolism of Reason, Rite and Art*, Cambridge, Mass. : Harvard University Press, 1942, p. 292.

16 T. Nagel, *Mortal Questions*, p. 197.

17 Ibid., p. 197.

18 In Cohen's view Aristotle's suggestion that metaphor is close to genius seems a way to avoid Plato's castigation of art inasmuch as it lacks a direct relation to knowledge; in this perspective the sharpest possible rebuttal would seem to be one which asserts that art *is* an implement of knowing. 'But in this response's implication that art is, therefore, worthwhile, there is the further implication that Plato was right about the main point, that knowledge is what matters. Should we accept that point? Should we accept the correlate point about metaphor? Even if we did, and supposed that metaphors could share in the preeminent philosophical prize only if they partook of meaning, truth and knowledge, it would still be worth knowing whether they serve a lesser good. To learn this we will have to understand better than we do how metaphors are actually created and reacted to, whether or not these are matters of meaning' (T. Cohen, 'Metaphor and the cultivation of intimacy', *Critical Inquiry*, 1(5), 1978, pp. 3–12. The work also appears in S. Sacks (ed.), *On Metaphor*, Chicago and London: University of Chicago Press, 1979.

19 In the chapter entitled 'Unfamiliar noises: Hesse and Davidson on metaphor', Rorty argues that it is possible unwittingly to share a number of background assumptions, such as 'the Kantian presumption that there is some sort of inviolable "metaphysical" break between the formal and the material, the logical and the psychological, the non-natural and the natural – between, in short, what Davidson calls "scheme and content"' (R. Rorty, *Objectivity, Relativism and Truth*, p. 168).

20 Studies in contemporary branches of research are sufficient to radically question logocratic views of meaning and rationality. Taken together they are even more significant. This vast network of related empirical studies, in conjunction with logical arguments voiced by eminent thinkers indicate that any comprehensive accounts of meaning and rationality should allow for the joint synergy of affectual and metaphoric structures by which we shape and know our world (M. Johnson, *The Body in the Mind*, p. xiii). Labouvie-Vief points out in this connection that a disquieting aspect of the literalist bias is equally evident in those theories of intellectual development deriving from the

assumption that thought is grounded in the nature of our being as an organism. According to Labouvie-Vief an example of this difficulty could be illustrated with Piaget's theories of intelligence, based on the assumption that it arises out of organic schemata which provide adaptations for basic biological needs such as nourishment, contact and exploration. Nevertheless, his account of development highlights the organicity of thought only early in the life span and regards later intelligence as capable of entirely freeing itself from that organic ground (G. Labouvie-Vief, 'Wisdom as integrated thought: historical and developmental perspectives', in R. J. Sternberg (ed.), *Wisdom: Its Nature, Origins and Development*, Cambridge: Cambridge University Press, 1990, pp. 32–83.

21 J. Bruner, *Acts of Meaning*, Cambridge, Mass. and London: Harvard University Press, 1990, p. xiii.

22 Aristotle, *Politics*, Book I, 1252b 1, *The Complete Works of Aristotle*, Revised Oxford Translation, edited by Jonathan Barnes, vol. II, Bolliugen Series LXXI. 2; Princeton, N.Y.: Princeton University Press, 1985, p. 1986–7. It is perhaps appropriate to quote a sample piece of testimonony from Aristotle: 'For where there is nothing in common to ruler and ruled, there is no friendship either, since there is no justice; e.g. between craftsman and tool, soul and body, master and slave; the latter in each case is benefited by that which uses it, but there is no friendship nor justice towards lifeless things' *Nicomachean Ethics*, Book VIII, 1161a 31 – 1161b 2, p. 1835).

23 As has been pointed out in Chapter 1, he says, for instance, that 'It is not quite appropriate that fine language should be used by a slave or a very young man' (Aristotle, *Rhetoric*, Book III, 10–15, p. 2239).

24 Significantly Aristotle remarks, 'I will hereafter explain what is the proper treatment of slaves, and why it is expedient that liberty should be always held out to them as the reward of their services' (*Politics*, Book VII, 1330a 30, p. 2111).

25 As Barth points out, much of our philosophy cognitively operates in a 'social-solipsistic' style in which objects 'may be of importance as such but where *no* verbal contact or other sign contact between humans occur, or are taken into consideration' (E. M. Barth, 'Waiting for Godot: on attitudes towards artefacts vs. entities, as related to different phases of operation in cognition', *Epistemologia*, XIV, 1991, pp. 77–104, italics added).

26 D. Leder, *The Absent Body*, Chicago and London: University of Chicago Press, 1990, p. 122.

27 Ibid., p. 124.

28 J. Derrida, *Speech and Phenomena*, translated by D. B. Allison, Evanston, Ill.: Northwestern University Press, 1973, p. 77.

29 R. Rorty, *Philosophy and the Mirror of Nature*, Oxford: Blackwell, 1980. See especially part 2, 'Mirroring', pp. 129–306.

30 Plato, *Republic*, 533d; E. Hamilton and H. Cairns (eds), *The Collected Dialogues*, Princeton, N. J.: Princeton University Press, 1961, p. 765.

31 R. Descartes, *Philosophical Letters*, translated and edited by A. Kenny, Minneapolis, Minn.: University of Minnesota Press, 1970, p. 67.

32 R. Descartes, *The Philosophical Works of Descartes*, vol. 1, edited by E. Haldane and G. R. T. Ross, Cambridge: Cambridge University Press, 1911, p. 101.

33 B. Bettelheim, *The Uses of Enchantment*, New York: Alfred A. Knopf, 1976, pp. 74–5.

34 And if we ask what can be lost in this approach – in the language of Rorty – the answer is: 'Everything that makes it possible to draw a philosophically interesting distinction between explanation and understanding or between explanation and interpretation. That is, of course, just the sort of thing we anti-essentialists *want to lose*' (R. Rorty, *Objectivity, Relativism, and Truth*, p. 109).

35 M. Arbib and M. B. Hesse, *The Construction of Reality*, p. 37.

36 Aspects of this function of metaphor are discussed by Cohen in 'Metaphor and the cultivation of intimacy'.

37 Rorty further suggests that as 'metaphors get picked up, bandied about, and begin to die, and as paradoxes begin to function as conclusions, and later as premises, of arguments

... noises start to convey information. The process of becoming stale, familiar, unpara-
doxical and platitudinous is the process by which such noises cross the line from "mere"
causes of belief to reasons for belief' (R. Rorty, *Objectivity, Relativism, and Truth*, p.
171).
38 D. E. Cooper, *Metaphor*, Aristotelian Society Series, vol. 5, Oxford: Blackwell, 1986,
p. 165.
39 See on this topic A. M. Muratori, 'Dal ''non comunicato'' alla comunicazione', in A. M.
Muratori (ed.), *La relazione analitica*, Rome: Borla, 1981, pp. 135–40.
40 R. Rorty, *Objectivity, Relativism, and Truth*, p. 171.

8   THE AWARENESS OF METAPHORIC PROJECTIONS

1 Aristotle, *Poetics*, paragraph 22, 1459a 5–8, pp. 2234–5. *The Complete Works of
Aristotle*, Revised Oxford Translation, edited by Jonathan Barnes, vol. II, Bollingen
Series LXXI.2, Princeton, N. J.: Princeton University Press, 1985.
2 Ibid., 1459a 5–8.
3 Ibid., 1459a 5–8.
4 P. F. Strawson, 'Imagination and Perception', in *Freedom and Resentment and Other
Essays*, London and New York: Methuen, 1974, p. 53, italics added. As the idea of
rational activity is customarily associated with mental processes aimed at decision-
making, whatever inner dynamics are independent of decisions tend to be regarded as
passive or irrational. In this general perspective of rational activity affectual experiences
are taken as passive and therefore irrational. And yet it is not clear why 'passive' attitudes
must also be irrational or why affectual processes are necessarily passive, or detached
from any rational thought. The 'seeing as' dynamics involved in seeing things in a
different way requires the application of concepts or thoughts which, therefore, somehow
become part of attitudes, feelings and emotions. To avoid these considerations is to insist
on an obsolete and misguiding dichotomy between what is to count as rational, or
irrational, on the basis of criteria which are not related to, or strictly implied by, the
structure of any current epistemology (F. M. Berenson, *Understanding Persons: Personal and Impersonal Relationships*, Brighton: Harvester Press, 1981, pp. 120–1).
5 Aristotle, *Poetics*, 1457b 8–9, p. 1457.
6 To try to insist on purely intellectual accounts requires that we blind ourselves to
important features about our arguments and discussions. We should, for instance, ignore
the question whether we could make sense of the general notion of human agency without
any reference to affectual concepts; we should not even ask whether we could grasp as
intelligible the notion of a calculating, rational, dispassionate agent – ultimately a lifeless
agent. Such an account of 'agency' would be immediately called into question inasmuch
as we regard an agent as someone engaging in activities which to a lesser or greater extent
he cares about. And there is no sufficient reason for regarding such a purely calculating
subject as a proper human agent. Central features of human agency thus cannot be
adequately understood independently of some ultimate connection with our roots as
organisms.
7 N. Goodman, *Languages of Art*, Brighton: Harvester Press, 1977, p. 7.
8 L. Wittgenstein, *The Blue and Brown Books. Preliminary Studies for the 'Philosophical
Investigations'*, Oxford: Blackwell, 1989, p. 117, italics added.
9 In Strawson's inimitable language this is the general picture of the (Cartesian) schism:
'It is not enough to acknowledge that a person has two sides to his nature and his history,
a mental or conscious side and a material or corporeal side. For really the history of a
human being is not the history of one two-sided thing, it is the history of two one-sided
things. One of these things is a material object, a body; the other is an immaterial object,
a soul or mind or spirit or individual consciousness . . . None of the predicates which
properly apply to bodies . . . apply to minds; and none of the predicates which properly

apply to consciousness . . . apply to bodies. During the lifetime of a human being, two of these things, one of each kind, are peculiarly intimately related; but the intimacy of their union does not count against or diminish the essential independence of their nature' (P. F. Strawson, 'Self, mind and body', in *Freedom and Resentment and Other Essays*, p. 170.

10 'It has often been observed that modern Western society is typified by a certain "disembodied" style of life . . . Furthermore, far from being indigenous just to modern society, a certain telos toward disembodiment is an abiding strain of Western intellectual history. The Platonic emphasis on the purified soul, the Cartesian focus on the "cogito" experience, pull us toward a vision of self within which an immaterial rationality is central. The body has frequently been relegated to a secondary oppositional role, while an incorporeal reason is valorized' (D. Leder, *The Absent Body*, Chicago and London: University of Chicago Press, 1990, pp. 2–3).

11 See M. J. Apter, 'Metaphor as synergy', in D. Miall (ed.), *Metaphor: Problems and Perspectives*, Brighton: Harvester Press, 1982, p. 65.

12 For an extended discussion of this topic see 'The power of discourse and the strength of listening' in G. Corradi Fiumara, *The Other Side of Language: A Philosophy of Listening*, London and New York: Routledge, 1990, pp. 52–71.

13 Leder significantly remarks that 'Cartesian categories of mind and body merely reify and segregate classes of experience that stand in ceaseless interchange. Times in which the body is most tacit and self-transcending are collected under the rubric of rational "mind". Other experiences, where corporeality comes to strong thematic presence, are collected under the rubric of "body".' He also argues that 'It is true that splitting the self into *res cogitans* and *res extensa* is incongruent with many aspects of lived experience. As such, the Cartesian account is often assumed to arise from metaphysical or epistemological commitments to the detriment of attending to the life-world. I have suggested a different interpretation; it is from the very immediacy of the life-world that this dualism is first brought forth and by which it is continually sanctioned. The onto-valuational opposition of rational mind and body may be a misreading, but one motivated by the lived body itself' (D. Leder, *The Absent Body*, p. 149).

14 'Philosophy is a battle against the bewitchment of our intelligence by means of language' (L. Wittgenstein, *Philosophical Investigations*, translated by G. E. M. Anscombe, Oxford: Blackwell, 1988, paragraph 109, p. 47e).

15 L. Wittgenstein, *Blue and Brown Books. Preliminary Studies for the 'Philosophical Investigations'*, p. 6.

16 Indeed the examination of latent, pre-emptive assumptions can be one of the more fruitful ways of approaching the epistemic trends of our culture; it is a seminal dimension which rests hardly acknowledged in philosophy. 'In a certain sense, therefore, the distinction involved in some, at least, of the categories, *viz.*, space, time, thing and person, are present in the sense percepts of animals . . . It is clear that historically and phylogenetically perceptual elements anticipatory of some of the categories existed prior to the genesis of thought' (William K. Wright, 'The genesis of the categories', *Journal of Philosophy, Psychology and Scientific Methods*, 10, 1913, pp. 645–57).

'Metaphor is not an isolated phenomenon of passing interest – just the reverse: it raises deep epistemological and ontological issues and challenges many traditional assumptions especially those of Anglo-American philosophy' (M. Johnson (ed.), *Philosophical Perspectives on Metaphor*, Minneapolis, Minn.: University of Minnesota Press, 1981, p. 4).

There is also perhaps a challenge to the visual metaphor of western philosophy, namely to the pre-emptive assumption that language serves to produce accurate representations – 'mirror images', almost – of reality. The challenge consists in demonstrating that there actually is such a metaphor at work and that it is no more than a fairly stable seminal metaphor.

17 M. Johnson, *The Body in the Mind: The Bodily Basis of Meaning, Imagination and Reasoning*, Chicago and London: University of Chicago Press, 1987, p. xv.
18 In Quine's view the philosopher's task differs from the others' only in detail and 'in no such drastic way as those suppose who imagine for the philosopher a vantage point outside the conceptual scheme that he takes in charge. *There is no such cosmic exile.* He cannot study . . . the fundamental . . . scheme of . . . common sense without having some conceptual scheme, whether the same or another . . . , in which to work' (W. V. O. Quine, *Word and Object*, Cambridge, Mass.: MIT Press, 1981, pp. 275–6).
19 G. Corradi Fiumara, *The Symbolic Function: Psychoanalysis and the Philosophy of Language*, Oxford and Cambridge, Mass.: Blackwell, 1992; see chapter 11, 'From biological life to dialogic relations' and especially the paragraphs 'On interactive interpretations', 'The interpretative effort', and 'Reciprocity in early dialogue', pp. 154–77.
20 M. Johnson, 'The emergence of meaning through schematic structure', in *The Body in the Mind*, pp. 18–40.
21 Ibid., p. 75.
22 Ibid., p. 87.
23 Ibid., pp. 95–6.
24 Ibid., chapter 4, 'Metaphorical projections of image schemata', pp. 65–100.
25 J. Bruner, *Acts of Meaning*, Cambridge, Mass. and London: Harvard University Press, 1990, p. xv.
26 M. Johnson, *The Body in the Mind*, p. 169.
27 Ibid., p. 169.
28 D. Leder, *The Absent Body*, p. 155.
29 P. F. Strawson, *Freedom and Resentment and Other Essays*, p. 168.
30 Ibid., pp. 126–48. The idea of a pure mind which is subjective and prior to the objective – logically severed from 'reality' – is lucidly criticized by Davidson in 'The varieties of knowledge'; he concludes with the suggestion that 'the thoughts we form and entertain are located conceptually in the world we inhabit, and know we inhabit, with others'. The picture of thought which be sketches here 'leaves no room for such priority since it predicates self-knowledge on knowledge of other minds and of the world. The objective and the inter-subjective are thus essential to anything we can call subjectivity, and constitute the context in which it takes form' (p. 8, unpublished).
31 M. J. Apter, 'Metaphor as synergy', in D. Miall (ed.), *Metaphor: Problems and Perspectives*, p. 65.
32 H. A. Wolfson, *Philo: Foundations of Religious Philosophy in Judaism, Christianity, and Islam*, vol. I, Cambridge, Mass.: Harvard University Press, 1947, pp. 106–7.
33 Aristotle, *Politics*, Book I, 1252b 1, pp. 1986–7.
34 Aristotle, *Nicomachean Ethics*, Book VIII, 1161a 31–1161b 2, p. 1835.
35 Aristotle, *Posterior Analytics*, b 37, p. 162.
36 J. Kepler, quoted by D. Gentner in D. S. Miall (ed.), *Metaphor: Problems and Perspectives*, p. 106. Also quoted in G. Polya, *Mathematics and Plausible Reasoning*, vol.I, Princeton, N. J. : Princeton University Press, 1973.
37 M. Arbib and M. B. Hesse, *The Construction of Reality*, Cambridge: Cambridge University Press, 1986, p. 83.
38 L. Wittgenstein, *Philosophical Investigations*, translated by G. E. M. Anscombe, Oxford: Blackwell, 1988, p. 220 e.
39 J. Habermas, *Theory of Communicative Action*, vol. I, Boston, Mass.: Beacon Press, 1984, p.110.

9 THE METAPHORIC FUNCTION

1 The popular idea of timelessness which seems embedded in much of the philosophy of

language can be deceptive in the sense that it leads us to ignore the language of infancy and senescence. Our philosophy seems to depend upon a language of self-affirmation even in the awareness of one's having to die, so that ultimately only the language of a 'permanent' philosophical life is considered. Interest in metaphors seems somehow to reflect such invisible philosophical constraints.

2 For an introductory discussion of this topic see T. Cohen, 'Metaphor and the cultivation of intimacy', *Critical Inquiry* 5(1), 1978, pp. 3–12. The essay also appears in S. Sacks (ed.), *On Metaphor (based on a Symposium 'Metaphor: the Conceptual Leap')*, Chicago and London: University of Chicago Press, 1981.

3 D. E. Cooper, *Metaphor*, Aristotelian Society Series, vol. 5, Oxford: Blackwell, 1986, p. 141.

4 Ibid., p. 141.

5 Aristotle, *Poetics*, paragraph 22, 1459a 5–8. *The Complete Works of Aristotle*, Revised Oxford Translation, edited by J. Barnes, vol. II, Bollingen Series LXXI.2; Princeton, N.J.: Princeton University Press, 1985, pp. 2234–5.

6 Oedipus, Hamlet, and Smerdyakov 'know' precisely the things that they cannot propositionally enunciate. This general topic is discussed in a psychoanalytic perspective by C. Bollas in *The Shadow of the Object: Psychoanalysis of the Unthought Known*, London: Free Association Books, 1987.

7 For an innovative philosophical discussion of this issue see P. Ricoeur, *Soi-même comme un autre*, Paris: Editions du Seuil, 1990.

8 See J. Fernandez, 'The mission of metaphor in expressive culture', *Current Anthropoloy*, 15(2), 1974, pp. 119–33.

9 The issue is discussed in O. Kitayama, 'Metaphorization – making terms', *International Journal of Psycho-Analysis*, 1987, 68(4), pp. 499–509.

10 R. Rorty, *Philosophy and the Mirror of Nature*, Oxford: Blackwell, 1980, Introduction, pp. 3–13.

11 'It is true that we compare a picture that is firmly rooted in us to a superstition; but it is equally true that we *always* eventually have to reach some firm ground, either a picture or something else, so that a picture which is the root of all our thinking is to be respected and not treated as a superstition' (L. Wittgenstein, *Culture and Value*, translated by P. Winch, edited by G. H. von Wright in collaboration with H. Nyman, Oxford: Blackwell, 1980, p. 83e).

12 O. Kitayama, 'Metaphorization – making terms', pp. 499–509.

13 L. Wittgenstein, *Culture and Value*, p. 73.

14 O. Kitayama, 'Metaphorization – making terms', p. 507.

15 J. R. Eiser, *Attitudes, Chaos and the Connectionist Mind*, Oxford and Cambridge, Mass.: Blackwell, 1994, p. 209.

16 Ibid., pp. 211–12.

17 The complex experiences of early affectual and cognitive investments induce the nascent mind to equate objects with other objects and thus to make ever new equations, which form the basis of interest in world and language. Our earliest forms of metaphoricity rescue the developing self from stagnant contexts of significance and thus enhance opportunities for ever new openings: inasmuch as early 'metaphor' leads to the construction of experiences, to which one could not otherwise gain access, an original propensity to metaphorize cannot be reduced to a mere transfer of meanings. For a discussion of symbolic equations, embryonic metaphoricity and primal dialogue see G. Corradi Fiumara, *The Symbolic Function: Psychoanalysis and the Philosophy of Language*, especially chapters 9, 10 and 11, Oxford and Cambridge, Mass.: Blackwell, 1992.

18 M. J. Apter, 'Metaphor as synergy', in D. Miall (ed.), *Metaphor: Problems and Perspectives*, Brighton: Harvester Press, 1982, pp. 55–70.

19 Ibid., p. 67.

20 J. Bruner and C. Fleisher Feldman, 'Metaphors of consciousness and cognition in the

history of psychology', in D. E. Leary (ed.), *Metaphors in the History of Psychology*, Cambridge: Cambridge University Press, 1990, p. 231.

21 Ibid., p. 231.

22 Ibid., p. 235.

23 F. Nietzsche, *Die fröhliche Wissenschaft*, in *Opere di F. Nietzsche*, vol. V, translated by F. Masini and M. Montinari, edited by G. Colli and M. Montinari, Milan: Adelphi, 1965, p. 329.

24 W. V. O. Quine, 'A Postscript on Metaphor', *Critical Inquiry*, 5(1), 1978, pp. 161–2.

25 Heraclitus, fragment 52. See K. Freeman, *Ancilla to the Pre-Socratic Philosophers: Complete Translation of the Fragments in Diels 'Fragmente des Vorsokratiker'*, Oxford: Blackwell, 1956, p. 28.

26 M. Heidegger, *Der Satz vom Grund*, Pfullingen: Neske, 1971, p. 187.

27 L. Wittgenstein, *Philosophical Investigations*, translated by G. E. M. Anscombe, Oxford: Blackwell, 1988, paragraphs 45–7, pp. 132e–33e.

28 E. V. M. Lieven, 'Conversations between mothers and young children: individual differences and their possible implication for the study of language learning', in N. Waterson and C. Snow (eds), *The Development of Communication*, Chichester and New York: John Wiley and Sons, 1978, pp. 173–87.

29 Ibid., p. 173.

30 Lieven remarks that considerable discussion has centred on the very high proportion of questions in adults' speech to young children, relative to their normal speech. Questions, at least in speech among adults, presuppose answers and are a device for ensuring continued turn-taking in conversation. Such a high proportion of questions may indicate interest, curiosity or a disposition to listen (p. 174).

31 'No more fiendish punishment could be devised, were such a thing physically possible, than that one should be turned loose in society and remain absolutely unnoticed by all the members thereof. If no one turned round when we entered, answered when we spoke, or minded what we did, but if every person we met "cut us dead", and acted as if we were non-existing things, a kind of rage and impotent despair would ere long well up in us, from which the cruellest bodily tortures would be a relief; for those who would make us feel that, however bad might be our plight, we had not sunk to such a depth as to be unworthy of attention at all' (W. James, *Principles of Psychology*, New York: Henry Holt, 1980, pp. 293–4).

32 E. Winner, 'Early metaphors in spontaneous speech', in C. Cacciari (ed.), *Teorie della metafora. L'acquisizione, la comprensione e l'uso del linguaggio figurato*, Milan: Raffaello Cortina Editore, 1991, p. 36. Winner's article first appeared in *The Point of Words. Children's Understanding of Metaphor and Irony*, Cambridge: Cambridge University Press, 1988, pp. 90–109.

33 J. Piaget, *Play, Dream and Imitation in Childhood*, New York: Norton, 1962, pp. 227–8; quoted in E. Winner, 'Early metaphors in spontaneous speech', p. 37.

34 E. Winner, 'Early metaphors in spontaneous speech', p. 41.

35 Ibid., p. 40.

36 Ibid., p. 40.

37 Ibid., p. 40.

38 Ibid., pp. 43–4.

39 M. J. Apter, 'Metaphor as synergy', p. 57.

40 Ibid., p. 57.

41 Ibid., p.58.

42 The issue of symmetries and asymmetries constitutes the core of Matte Blanco's contributions to the theory of psychoanalysis. There is a further corollary to the operation of the principle of symmetry: when this principle holds, a *part* of something is equal to the *whole* and is therefore indistinguishable from it. The equation – that is, the symmetrization of the relationship – between the part and the whole of any object is frequently observed in clinical practice and ordinary life (I. Matte Blanco, *Thinking, Feeling and*

Being: Clinical Reflections on the Fundamental Antinomy of Human Beings and World, The New Library of Psychoanalysis, no.5, London and New York: Routledge, 1989, p. 21. This work should be seen in conjunction with *The Unconscious as Infinite Sets: an Essay in Bi-logic*, London: Duckworth, 1975.

43 M. J. Apter, 'Metaphor as synergy', p. 58.

44 Ibid., p. 59.

45 Ibid., p. 61.

46 I. Matte Blanco, *The Unconscious as Infinite Sets*, pp. 93–4.

47 I. Matte Blanco, *Thinking, Feeling and Being*, p. 20.

48 L. Woolley, *The Beginnings of Civilization*, New York: Mentor Books, 1963; quoted in J. C. Eccles, *The Human Mystery*, Berlin and Heidelberg: Springer International, 1979, p. 110.

49 G. Galilei, *Dialogue on the Great World Systems*, the Salisbury translation, revised, annotated and with an introduction by G. de Santillana, Chicago: University of Chicago Press, 1953, pp. 116–17.

50 L. Wittgenstein, *Philosophical Investigations*, paragraph 122, p. 49e, emphasis added.

51 M. Arbib and M. B. Hesse, *The Construction of Reality*, Cambridge: Cambridge University Press, 1986, p. 154.

52 Aristotle, *Poetics*, 1457b, 6–9.

53 I. A. Richards, *The Philosophy of Rhetoric*, Oxford: Oxford University Press, 1936. In the 1965 edition printed in New York, this passage appears at p. 93.

54 R. Rorty, *Objectivity, Relativism and Truth: Philosophical Papers*, vol. I, Cambridge: Cambridge University Press, 1991, p. 93.

55 Ibid., p. 94.

56 The metaphoric linking of one term with another may repeat itself indefinitely thoughout the life cycle of the individual and of the phatic community. As a concept emerges more distinctly from its vehicle and acquires firm referential boundaries it can enter into metaphoric relations of its own. In our linguistic lives literal and figurative senses will interpenetrate and shape each other at every stage.

57 J. Hornsby, 'Speech acts and pornography', *Women's Philosophy Review*, 10, 1993, pp. 38–45.

58 J. L. Austin, *How to Do Things with Words*, William James Lectures delivered at Harvard University in 1955, edited by J. O. Urmson and M. Sbisà, Oxford: Clarendon Press, 1975. Italian translation by M. Gentile and M. Sbisà, *Quando dire è fare*, Turin: Marietti, 1974, p. 189.

59 J. Hornsby, 'Speech acts and pornography', p. 50. J. R. Searle, *Speech Acts*, London: Cambridge University Press, 1969, p. 58.

60 Ibid., p. 42.

61 Ibid., p. 41.

62 Ibid., p. 40.

63 D. Davidson, *Inquiries into Truth and Interpretation*, Oxford: Clarendon Press, 1985, p. 197.

64 Ibid., p. 153.

65 Ibid., p. 153.

66 J. Hornsby, 'Speech acts and pornography', p. 41.

67 Ibid., p. 41.

68 Ibid., p. 42. Hornsby specifies that the quotation from Judge Wild is from a summing up, as reported in *The Sunday Times* of 12 December 1982.

69 M. Johnson, *The Body in The Mind: The Bodily Basis of Meaning, Imagination and Reasoning*, Chicago and London: University of Chicago Press, 1987.

70 Ibid., p. 1.

71 Ibid., p. 1.

72 Ibid., pp. xiv–xv.

73 Ibid., p. xvi.

74 R. Descartes, 'The principles of philosophy', in E. Haldane and G. R. T. Ross (eds), *The Philosophical Works of Descartes*, vol. I, Cambridge: Cambridge University Press, 1911, p. 237.
75 M. Johnson, *The Body in the Mind*, pp. 21–2.
76 Ibid., p. 30.
77 Ibid., p. 22.
78 Ibid., p. 22.
79 Ibid., p. 28.
80 Ibid., p. 74.
81 Ibid., p. 75.
82 Ibid., p. 76.
83 Ibid., p. 74.
84 Salimbene de Adam of Parma, 'Chronicon parmense: avvenimenti tra il 1167 e il 1287', in A. Viscardi, B. and T. Nardi, G. Vidossi and F. Arese (eds), *La letteratura italiana: Storia e testi. Le origini*, Milan and Naples: Riccardo Ricciardi Editore, 1946, p. 979.

10 VICISSITUDES OF SELF-FORMATION

1 H. Putnam, *Renewing Philosophy*, Cambridge, Mass.: Harvard University Press, 1992, p. 13.
2 M. Arbib and M. B. Hesse, *The Construction of Reality*, Cambridge: Cambridge University Press, 1986, p. 39.
3 D. Davidson, 'Communication and convention', in *Inquiries into Truth and Interpretation*, Oxford: Clarendon Press, 1985, p. 280.
4 For more relevant, related discussion see J. Bruner, *Acts of Meaning*, Cambridge, Mass. and London: Harvard University Press, 1990, p. 12.
5 On this topic see P. Lepenne, *On Autobiography*, Minneapolis, Minn.: University of Minnesota Press, 1989, p. 132.
6 M. Arbib and M. B. Hesse, *The Construction of Reality*, p. 39. Davidson argues that various theories labouring on the problem of 'how metaphors work' ultimately do not 'provide a method for deciphering an encoded content'; they rather tell us (or try to tell us) something about the *effects* metaphors have on us (D. Davidson, 'What metaphors mean', in *Inquiries into Truth and Interpretation*, p. 245). Rorty comments that 'Davidson can cheerfully agree with the positivists that those effects are "psychological" rather than "logical". But the acquisition of knowledge is, after all, a psychological matter' (R. Rorty, *Objectivity, Relativism and Truth: Philosophical Papers*, vol. I, Cambridge: Cambridge University Press, 1991, p. 168).
7 With reference to this passage see T. Nagel, *Mortal Questions*, Cambridge: Cambridge University Press, 1979 p. 7. Relevant, related material is also to be found in T. Nagel, *The View from Nowhere*, Oxford: Oxford University Press, 1986. As a corollary we could say that the living complexity of inner life constitutes an irreducible feature of reality, a cognitive factor without which we could not even do physics, a factor which should occupy as important a place in any credible approach to reality as verification, quantification and formalization.
8 D. E. Cooper, *Metaphor*, Aristotelian Society Series, vol. 5, Oxford: Blackwell, 1986, p. 223.
9 Wheelwright suggests that the essential possibility of metaphor lies in the broad ontological fact that new qualities and new meanings can emerge, simply come into being, out of some hitherto ungrouped combination of elements. 'If one can imagine a state of the world, perhaps a trillion years ago, before hydrogen atoms and oxygen atoms had ever come together, it may be presumed that up to that time water did not exist. Somewhere in the later vastitude of time, then, water first came into being – when just those two necessary elements came together at last under the right conditions of

temperature and pressure. Analogous novelties occur in the sphere of meanings as well. As in nature new qualities may be engendered by the coming together of elements in new ways, so too in poetry new suggestions of meaning can be engendered by the juxtaposition of previously unjoined words and images' (P. Wheelwright, *Metaphor and Reality* Bloomington, Ind.: Indiana University Press, 1962, pp. 85–6.

10 G. Bateson, *Steps to an Ecology of Mind*, New York: Ballantine Books, 1972, pp. 323–37.

11 It is the quality of a dialogue stemming from the relationship itself which permits freer transitions from the abstract to the concrete, from the general to the particular, and vice versa.

12 Paradoxically, the more our thinking potential can be described as 'intimate', 'profound', 'subjective', the more its development is dependent upon the quality of the interpersonal relationship in which the transformation from simply being to existing, from 'knowing' something to thinking it, is either aided or hindered. In fact, only if the nascent self is able to perceive himself as a party to a relationship of mutual recognition can he face the challenge of self-awareness.

13 J. Bruner, *Acts of Meaning*, p. 72.

14 What the utterer intends his hearer to understand is not only his meaning but the fact that this meaning is intended, aimed to, sought out. In his introduction to *Word and Object*, Quine stresses that 'Language is a *social art*' (W. V. O. Quine, *Word and Object*, Cambridge, Mass.: MIT Press, 1981, p. ix (emphasis added)).

15 C. Bollas, *The Shadow of the Object: Psychoanalysis of the Unthought Known*, London: Free Association Books, 1987.

16 Black remarks that 'Every implication complex supported by a metaphor's secondary subject . . . is a *model* of the ascriptions imputed to the primary subject. Every metaphor is the tip of a submerged model' (M. Black, 'More about metaphor', in A. Ortony (ed.), *Metaphor and Thought*, Cambridge: Cambridge University Press, 1980, p. 31).

17 G. Lakoff, and M. Johnson, *Metaphors We Live By*, Chicago and London: University of Chicago Press, 1980, p. 236.

18 J. Laplanche and J. B. Pontalis, *The Language of Psychoanalysis*, translated by D. Nicholson-Smith, London: Hogarth Press, 1973, p. 166.

19 Only recently have children been studied in the world in which their interactive development takes place, or in a context in which we can be sensitive to the subtleties of their social lives. But this is no more a plea for an 'ecological situatedness' in developmental research. The point is that an understanding of human interactions, however formalized it may eventually become, always begins with a practice in which the immature person is involved as an agent, a victim, an accomplice or in any other role. With reference to the above see J. Bruner, *Acts of Meaning*, p. 85, and J. Dunn, *The Beginnings of Social Understanding*, Cambridge, Mass.: Harvard University Press, 1988, p. 5. Bruner also remarks that there are certain generalized communicative skills crucial to language which seem in place before language proper begins and which are later incorporated into the child's speech once it begins: 'Joint attention to a putative referent, turn taking, mutual exchange, to mention the most prominent'. And one cannot avoid wondering what language would be like if these crucial skills were not previously at work (J. Bruner, *Acts of Meaning*, p. 71).

20 In this connection see the distinction between meta-bolic and dia-bolic processes in G. Corradi Fiumara, *The Symbolic Function. Psychoanalysis and the Philosophy of Language*, Oxford and Cambridge, Mass.: Blackwell, 1992, p. 149.

21 P. Wheelwright, *Metaphor and Reality*, p. 71.

22 It is important also to recognize the creative experiences of the individual in his own terms, that is, with a measure of freedom from the compulsion to automatically translate them in terms of whatever theories are at work in any local culture and with a continual interest in the construal of whatever world-views they propagate.

23 Some humans almost seem to develop a fixation for seeking 'parental', 'interpretative' roles. As long as they can stage cultural interactions in which dependent figures look up

at them as linguistic referents, or irreplaceable sources of cognitive life, they may well dispense with their own journey to maturity; the sufficient condition for their identity may amount to no more than exhibiting features of parental 'authority', however circumscribed. For a discussion of the usurpation of one's symbolic potential see G. Corradi Fiumara, 'Reciprocity in early dialogue', in *The Symbolic Function: Psychoanalysis and the Philosophy of Language*, pp. 174–7.

24 This issue is also discussed in 'The logocentric system of culture' and 'A philosophy of listening within a tradition of questioning' in G. Corradi Fiumara, *The Other Side of Language: A Philosophy of Listening*, London and New York: Routledge, 1990, pp. 18–27 and 28–51.
25 For a discussion of this problem see 'Pseudosymbols and the philosophy of education', in G. Corradi Fiumara, *The Symbolic Function*, pp. 106–8.
26 This concept has been extensively developed by C. Bollas, *The Shadow of the Object*, 'Extractive introjection', pp. 157–69.
27 This clinical hypothesis also originates in C. Bollas, ibid., p. 19.
28 F. Nietzsche, 'On truth and lies in a nonmoral sense', in *Philosophy and Truth: Selection from Nietzsche's Notebooks of the early 1870s*, Atlantic Hyland, N.J.: Humanities Press, 1979, p. 89.
29 W. R. Bion, *Attention and Interpretation: A Scientific Approach to Insight in Psychoanalysis and Groups*, London: Tavistock, 1970, p. 105.
30 E. F. Kittay, *Metaphor: Its Cognitive Force and Linguistic Structure*, Oxford: Clarendon Press, 1987, p. 312.
31 See C. Bollas, *The Shadow of the Object*, pp. 15–18.
32 The basic ideas of this discussion are stated in G. Corradi Fiumara, *The Other Side of Language: A Philosophy of Listening*, expecially in the paragraphs entitled 'Circular causality in the dialogic field', pp. 117–20, 'The listening experience as event', pp. 120–3, and in chapter 10, 'Midwifery and philosophy', pp. 143–68.
33 See G. Corradi Fiumara, paragraph entitled 'Pseudosymbols and the philosophy of education', in *The Symbolic Function*, pp. 103–6.
34 D. E. Cooper, *Metaphor*, p. 164.
35 Ibid., pp. 157–8.
36 T. Cohen, 'Metaphor and the cultivation of intimacy', *Critical Inquiry*, 5(1), 1978, pp. 3–12.
37 See G. Corradi Fiumara, *The Symbolic Function*, pp. 122, 132, 143, 149.

Bibliography

Aarts, J. P. and Colbert, J., *Metaphor and Non-Metaphor: The Semantics of Adjective–Noun Combinations*. Tübingen: Niemeyer, 1979.

Abercrombie, L., *The Theory of Poetry*. New York: Harcourt Brace, 1926.

Allen, B., *Truth in Philosophy*. Cambridge, Mass. and London: Harvard University Press, 1993.

Amati Mehler, J., Argentieri, S., Canestri, J., 'The Babel of the unconscious', *International Journal of Psycho-Analysis*, 71, 1990, pp. 569–83.

Apter, M. J., 'Metaphor as synergy', in D. Miall (ed.), *Metaphor: Problems and Perspectives*. Brighton: Harvester Press, 1982, pp. 55–70.

Arbib, M. and Hesse, M. B., *The Construction of Reality*. Cambridge: Cambridge University Press, 1986.

X Arbib, M., *The Metaphorical Brain*. New York: Wiley-Interscience, 1972.

Aristotle, *The Complete Works of Aristotle*. Revised Oxford Translation, edited by J. Barnes, vols I and II, Bollingen Series LXXI.2. Princeton, N. J.: Princeton University Press, 1985.

Aristotle, *Metaphysics*, Books I–I, trans. H. Tredennick. Cambridge, Mass.: Harvard University Press, 1980.

Audi, R., *Practical Reasoning*. London: Routledge, 1989.

Austin, J. L., *How to Do Things with Words*. William James Lectures delivered at Harvard University in 1955, ed. J. O. Urmson and M. Sbisà, Oxford: Clarendon Press, 1975.

Aylwin, S., *Structure in Thought and Feeling*. London: Methuen, 1985.

Ayala, F. J., 'The concept of biological progress', in F. J. Ayala and T. Dobzhansky (eds), *Studies in Philosophy of Biology*. Berkeley, Calif.: University of California Press, 1974, pp. 339–54.

Bachelard, G., *La poétique de l'espace*. Paris: Presses Universitaires de France, 1957.

Barfield, O., 'The meaning of the word "Literal" ', in L. C. Knights and C. Basil (eds), *Metaphor and Symbol*. London: Butterworth Scientific Publications, 1960.

Barfield, O., 'Poetic diction and legal fiction', in M. Black (ed.), *The Importance of Language*. Englewood Cliffs, N. J.: Prentice Hall, 1962, pp. 57–71.

Barfield, O., *Poetic Diction: A study in Meaning*. New York: Mc Graw Hill, 1964.

Baron, J., *Rationality and Intelligence*. Cambridge: Cambridge University Press, 1985.

Barth, E. M., *The Logic of Articles in Traditional Philosophy*. Dordrecht: Reidel, 1974.

Barth, E. M., *Perspectives on Analytic Philosophy*. Amsterdam: North Holland Publishing Company, 1979.

Barth, E. M., 'Waiting for Godot: on attitudes towards artefacts vs. entities, as related to different phases of operation in cognition', *Epistemologia*, XIV, 1991, pp. 77–104.

Barth, E. M. and Krabbe, E. C. W., *From Axiom to Dialogue*. Berlin: De Gruyter, 1982.

Barth, E. M. and Martens, J. L. (eds), *Argumentation: Approaches to Theory Formation*. Amsterdam: John Benjamins, 1982.

Barth, E. M. and Wiche, R. T. P., *Problems, Functions and Semantic Roles*. Berlin: De Gruyter, 1986.

Bateson, G., *Steps to an Ecology of Mind*. New York: Ballantine Books, 1972.

Bateson, G., *Mind and Nature: A Necessary Unity*. New York: Bantam Books, 1979.

Bateson, M. C., *Our Own Metaphor*. New York: Knopf, 1972.

Baynes, K., Bohman, J. and McCarthy, T. (eds), *After Philosophy: End or Transformation?*, Cambridge, Mass.: MIT Press, 1987.

Beardsley, M. C., Metaphor, *Encyclopaedia of Philosophy*, vol.5, New York: Macmillan, 1967, pp. 284–9.

Beardsley, M. C., ' Metaphorical senses', *Noûs*, 12, 1978, pp. 3–16.

Beardsley, M. C., 'The metaphorical twist', *Philosophy and Phenomenological Research*, 22(3), 1962, pp. 293–307.

Beavin Bavelas, J., Black, A., Chovil, N. and Mullett, J., *Equivocal Communication*. London: Sage Publications, 1990.

Beck, B. E., 'The metaphor as a mediator between semantic and analogic modes of thought', *Current Anthropology*, 19, 1978, pp. 83–94.

Bedini, S., 'The instruments of Galileo Galilei', in E. McMullin (ed.), *Galileo, Man of Science*. New York: Basic Books, 1967, pp. 257–67.

Benhabib, S., *Critique, Norm and Utopia: A Study of the Foundations of Critical Theory*. New York: Columbia University Press, 1986.

Berenson, F. M., *Understanding Persons: Personal and Impersonal Relationships*. Brighton: Harvester Press, 1981.

Berggren, D., 'The use and abuse of metaphor', *Review of Metaphysics*, 16(2), 1962, pp. 237–58; and 16(3), 1963, pp. 450–72.

Best, C. T., *Hemispheric Function and Collaboration in the Child*. Orlando, Fla.: Academic Press, 1985.

Bettelheim, B., *The Uses of Enchantment*. New York: Alfred A. Knopf, 1976.

Bickerton, D., 'Prolegomena to a linguistic theory of metaphor', *Foundations of Language*, 5(1), 1969, pp. 34–52.

Binkley, T., 'On the truth and probity of metaphor', *Journal of Aesthetics and Art Criticism*, 33(2), 1974, pp. 171–80.

Bion, W. R., *All my Sins Remembered: The Other Side of Genius*. Abingdon, Berks.: Fleetwood Press, 1985.

Bion, W. R., *Attention and Interpretation: A Scientific Approach to Insight in Psychoanalysis and Groups*. London: Tavistock Publications, 1970.

Bion, W. R., 'A theory of thinking', *International Journal of Psycho-Analysis*, 43, 1962, pp. 306–10.

Black, M., *Models and Metaphors: Studies in Language and Philosophy*. Ithaca, N. Y.: Cornell University Press, 1962.

Black, M., 'Metaphor', in M. Johnson (ed.), *Philosophical Perspectives on Metaphor*. Minneapolis, Minn.: University of Minnesota Press, 1981.

Black, M., 'Metaphor', *Proceedings of the Aristotelian Society*, 55, 1954–5, pp. 273–94.

Black, M., 'How metaphors work: a reply to Donald Davidson', in S. Sacks (ed.), *On Metaphor*. Chicago and London: University of Chicago Press, 1979, pp. 181–92.

Black, M., 'More about metaphor', *Dialectica*, 31 (3–4), 1977, pp. 431–57 and in A. Ortony (ed.), *Metaphor and Thought*, Cambridge: Cambridge University Press, 1980.

Blackburn, S., *Spreading the Word*. Oxford: Oxford University Press, 1984.

Blakemore, C. and Greenfield, S. (eds), *Mindwaves: Thoughts on Intelligence, Identity and Consciousness*. London: Blackwell, 1987.

Blumenberg, H., *Paradigmi per una metaforologia*. Bologna: Il Mulino, 1969.

Bolinger, D., *Language: The Loaded Weapon*. London: Longman, 1980.

Bollas, C., *The Shadow of the Object: Psychoanalysis of the Unthought Known*. London: Free Association Books, 1987.

Bohr, N., *Atomic Physics and Human Knowledge*. New York: John Wiley and Sons, 1958.

Brandon, R., 'Reference explained away', *Journal of Philosophy*, 81(9), 1984, 469–92.

Briosi, S., *Il senso della metafora*. Naples: Liguori, 1985.

Brown, R. W., *A First Language: The Early Stages*. Cambridge, Mass.: Harvard University Press, 1973.

Brooke-Rose, C., *A Grammar of Metaphor*. London: Secker and Warburg, 1970.

Bruner, J., *On Knowing: Essays for the Left Hand*. Cambridge, Mass.: Harvard University Press, 1962 and New York: Atheneum, 1966.

Bruner, J., *Actual Minds, Possible Worlds*. Cambridge, Mass.: Harvard University Press, 1986.

Bruner, J., *Acts of Meaning*. Cambridge, Mass. and London: Harvard University Press, 1990.

Bruner, J. and Fleisher Feldman, C., 'Metaphors of consciousness and cognition in the history of psychology', in D. E. Leary (ed.), *Metaphors in the History of Psychology*. Cambridge: Cambridge University Press, 1990, pp. 230–8.

Bubner, R., *Essays in Hermeneutics and Critical Theory*. New York: Columbia University Press, 1988.

Budick, S., and Iser W. (eds), *Language of the Unsayable: The Play of Negativity in Literature and Literary Theory*. New York: Columbia University Press, 1989.

Burke, K., *A Grammar of Motives*. New York: Prentice Hall, 1945.

Burke, K., *The Philosophy of Literary Form*. New York: Vintage Books, 1957.

Cacciari, C. (ed.), *Teorie della metafora: L'acquisizione, la comprensione e l'uso del linguaggio figurato*. Milan: Raffaello Cortina Editore, 1991.

Cacciari, C., 'The place of idioms in a literal and metaphorical world', in C. Cacciari and P. Tabossi (eds), *Idioms: Processing, Structure and Interpretation*. Hillsdale, N.J.: Hove and London: Lawrence Erlbaum Associates, 1993, pp. 27–55.

Cacciari, C. and Tabossi, P., 'The comprehension of idioms', *Journal of Memory and Language*, 27, 1988 (Biblioteca di Psicologia).

Cacciari, C. and Tabossi, P. (eds) *Idioms: Processing, Structure and Interpretation*. Hillsdale, N.J.: Hove and London: Lawrence Erlbaum Associates, 1993.

Calvino, I., *Lezioni americane. Sei proposte per il prossimo millennio*. Milan: Garzanti, 1988.

Caplan, D. (ed.), *Biological Studies of Mental Processes* (Proceedings of the conference 'Maturational factors in cognitive development and the biology of language'). Cambridge, Mass. and London: MIT Press, 1980.

Caplan, D., Lecours, A. R. and Smith, A. (eds), *Biological Perspectives on Language*. Cambridge, Mass. : MIT Press, 1984.

Campbell, D. T., 'Evolutionary epistemology', in G. Radnitzky and W. W. Bartley (eds) *Evolutionary Epistemology, Rationality, and the Sociology of Knowledge*. La Salle, Ill.: Open Court, 1987, pp. 47–89.

Cascardi, A. J. (ed.), *Literature and the Question of Philosophy*. Baltimore, Md. and London: Johns Hopkins University Press, 1989.

Cassirer, E., *Language and Myth,*. ed. J. Cowan and J. F. Havier. Chicago and London: The University of Chicago Press, 1979.

Cavell, M., 'Metaphor, dreamwork and irrationality', in E. LePore (ed.), *Truth and Interpretation: Perspectives on the Philosophy of Donald Davidson*. Oxford: Blackwell, 1986, pp. 495–507.

Cavell, M., *The Psychoanalytic Mind: From Freud to Philosophy*. Cambridge, Mass.: Harvard University Press, 1993.

Charlton, W., 'Living and dead metaphors', *British Journal of Aesthetics*, 15(2), 1975, pp. 172–8.

Chastain, C., 'Reference and context', in K. Gunderson (ed.), *Language, Mind and Knowledge*, Minnesota Studies in the Philosophy of Science, 7. Minneapolis, Minn.: University of Minnesota Press, 1975, pp. 194–269.

Child, A., 'On the theory of the categories', *Philosophy and Phenomenological Research*, 7, 1946, pp. 316–35.

Chinen, A. B., 'Fairy tales and transpersonal development in later life', *Journal of Transpersonal Psychology*, 17, 1985, pp. 99–122.

Chomsky, N., *Language and Mind*. New York: Harcourt Brace, 1968.

Church, J., *Language and the Discovery of Reality*. New York: Vintage Books, 1961.

Cicero, *De Oratore*, III, XXXIX, 157, trans. E. W. Sutton and H. Rackham. 2 vols, Loeb Classical Library, 1942.

Clark, A. K., 'Metaphor and literal language', *Thought*, 52 (207), 1977, pp. 366–80.

Cohen, J., *Homo Psychologicus*. London: Allen and Unwin, 1970.

Cohen, T., 'Metaphor and the cultivation of intimacy', *Critical Inquiry*, 5(1), 1978, pp. 3–12, and in S. Sacks (ed.), *On Metaphor*. Chicago: University of Chicago Press, 1979.

Cole, M. and Means, B., *Comparative Studies of How People Think: An Introduction*. Cambridge, Mass. and London: Harvard University Press, 1981.

Commons, M. L., Richards, F. A. and Armon, C. (eds), *Beyond Formal Operations*. New York: Praeger, 1984.

Cooper, D. E., *Metaphor*, Aristotelian Society Series, vol. 5. Oxford: Blackwell, 1986.

Corradi, G., *Philosophy and Coexistence*. Leyden: Sijthoff, 1966.

Corradi Fiumara, G., 'The symbolic function, transference and psychic reality', *International Review of Psycho-Analysis*, 4, 1977, pp. 171–80.

Corradi Fiumara, G., *The Other Side of Language: A Philosophy of Listening*. London and New York: Routledge, 1990.

Corradi Fiumara, G., *The Symbolic Function: Psychoanalysis and the Philosophy of Language*. Oxford and Cambridge, Mass.: Blackwell, 1992.

Corradi Fiumara, G., 'The metaphoric function and the question of objectivity', in K. Lennon and M. Whitford (eds), *Knowing the Difference: Perspectives on Feminist Epistemology*. London and New York: Routledge, 1994.

Coulmas, F., 'Idiomaticity as a problem of pragmatics', in H. Parret and M. Sbisà (eds), *Possibilities and Limitations of Pragmatics*. Amsterdam: John Benjamins, 1981, pp. 139–51.

Danto, A. C., 'Philosophy as/and/of literature', in A. J. Cascardi (ed.), *Literature and the Question of Philosophy*. Baltimore, Md. and London: Johns Hopkins University Press, 1989, pp. 3–23.

Dascal, M., 'Defending literal meaning', *Cognitive Science*, 11, 1987, pp. 259–81.

Davidson, D., *Inquiries into Truth and Interpretation*. Oxford: Clarendon Press, 1985.

Davidson, D., 'The social aspect of language', unpublished paper presented at the University of Rome, 1993.

Davidson, D., 'Three varieties of knowledge', unpublished paper presented at the University of Rome, 1993.

Davies, M., 'Idiom and metaphor', *Proceedings of the Aristotelian Society*, 83, 1982–3, pp. 67–85.

de Man, P., 'The epistemology of metaphor', *Critical Inquiry*, 1, 1978, pp. 13–30.

Dennett, D. C., *Brainstorms: Philosophical Essays on Mind and Psychology*. Hassocks, Sussex: Harvester Press, 1981.

Deri, S. K., *Symbolization and Creativity*. London and Madison, Conn.: International Universities Press, 1984.

Derrida, J., *Speech and Phenomena*, trans. D. B. Allison. Evanston, Ill. : Northwestern University Press, 1973.

Descartes, R., 'The principles of philosophy', in E. Haldane and G. R. T. Ross (eds), *The Philosophical Works of Descartes*, vols 1 and 2. Cambridge: Cambridge University Press, 1911.

Descartes, R., *Discourse on Method*, part II, trans. J. Veitch. London: Dent and Dutton Everyman, 1937.

Descartes, R., *Philosophical Letters*, trans. and ed. A. Kenny. Minneapolis, Minn.: University of Minnesota Press, 1970.

Descartes, R., *Descartes' Conversation with Burman*, trans. and ed. J. Cottingham. Oxford: Clarendon Press, 1976.

Desmedt, J. E. (ed.), *Language and Hemispheric Specialization in Man: Cerebral Event – Related Potentials*. Basel: Karger, 1977.

De Sousa, R., 'The rationality of emotions', in A. O. Rorty (ed.), *Explaining Emotions*. Berkeley, Calif.: University of California Press, 1980, pp. 127–51.

Dewey, J., 'The influence of Darwin on philosophy', in J. A. Boydston (ed.), *The Middle Works of John Dewey*, vol. 4. Carbondale, Ill.: Southern Illinois University Press, 1977.

Dirven, R. and Poprotte, W. (eds), *The Ubiquity of Metaphor: Metaphor in Language and Thought*. Amsterdam and Philadelphia: J. Benjamins, 1985.

Dobzhansky, T. and Ayala, F. J., *Studies in Philosophy of Biology*. Berkeley, Calif.: University of California Press, 1974.

Donaldson, M. L., *Children's Explanations: A Psychoanalytic Study*. Cambridge: Cambridge University Press, 1986.

Douglas, M., *Purity and Danger*. London: Routledge and Kegan Paul, 1966.

Dretske, F. J., *Knowledge and the Flow of Information*. Cambridge, Mass.: MIT Press, 1983.

Dretske, F. J., 'Contrastive statements', *Philosophical Review*, 1(4), 1972, pp. 411–37.

Dummett, M., *Truth and Other Enigmas*. Cambridge, Mass. : Harvard University Press, 1978.

Dunn, J., *The Beginnings of Social Understanding*. Cambridge, Mass.: Harvard University Press, 1988.

Edelson, M., *Language and Interpretation in Psycho-Analysis*. New Haven, Conn. and London: Yale University Press, 1975.

Einstein, A., *Ideas and Opinions*. London: Souvenir Press, 1954.

Eiser, J. R., *Attitudes, Chaos and the Connectionist Mind*. Oxford and Cambridge, Mass.: Blackwell, 1994.

Elias, N., *La solitudine del morente*. Bologna: Il Mulino, 1985.

Elias, N., *The Symbol Theory*. London: Sage Publications, 1991.

Emonds, H., *Metaphern Kommunikation: zur Theorie des Verstehens von metaphorisch verwendaten der Sprache*. Goppingen: Kummerle, 1986.

Evans, J. (ed.), *Thinking and Reasoning: Psychological Approaches*. London: Routledge and Kegan Paul, 1983.

Feigl, H., 'Positivism in the twentieth century (Logical Positivism)', in P. P. Wiener (editor in chief), *Dictionary of the History of Ideas: Studies of Selected Pivotal Ideas*. New York: Charles Scribner's Sons, 1974, pp. 545–51.

Ferguson, C. A. and Snow, C. E. (eds), *Talking to Children: Language Input and Acquisition*. Cambridge: Cambridge University Press, 1977.

Fernandez, J., 'The mission of metaphor in expressive culture', *Current Anthropology*, 15(2), 1974, pp. 119–33.

Fisher, A., *The Logic of Real Arguments*. Cambridge: Cambridge University Press, 1988.

Fiumara, R., 'Il cervello come macchina darwiniana', *Bollettino di Psichiatria Biologica*, IV(3), 1988, pp. 63–6.

Fogelin, R. J., *Figuratively Speaking*. London: Yale University Press, 1988.

Fonagy, I., *La métaphore en phonétique*. Ottawa: Didier, 1979.

Fox Keller, E., *Reflections on Gender and Science*. New Haven, Conn.: Yale University Press, 1985.

Fraser, J. T., *Of Time, Passion and Knowledge: Reflections on the Strategy of Existence*. Princeton, N. J.: Princeton University Press, 1990.

Galilei, G., *Dialogue on the Great World Systems*, the Salisbury translation, revised, annotated and with an introduction by G. de Santillana. Chicago: University of Chicago Press, 1953.

Galilei, G., *Il saggiatore*, ed. L. Sosio. Milan: Feltrinelli, 1965.

Gardner, H. and Winner, E., 'The development of metaphoric competence: implications for humanistic disciplines', *Critical Inquiry*, 5(1), 1978, pp. 123–42.

Gatlin, L., *Information Theory and the Living System*. New York: Columbia University Press, 1972.

Gendlin, E., 'A philosophical critique of the concept of narcissism: the significance of the Awareness Movement', in D. Levin (ed.), *Pathologies of the Modern Self: Postmodern Studies on Narcissism, Schizophrenia and Depression*. New York: New York University Press, 1987.

Gentner, D. and Gentner, D., 'Flowing water or teeming crowds: mental models of electricity', in D. Gentner and A. Stevens (eds), *Mental Models*. Hillsdale, N. J.: Lawrence Erlbaum Associates, 1983, pp. 99–129.

George, F. H., *Precision, Language and Logic*. Oxford: Pergamon, 1977.

Gerhart, M. and Russell, A. M., *Metaphoric Process: The Creation of Scientific and Religious Understanding*. Fort Worth, Tex.: Texas Christian University Press, 1984.

Geyer, R. F. and Schweitzer, D. R. (eds), *Theories of Alienation: Critical Perspectives in Philosophy and the Social Sciences*. Leyden: Martinus Nijhoff Social Sciences Division, 1976.

Gibbs, R. W., 'Why idioms are not dead metaphors', in C. Cacciari and P. Tabossi (eds), *Idioms: Processing, Structure, and Interpretation*. Hillsdale, N. J.: Hove and London: Lawrence Erlbaum Associates, 1993, pp. 57–77.

Gilhooly, K. J., *Thinking: Directed, Undirected and Creative*. London: Academic Press, 1982.

Gilligan, C., *In a Different Voice: Psychological Theory and Women's Development*. Cambridge, Mass. : Harvard University Press, 1982.

Glucksberg, S., 'Idiom meanings and allusional content', in C. Cacciari and P. Tabossi (eds) *Idioms: Processing, Structure, and Interpretation*. Hillsdale, N. J.: Hove and London: Lawrence Erlbaum Associates, 1993, pp. 3–26.

Goffman, E., *Frame Analysis: An Essay on the Organization of Experience*. New York: Harper and Row, 1974.

Goodman, N., *Languages of Art*. Indianapolis, Ind.: Bobbs-Merrill, 1968 and Brighton: Harvester Press, 1977.

Gould, S. J., *Time's Arrow, Time's Cycle: Myth and Metaphor in the Discovery of Geological Time*. Cambridge, Mass. and London: Harvard University Press, 1987.

Graham, A. C., *Reason and Spontaneity*. London: Curzon, 1985.

Greenfield, S. and Blakemore, C. (eds), *Mindwaves: Thoughts on Intelligence, Identity and Consciousness*. London: Blackwell, 1987.

Griffin, S., *Woman and Nature*. New York: Harper and Row, 1978.

Gutting, G. (ed.), *Paradigms and Revolutions. Applications and Appraisals of Thomas Kuhn's Philosophy of Science*. Notre Dame and London: University of Notre Dame Press, 1980.

Hacker, P. M. S., *Insight and Illusion: Wittgenstein on Philosophy and the Metaphysics of Experience*. Oxford: Clarendon Press, 1972.

Hacking, J., *Why Does Language Matter to Philosophy?* Cambridge: Cambridge University Press, 1975.

Haken, H., *Synergetics, an Introduction. Nonequilibrium Phase Transitions and Self-Organization in Physics, Chemistry and Biology*. New York: Springer Verlag, 1978.

Harding, S., and Hintikka, M. B. (eds), *Discovering Reality: Feminist Perspectives on Epistemology, Metaphysics, Methodology and the Philosophy of Science*. Boston, Mass.: D. Reidel Publishing Co., 1983.

Harman, G., *Change in View: Principles of Reasoning*. Cambridge, Mass.: MIT Press, 1986.

Harries, K., 'Afterthoughts on metaphor', *Critical Inquiry*, 5(1), 1978, pp. 167–74.

Haverkamp, A., *Theorie der Metapher*. Darmstadt: Wissenschaftliche Buchgesellschaft, 1983.

Hawkes, T., *Metaphor*. London: Methuen, 1977.

Haynes, F., 'Metaphor as interactive', *Educational Theory*, 25(3), 1975, pp. 272–7.

Heisenberg, W., *Physics and Philosophy*. New York: Harper Torchbooks, 1958.

Heisenberg, W., *Physics and Beyond*. New York: Harper and Row, 1971.

Helman, D. H., *Analogical Reasoning: Perspectives of Artificial Intelligence, Cognitive Science and Philosophy*. Dordrecht: Kluwer, 1988.

Henle, P., 'Metaphor', in P. Henle (ed.), *Language, Thought and Culture*. Ann Arbor, Mich.: University of Michigan Press, 1958, reprinted 1965.

Hesse, M. B., *Models and Analogies in Science*. London: Sheed and Ward, 1963.

Hesse, M. B. and Arbib, M., *The Construction of Reality*. Cambridge: Cambridge University Press, 1986.

Hobbs, J., 'Metaphor, metaphor schemata and selective inferencing', Technical Note No. 204. Cambridge Computer Science Research, Menlo Park, Calif., 1979.

Hoenigswald, H. M. and Wiener, L. F. (eds), *Biological Metaphor and Cladistic Classification: An Interdisciplinary Perspective*. London: Pinter, 1987.

Hoffman, R. R., Cochran, E. L. and Nead, J. M., 'Cognitive metaphors in experimental psychology', in D. E. Leary (ed.), *Metaphors in the History of Psychology*. Cambridge: Cambridge University Press, 1990, pp. 173–229.

Hofstadter, D. R., *Goedel, Escher, Bach: An Eternal Golden Braid*. New York: Vintage Books, 1979.

Holton, G., *The Scientific Imagination: Case Studies*. Cambridge: Cambridge University Press, 1978.

Hookway, C. and Petitt, P. (eds), *Action and Interpretation: Studies in the Philosophy of the Social Sciences*. Cambridge: Cambridge University Press, 1978.

Hornsby, J., 'Speech acts and pornography', *Women's Philosophy Review*, 10, 1993, pp. 38–45.

Horsburgh, H. J. N., 'Philosophers against metaphor', *Philosophical Quarterly*, 8(32), 1958, pp. 231–45.

Humboldt, von W., *On Language: The Diversity of Human Language – Structure and Its Influence on the Mental Development of Mankind*, trans. P. Heath. Cambridge: Cambridge University Press, 1988.

Hume, D., *A Treatise on Human Nature*, ed. L. Selby-Bigge. Oxford and London: Oxford University Press, 1973.

Isenberg, A., 'On defining metaphor', *Journal of Philosophy*, 66(21), 1963, pp. 609–22.

Jacques, F., *Différence et intersubjectivité*. Paris: Aubier, 1982.

James, W., *Principles of Psychology*. New York: Henry Holt, 1980.

Jay, M., *The Dialectical Imagination*. Boston, Mass.: Little Brown and Co., 1973.

Jaines, J., *The Origin and History of Consciousness in the Breakdown of the Bicameral Mind*. Boston, Mass.: Houghton Mifflin, 1976.

Jocić, M., 'Adaptation in adult speech during communication with children', in N. Waterson and C. Snow (eds), *The Development of Communications*. Chichester and New York: John Wiley and Sons, 1978, pp. 159–71.

Johnson, M., 'A philosophical perspective on the problems of metaphor', in R. Hoffman and R. Honeck (eds), *Cognition and Figurative Language*. Hillsdale, N. J.: Lawrence Erlbaum Associates, 1980, pp. 47–67.

Johnson, M., *The Body in the Mind: The Bodily Basis of Meaning, Imagination and Reasoning*. Chicago and London: University of Chicago Press, 1987.

Johnson, M. (ed.), *Philosophical Perspectives on Metaphor*. Minneapolis, Minn.: University of Minnesota Press, 1981.

Johnson, M. and Erickson, G. W., 'Toward a new theory of metaphor', *Southern Journal of Philosophy*, 18(3), 1980, pp. 289–99.

Jones, R. S., *Physics as Metaphor*. London: Abacus, 1983.

Jongen, R. (ed.), *La métaphore. Approche pluridisciplinaire*. Bruxelles: Facultés Universitaires Saint Louis, 1980.

Kant, I., *Critique of Pure Reason*, trans. N. Kemp Smith. New York: St Martin's Press, 1965.

Katz, J. J. and Fodor, J., 'The structure of semantic theory', *Language*, 39, 1963, pp. 170–210.

Keane, M. T., *Analogical Problem Solving*. Chichester: Ellis Horwood, 1988.

Kemp, G. N., 'Metaphor and aspect–perception', *Analysis*, 51(2) (New series no. 229), March 1991, pp. 84–90.

Kermode, F., *The Genesis of Secrecy: On the Interpretation of Narrative*. Cambridge, Mass.: Harvard University Press, 1979.

Kittay, E. F., *Metaphor: Its Cognitive Force and Linguistic Structure*. Oxford: Clarendon Press, 1987.

Kitayama, O., 'Metaphorization – making terms', *International Journal of Psycho-Analysis*, 68(4), 1987, pp. 499–509.

Koch, S. and Leary, E.D. (eds), *A Century of Psychology as Science*. New York: McGraw-Hill, 1985.

Kofman, S., *Nietzsche and Metaphor*. London: Athlone Press, 1993.

Kövecses, Z., *Metaphors of Anger, Pride and Love: a Lexical Approach to the Structure of Concepts*. Amsterdam: John Benjamins, 1986.

Krabbe, E. C. W., Dalitz, R. J. and Smit, P. A. (eds), *Empirical Logic and Public Debate: Essays in honor of E. M. Barth*. Amsterdam and Atlanta, Ga.: Editions Rodopi, 1993.

Kristeva, J., *Language: The Unknown*, trans. A. M. Menke. New York: Columbia University Press, 1989.

Kübler-Ross, E., *Death, the Final Stage of Growth*. New York: Simon and Schuster, 1975.

Labouvie-Vief, G., 'Wisdom as integrated thought: historical and developmental perspectives', in R. J. Sternberg (ed.), *Wisdom: Its Nature, Origins and Development*. Cambridge: Cambridge University Press, 1990, pp. 52–83.

Laing, R. D., *Self and Others*. London: Tavistock Publications, 1969.

Lakatos, J., *Proofs and Refutations: The Logic of Mathematical Discovery*. Cambridge: Cambridge University Press, 1976.

Lakoff, G., *Women, Fire and Dangerous Things: What Categories Reveal about Mind*. Chicago and London: University of Chicago Press, 1987.

Lakoff, G. and Johnson, M., *Metaphors We Live By*. Chicago and London: University of Chicago Press, 1980.

Lakoff, G. and Johnson, M., 'Conceptual metaphor in everyday language', *Journal of Philosophy*, 77(8), 1980, pp. 452–86.

Langer, S., *Philosophy in a New Key: A Study of the Symbolism of Reason, Rite and Art*. Cambridge, Mass.: Harvard University Press, 1942.

Laplanche, J. and Pontalis, J. B., *The Language of Psychoanalysis*. trans. D. Nicholson-Smith. London: Hogarth Press, 1973.

Leach, E., *Culture and Communication*. Cambridge: Cambridge University Press, 1976.

Leary, D. E. (ed.), *Metaphors in the History of Psychology*. Cambridge: Cambridge University Press, 1990.

Leary, D. E., 'Psyche's muse: the role of metaphor in the history of psychology', in D. E. Leary (ed.), *Metaphors in the History of Psychology*. Cambridge: Cambridge University Press, 1990, pp. 1–78.

Lebrun, J. and Raffler-Engel, von W. (eds), *Baby Talk and Infant Speech*. Amsterdam: Swets and Zeitlingen, 1976.

Leder, D., *The Absent Body*. Chicago and London: University of Chicago Press, 1990.

Leman, G., 'Words and worlds', in D. Bannister (ed.), *Perspectives in Personal Construct Theory*. London: Academic Press, 1970.

Leondar, B., 'Metaphor and infant cognition', *Poetics*, 4, 1975, pp. 273–87.

Lepenne, P., *On Autobiography*. Minneapolis, Minn.: University of Minnesota Press, 1989.

LePore, E., and Fodor, J., *Holism: A Shopper's Guide*. Oxford: Blackwell, 1992.

LePore, E. (ed.), *Truth and Interpretation: Perspectives on the Philosophy of Donald Davidson*. Oxford: Blackwell, 1986.

LePore, E., 'Truth and meaning', in E. Le Pore (ed.), *Truth and Interpretation: Perspectives on the Philosophy of Donald Davidson*. Oxford: Blackwell, 1986, pp. 3–26.

Levin, D. M., *The Listening Self: Personal Growth, Social Change and the Closure of Metaphysics*. London and New York: Routledge, 1989.

Levin, D. M. (ed.), *Pathologies of the Modern Self: Postmodern Studies on Narcissism, Schizophrenia and Depression*. New York: New York University Press, 1987.

Levin, S. R., *The Semantics of Metaphor*. Baltimore, Md. and London: Johns Hopkins University Press, 1977.

Levins, R. and Lewontin, R., *The Dialectical Biologist*. Cambridge, Mass. and London: Harvard University Press, 1985.

Lieven, E. V. M., 'Conversations between mothers and young children: individual differences and their possible implication for the study of language learning', in N. Waterson and C. Snow (eds), *The Development of Communication*. Chichester and New York: John Wiley and Sons, 1978, pp. 173–87.

Lloyd, G., *The Man of Reason: 'Male' and 'Female' in Western Philosophy*. London: Methuen, 1984.

Loewenberg. J., 'Truth and consequences of metaphor', *Philosophy and Rhetoric*, 6, 1973, pp. 30–45.

Longino, H. E., *Science as Social Knowledge: Values and Objectivity in Scientific Inquiry*. Princeton, N.J.: Princeton University Press, 1990.

Lotman, J., *La semiosfera*. Venice: Marsilio, 1985.

Lowen, W., *Dichotomies of the Mind: A System of Science Models of the Mind and Personality*. New York and Chichester: John Wiley and Sons, 1982.

McCanney Gergen, M. (ed.), *Feminist Thought and the Structure of Knowledge*. New York: New York University Press, 1988.

Mach, E., 'On the part played by accident in invention and discovery', *The Monist*, 6, 1896, pp. 161–75.

McCornac, E. R., *Metaphor and Myth in Science and Religion*. Durham, N.C.: Duke University Press, 1976.

McCornac, E. R., *A Cognitive Theory of Method*. Cambridge, Mass.: MIT Press, 1985.

McGuinness, B., *Wittgenstein, a Life. Young Ludwig (1889–1921)*. London: Duckworth, 1988.

McReynolds, P., 'Motives and metaphors: a study in scientific creativity', in D. E. Leary (ed.), *Metaphors in the History of Psychology*. Cambridge: Cambridge University Press, 1990, pp. 133–72.

Malcolm, N., *Ludwig Wittgenstein: A Memoir*. London: Oxford University Press, 1958.

Marjanovich, A., 'Criteria of metaphoricity of children's utterances', Report presented at the annual meeting of the American Psychological Association, Anaheim, California, 1983.

Matte Blanco, I., *Thinking, Feeling and Being: Clinical Reflections on the Fundamental Antinomy of Human Beings and World*, New Library of Psychoanalysis, no.5, London and New York: Routledge, 1989.

Matte Blanco, I., *The Unconscious as Infinite Sets: An Essay in Bi-Logic*. London: Duckworth, 1975.

Means, B. and Cole, M., *Comparative Studies of How People Think: An Introduction*. Cambridge, Mass. and London: Harvard University Press, 1981.

Melandri, E., 'Per una filosofia della metafora', introduzione all'edizione italiana di H. Blumenberg, *Paradigmi per una metaforologia*. Bologna: Il Mulino, 1969, pp. vii–xiv.

Memmi, A., *The Colonizer and the Colonized*. Boston, Mass.: Beacon Press, 1967.

Meniuk, P., *Language and Maturation*. Cambridge, Mass.: MIT Press, 1977.

Merchant, C., *The Death of Nature: Women, Ecology and Scientific Revolution*. San Francisco: Harper and Row, 1980.

Merleau Ponty, M., *The Visible and the Invisible*, trans. A. Lingus. Evanston, Ill. : Northwestern University Press, 1968.

Mew, P., 'Metaphor and truth', *British Journal of Aesthetics*, 11, 1971, pp. 189–95.

Miall, D. S. (ed.), *Metaphor: Problems and Perspectives*. Brighton: Harvester Press, 1982.

Midgley, M., *Wisdom, Information and Wonder: What is Knowledge For?* London and New York: Routledge, 1989.

Midgley, M., *Science as Salvation: a Modern Myth and its Meanings*. London and New York: Routledge, 1992.

Miller, A., *For Your Own Good: The Roots of Violence in Child-rearing*. London: Virago Press, 1987.

Miller, A. J., *Imagery in Scientific Thought: Creating 20th-Century Physics*. Boston, Basle and Stuttgart: Birkhauser, 1984.

Miller, J. G., *Living Systems*. New York: Mc Graw-Hill, 1978.

Mooij, J. J., *A Study of Metaphor: On the Nature of Metaphorical Expressions, with Special Reference to their Reference*. Amsterdam and Oxford: North Holland Publishing Company, 1976.

Moulton, J., 'A paradigm of philosophy: the adversary method', in S. Harding and M. B. Hintikka (eds), *Discovering Reality: Feminist Perspectives on Epistemology, Metaphysics, Methodology and Philosophy of Science*. Boston, Mass.: D. Reidel Publishing Co., 1983.

Munitz, M. K., *The Question of Reality*. Princeton, N.J.: Princeton University Press, 1990.

Munitz, M. K., *Cosmic Understanding. Philosophy and Science of the Universe*, Princeton, N.J.: Princeton University Press, 1990.

Muratori, A. M., 'Dal "non comunicato" alla comunicazione', in A. M. Muratori (ed.), *La relazione analitica*. Rome: Borla, 1981, pp. 135–40.

Muratori, A. M. (ed.), *Il 'continuo' e il 'discreto' in psicoanalisi*. Rome: Borla, 1987.

Naess, A., *Interpretation and Preciseness*. Oslo: Dybwad, 1953.

Nagel, T., *Mortal Questions*. Cambridge: Cambridge University Press, 1979.

Nagel, T., *The View from Nowhere*. New York and Oxford: Oxford University Press, 1986.

Nelson, K. (ed.), *Narratives from the Crib*. Cambridge, Mass. and London: Harvard University Press, 1989.

Nicholson, L. J. (ed.), *Feminism – Postmodernism*. New York and London: Routledge, 1990.

Nietzsche, F., 'On truth and lies in the nonmoral sense', in *Philosophy and Truth: Selections from Nietzsche's Notebooks of the early 1870s*. Atlantic Hyland, N.J.: Humanities Press, 1979.

Nisbet, R., *Social Change and History*. New York: Oxford University Press, 1968.

Nolan, R., *Cognitive Practices: Human Language and Human Knowledge*. Oxford, and Cambridge, Mass.: Blackwell, 1994.

Noppen van, J. P., *Metaphor: A Bibliography of post-1970 Publications*. Amsterdam and Philadelphia: John Benjamins, 1985.

Norris, C., *The Deconstructive Turn: Essays in the Rhetoric of Philosophy*. London and New York: Methuen, 1983.

Nozick, R., *Philosophical Explanations*. Oxford: Clarendon Press, 1981.

Nozick, R., *The Nature of Rationality*. Princeton, N.J.: Princeton University Press, 1993.

Ochse, R., *Before the Gates of Excellence: the Determinants of Creative Genius*. Cambridge: Cambridge University Press, 1990.

Ogden, C. K., *Opposition: A Linguistic and Psychological Analysis*, Introduced by J. A. Richards. Bloomington, Ind. and London: Indiana University Press; New York: Midland Books, 1967.

Olscamp, P. J., 'How some metaphors may be true or false', *Journal of Aesthetics and Art Criticism*, 29(1), 1970, pp. 77–86.

Ong, W., *Ramus, Method and the Decay of Dialogue*. Cambridge, Mass.: Harvard University Press, 1958.

Oppenheimer, J. R., *Science and the Common Understanding*. New York: Oxford University Press, 1954.

Orbach, S., *Hunger Strike: The Anorectic's Struggle as a Metaphor for our Age*. London: Faber, 1986.

Ortony, A., 'Why metaphors are necessary and not just nice', *Educational Theory*, 25(1), 1975, pp. 45–53.

Ortony, A. (ed.), *Metaphor and Thought*. Cambridge: Cambridge University Press, 1980.

Owsey, T., *Galenism: Rise and Decline of a Medical Philosophy*. Ithaca, N.Y. and London: Cornell University Press, 1973.

Ozick, C., *Metaphor and Memory: Essays*. New York: Knopf, 1989.

Paprotte, W. and Dirven, R. (eds), *The Ubiquity of Metaphor: Metaphor in Language and Thought*. Amsterdam and Philadelphia: John Benjamins, 1985.

Parker, P. A., 'The metaphorical plot', in D. S. Miall (ed.), *Metaphor: Problems and Perspectives*. Brighton: Harvester Press, 1982, pp. 133–57.

Parret, H. and Sbisà, M. (eds), *Possibilities and Limitations of Pragmatics*. Amsterdam: John Benjamins, 1981.

Pears, D., *Motivated Irrationality*. Oxford: Clarendon Press, 1984.

Peirce, C. S., *Writings of Charles S. Peirce: A Chronological Edition*, general editor, M. H. Fisch, vol. 1, 1857–1866; Bloomington, Ind.: Indiana University Press, 1982.

Pepper, S. C., 'Metaphor in philosophy', in P. P. Wiener (editor in chief) *Dictionary of the History of Ideas: Studies of Selected Pivotal Ideas*. New York: Charles Scribner's Sons, 1974, pp. 196–201.

Perkins, D. N., *The Mind's Best Work*. Cambridge, Mass. and London: Harvard University Press, 1981.

Piaget, J., *Play, Dreams and Imitation in Children*. New York: Norton, 1962.

Piattelli Palmarini, M., 'L'entrepôt biologique et le démon comparateur', *Nouvelle Revue de Psychanalyse*, 15, 1977, pp. 105–23.

Putnam, H., *Representation and Reality*. Cambridge, Mass.: MIT Press, 1988.

Putnam, H. *Realism with a Human Face*, edited and introduced by J. Conant. Cambridge, Mass.: Harvard University Press, 1990.

Putnam, H., *Renewing Philosophy*. Cambridge, Mass.: Harvard University Press, 1992.

Quine, W. V. O., 'Speaking of objects', *Ontological Relativity and Other Essays*. New York: Columbia University Press, 1969.

Quine, W. V. O., 'A postscript on metaphor', *Critical Inquiry*, 5(1), 1978, pp. 161–2.

Quine, W. V. O., *Word and Object*. Cambridge, Mass.: MIT Press, 1981.

Quine, W. V. O., 'Indeterminacy of translation again', in D. Davidson and J. Hintikka (eds), *Words and Objections: Essays on the Work of W. V. O. Quine*. Dordrecht: Reidel, 1969.

Radnitzky, G. and Bartley, W. W. (eds), *Evolutionary Epistemology, Rationality, and the Sociology of Knowledge*. La Salle, Ill. : Open Court, 1987.

Raffler-Engel, von W. and Lebrun, J. (eds), *Baby Talk and Infant Speech*. Amsterdam: Swets and Zeitlinger, 1976.

Rayner, E. and Tuckett, D., 'An introduction to Matte Blanco's reformulation of the Freudian unconscious and his conceptualization of the internal world', in I. Matte Blanco (ed.), *Thinking, Feeling, and Being*, New Library of Psychoanalysis, no. 5, London: Routledge, 1988, pp. 3–42.

Recanati, F., *Meaning and Force: The Pragmatics of Performative Utterances*. Cambridge: Cambridge University Press, 1988.

Remortel, van M., *Literalness and Metaphorization: The Case of 'Turn'*. Wilrijk, Belgium: Universiteit Antwerpen, Universitaire Instelling Antwerpen, Dep. Germaanse, Afdeling Linguistiek, 1986.

Richards, A., *The Philosophy of Rhetoric*. Oxford: Oxford University Press, 1936.

Ricoeur, P., 'Creativity in Language', *Philosophy Today*, 17, 1973, pp. 97–111.

Ricoeur, P., *The Rule of Metaphor*, trans. R. Czerny with K. McLaughlin and J. Costello. Toronto: University of Toronto Press, 1977.

Ricoeur, P., 'The metaphorical process as cognition, imagination, feeling', *Critical Inquiry*, 5(1), 1978, pp. 143–60.

Ricoeur, P., *Soi-même comme un autre*. Paris: Éditions du Seuil, 1990.

Riedl, R., *Order in Living Organisms*. New York: John Wiley and Sons, 1978.

Riedl, R., *Biologia della conoscenza. I fondamenti evoluzionistici della ragione*. Milan: Longanesi, 1981.

Rogers, R., *Metaphor: A Psychoanalytic View*. Berkeley, Calif. and London: University of California Press, 1978.

Romanyshyn, R. D., *Psychological Life: From Science to Metaphor*. Milton Keynes: Open University Press, 1982.

Rorty, A. O. (ed.), *Explaining Emotions*. Berkeley, Calif.: University of California Press, 1980.

Rorty, R., *Philosophy and the Mirror of Nature*. Oxford: Blackwell, 1980.

Rorty, R., *Contingency, Irony and Solidarity*. Cambridge: Cambridge University Press, 1989.

Rorty, R., *Objectivity, Relativism and Truth: Philosophical Papers*, vol. I. Cambridge: Cambridge University Press, 1991.

Rosaldo, M., *Knowledge and Passion*. Cambridge: Cambridge University Press, 1980.

Russell, A. M. and Gerhart, M., *Metaphoric Process: The Creation of Scientific and Religious Understanding*. Fort Worth, Tex.: Texas Christian University Press, 1984.

Russell, B., *Autobiography*, vol. I. London: Allen and Unwin, 1967.

Ryle, G., *The Concept of Mind*. London: Hutchinson, 1949.

Sacks, S. (ed.), *On Metaphor*. Chicago: University of Chicago Press, 1979.

Sacks, S. (ed.), *On Metaphor*, based on the symposium 'Metaphor: The conceptual leap'. Chicago and London: University of Chicago Press, 1981.

Scheffler, I., *Beyond the Letter: A Philosophical Inquiry into Ambiguity, Vagueness and Metaphor in Language*. London: Routledge and Kegan Paul, 1979.

Schmid Kitsikis, E., *Legami creatori e legami distruttori dell'attività mentale*. Rome: Borla, 1993.

Schwaber, E. A., 'Interpretation and the therapeutic action of psychoanalysis', *International Journal of Psycho-Analysis*, 71, 1990, pp. 229–40.

Sciama, D. W., *The Unity of the Universe*. London: Faber, 1959.

Searle, J. R., *Speech Acts: An Essay in Philosophy of Language*. Cambridge: Cambridge University Press, 1969.

Searle, J. R., 'Metaphor', in A. Ortony (ed.), *Metaphor and Thought*. Cambridge: Cambridge University Press, 1980, pp. 92–123.

Searle, J. R., *The Rediscovery of the Mind*. Cambridge, Mass.: MIT Press, 1992.

Shapiro, J. and Sica, A. (eds.), *Hermeneutics: Questions and Prospects*. Amherst, Mass.: University of Massachusetts Press, 1984.

Shell, M., *Moneta, linguaggio e pensiero*. Bologna: Il Mulino, 1988.

Shibbles, W., 'The metaphorical method', *Journal of Aesthetic Education*, 7, 1974, pp. 23–36.

Siegelman, E. Y., *Metaphor and Meaning in Psychotherapy*. Hove, East Sussex: Guilford Press, 1990.

Smith, L. D. 'Metaphors of knowledge and behaviour in the behaviorist tradition', in D. E. Leary (ed.) *Metaphors in the History of Psychology*. Cambridge: Cambridge University Press, 1992, pp. 239–66.

Smith, P., *The Philosophy of Mind: An Introduction*. Cambridge: Cambridge University Press, 1986.

Snow, C. E., 'Mothers' speech research: from input to interaction', in C. E. Snow and C. A. Ferguson (eds), *Talking to Children: Language Input and Acquisition*. Cambridge: Cambridge University Press, 1977.

Snow, C. E. and Ferguson, C. A. (eds), *Talking to Children: Language Input and Acquisition*. Cambridge: Cambridge University Press, 1977.

Snow, C. and Waterson, N. (eds), *The Development of Communication*. Chichester and New York: John Wiley and Sons, 1978.

Solomon, R., *Love, Emotion, Myth and Metaphor*. New York: Anchor Press Doubleday, 1981.

Sontag, S., *Illness as Metaphor*. Harmondsworth: Penguin Books, 1983.

Soskice, J. Martin, *Metaphor and Religious Language*. Oxford: Clarendon Press, 1985.

Spence, D. D., *The Freudian Metaphor: Toward Paradigm Change in Psychoanalysis*. New York and London: Norton, 1987.

Sperry, R. W., *Science and Moral Priority: Merging Mind, Brain and Human Values*. New York: Columbia University Press, 1983; Oxford: Blackwell, 1983.

Srzednicki, J., 'On metaphor', *Philosophical Quarterly*, 10, 1960, pp. 228–37.

Stebbins, G. L., *The Basis of Progressive Evolution*. Chapel, N.C.: University of North Carolina Press, 1969.

Stern, D. N., *The Interpersonal World of the Infant*. New York: Basic Books, 1985.

Stern, K., *The Flight from Woman*. New York: Farrar, Strauss and Giroux, 1965.

Sternberg, R. J., *Intelligence, Information Processing and Analogical Reasoning: The Componential Analysis of Human Abilities*. Hillsdale, N.Y.: Erlbaum, distributed by Wiley, 1977.

Sternberg, R. J., *Metaphors of Mind: Conceptions of the Nature of Intelligence*. Cambridge: Cambridge University Press, 1990.

Sternberg, R. J. (ed.), *Wisdom: Its Nature, Origins and Development*. Cambridge: Cambridge University Press, 1990.

Stewart, J., 'Concepts of language and meaning: a comparative study', *Quarterly Journal of Speech*, 58, 1972, pp. 123–33.

Strawson, P. F., 'Imagination and perception', *Freedom and Resentment and Other Essays*. London and New York: Methuen, 1974, pp. 45–65.

Swanson, D. R., 'Toward a psychology of metaphor', *Critical Inquiry*, 5(1), 1978, pp. 163–6.

Tappa, G., 'L'interazione in psicoanalisi. Una ricerca attraverso i concetti di "continuo", "discontinuo", "discreto"', in A. M. Muratori (ed.), *Il 'continuo' e il 'discreto' in psicoanalisi*. Rome: Borla, 1987.

Toulmin, S., *Human Understanding*, vol.1. Princeton, N.J.: Princeton University Press, 1972.

Taylor, M., *The Possibility of Cooperation: Studies in Rationality and Social Change*. Cambridge: Cambridge University Press, 1987.

Tuckett, D. and Rayner, E., 'An introduction to Matte Blanco's reformulation of the Freudian unconscious and his conceptualization of the internal world', in I. Matte Blanco, *Thinking, Feeling, and Being*, New Library of Psychoanalysis, no. 5, London: Routledge, 1988, pp. 3–42.

Turbayne, C., *The Myth of Metaphor*. Columbia, S.C.: University of South Carolina Press, 1970.

Turner, V., *The Forest Symbols*. Ithaca, N.Y.: Cornell University Press, 1967.

Tyler, S. A., *The Said and the Unsaid: Mind, Meaning and Culture*. New York and London: Academic Press, 1978.

Tymieniecka, A. T., *Logos and Life: The Passions of the Soul and the Elements in the Onto-Poiesis of Culture*, vol. III. Dordrecht: Kluwer, 1990.

Van Buren, P. M., *The Edges of Language*. London: SCM Press, 1972.

Varela, F. J., 'Il circolo creativo: abbozzo di una storia naturale della circolarità', in P. Watzlawick (ed.), *La realtà inventata:Contributi al costruttivismo*. Milan: Feltrinelli, 1988, pp. 259–72.

Velikovsky, E., 'Can a newly acquired language become the speech of the unconscious? Word-plays in the dreams of Hebrew-thinking persons', *Psychoanalytical Review*, 21, 1934, pp. 329–35. Published in 1938 as 'Jeu de mots hébraïques', *Révue Française de Psychanalyse*, 10, 1938, pp. 66–71.

Vernon, R., 'Politics as metaphor: Cardinal Newman and Professor Kuhn', in G. Gutting (ed.), *Paradigms and Revolutions: Applications and Appraisals of Thomas Kuhn's Philosophy of Science*. Notre Dame, Ind. and London: University of Notre Dame Press, 1980, pp. 246–67.

Vesey, G. N. A., *The Embodied Mind*. London: Allen and Unwin, 1965.

Vollmer, G., *Evolutionäre Erkenntnistheorie*, 3rd edn., Stuttgart: S. Hirzel Verlag, 1981.

Waterson, N. and Snow, C. (eds), *The Development of Communication*. Chichester and New York: John Wiley and Sons, 1978.

Watzlawick, P., 'Le profezie che si autodeterminano', in P. Watzlawick (ed.), *La realtà inventata. Contributi al costruttivismo*. Milan: Feltrinelli, 1988.

Weiss, P., *Life, Order and Understanding*. New York: McGraw-Hill, 1978.

Weissman, D., *Truth's Debt to Value*. New Haven, Conn. and London: Yale University Press, 1993.

Werner, M., *Philosophical Finesse: Studies in the Art of Rational Persuasion*. Oxford: Clarendon Press, 1989.

Wheelwright, P., *Metaphor and Reality*. Bloomington, Ind.: Indiana University Press, 1962.

Wheelwright, P., *Symbolism*. Bloomington, Ind.: Indiana University Press, 1962.

Wicker, B., *The Story-Shaped World*. London: Athlone Press, 1975.

Wiener, L. and Hoenigswald, H. M. (eds), *Biological Metaphor and Cladistic Classification: An Interdisciplinary Perspective*. London: Pinter, 1987.

Winner, E., 'Early metaphors in spontaneous speech', in *The Point of Words: Children's Understanding of Metaphor and Irony*. Cambridge: Cambridge University Press, 1988, pp. 90–109.

Winnicott, D. W., *Playing and Reality*. New York: Basic Books, 1971.

Winson, J., *Brain and Psyche: The Biology of the Unconscious*. Garden City, N.Y.: Anchor Press/Doubleday, 1985.

Wilson, D. B., *The Figure of Transport: An Inaugural Lecture (17 May 1984). Durham: University of Durham Press, 1985.*

Wittgenstein, L., *Culture and Value*, trans. P. Winch, ed. G. H. von Wright, in collaboration with H. Nyman. Oxford: Blackwell, 1980.

Wittgenstein, L., *Remarks on the Philosophy of Psychology*. vol. I, trans. G. E. M. Anscombe, ed. G. E. M. Anscombe and G. H. von Wright. Oxford: Blackwell, 1980.

Wittgenstein, L., *Philosophical Investigations*, trans. G. E. M. Anscombe. Oxford: Blackwell, 1988.

Wittgenstein, L., *The Blue and Brown Books: Preliminary Studies for the 'Philosophical Investigations'*. Oxford: Blackwell, 1989.

Wolfson, H. A., *Philo: Foundations of Religious Philosophy in Judaism, Christianity and Islam*, vol. I, Cambridge, Mass.: Harvard University Press, 1947.

Woolley, L., *The Beginnings of Civilization*. New York: Mentor Books, 1963.

Zlotnic, J., 'Physical Chemistry: The Interface and the Metaphor' (an inaugural lecture given in the University of Fort Hare on 5 August 1981). Fort Hare: Fort Hare University Press, 1983.

Index

Martin-Soskice, J.: definitions of
  metaphor 9
masters and slaves 1–2, 3; Aristotle on 1,
  88, 101
mastery of language 3, 36, 53
Matte Blanco, I.: higher-dimensional logic
  66; symmetrical logic 114
maturation: intellectual 70, 91; of
  knowledge 52–63, 68; of rationality 36,
  41; of thinking 36, 68
maturity: and cognition 61–3, 68, 70,
  91–2; philosophical 21; self-formation
  and 61–3
meaning: assignment of 110; background
  distinguished 69; changing of 14;
  cognitive content and 36; concept of
  20; Davidson on 20, 30, 43; equivocal
  55; hierarchization of meanings 53;
  interactive 110; intersubjective
  appreciation of 134; linguistic meaning
  121; literalness and 34; metaphor as
  transference of 116; official meanings
  52; physiological transformations of
  55; primacy of literal meaning 52, 54;
  Putnam on 14; representationalist
  perspective 6–7; Ricoeur on 56; search
  for 3; sentence structure and 121;
  stability and permanence 14, 27, 34,
  54, 75; surplus of meanings 56;
  transfer of 129; Wittgenstein on 110
mental illness 56, 140
metaphor: Aristotle on 1, 11, 95;
  asymmetry and 113; attempts to define
  6, 9; biology and 13; circulation of
  metaphors 100–3;
  computational/computer metaphor *see*
  computational/computer metaphor;
  construction and construal of 92, 133,
  138; cybernetic metaphor 27; dead
  metaphors *see* dead metaphors;
  deconstructive metaphors 58–9, 81;
  disintegrative metaphors 81;
  emigration/immigration of 77;
  extended metaphors 85; freedom to
  create 89; Freud on use of 78;
  generation and use of links between
  115–18; heuristic use of 11–12, 76–9;
  Hobbes and 4, 5; of illumination 110;
  implicit 27; improper use of terms and
  111; inchoative 12; life-cycle of 15–16;
  in literature 136; logical positivist view
  4–5; nonsense and 117; oppositional
  see oppositional metaphor; oracular
  127; as paradigm of linguistic

interpretation 35; paradigm and root
  metaphor 11; paradox of 11; perception
  and 31; picture metaphor 72; as plot
  73–4; poetical metaphors 12; predictive
  127; as process 6–9; proposition
  metaphor 72; reception of 139–42;
  reciprocity and 119;
  recontextualizations and 37;
  redescription and 37; revelatory power
  of 32; root metaphor and paradigm 11;
  seminal metaphors 27, 34;
  thematization of 33; as transference of
  meaning 116; transmission of 139–42;
  visual metaphor of mind 90
metaphoric imagination 11, *see also*
  imagination
metaphoric revolutions 28
metaphoric thinking 10
metaphorical projections 2, 28, 94–5;
  bodily projections 121–4; circulation of
  metaphors 100–3; cognitive
  propensities 96–8; embodied
  experience 98–100; Johnson on 99,
  121, 123
metaphoricity 5, 10, 11, 14, 27; biology
  and 16; genius of 1, 2, 10, 37, 38, 88,
  94, 105; interaction with literalness
  74–6; interpersonal approach to 1–4;
  life and 24; psychic depth 14
metaphysics 4–5, 45
Midgley, M. 50–1, 63; interepistemic
  approach 41; isolationism 38
mind: as computer *see*
  computational/computer metaphor;
  disembodied *see* disembodiment; as
  mirror 6, 8; playful 110–11; visual
  metaphor of 90
mind–body dualism 23, 29, 73, 91, 125
mirror: mind as 6, 8
models: implicit 10; interactive
  metaphoric view of 27–8; predictive
  power 10, *see also* theory
Moulton, J.: adversarial process 42;
  aggressiveness 48; oppositional
  metaphor 49
Muratori, A.M.: continuity and discretion
  73
mythology 52, 61, 75; Babel myth 3

Nagel, T.: objectivity 70, 128
narrative mode of knowing 65–6
natural selection 78
nature: interactions with 126; richness of
  128